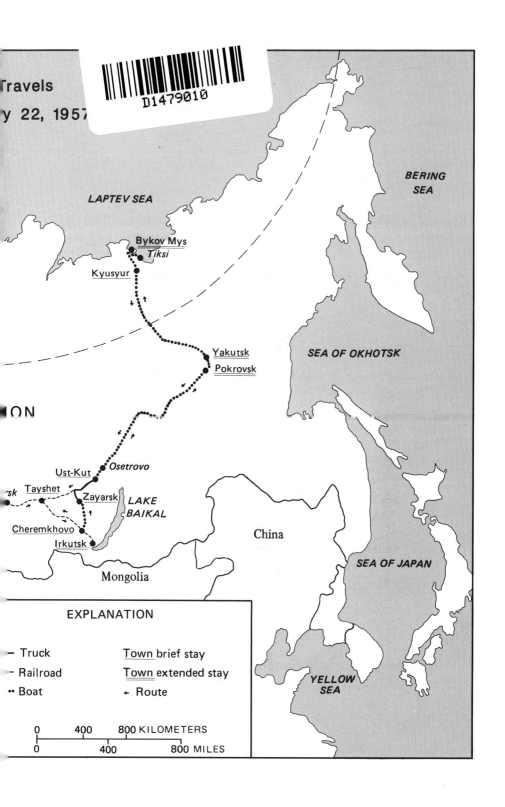

Travels

y 22, 1957

LAPTEV SEA

BERING
SEA

Bykov Mys
Tiksi

Kyusyur

SEA OF OKHOTSK

Yakutsk
Pokrovsk

ON

Ust-Kut Osetrovo

sk Tayshet

Zayarsk LAKE
BAIKAL

Cheremkhovo

Irkutsk

China

Mongolia

SEA OF JAPAN

EXPLANATION

— Truck   Town brief stay
— Railroad   Town extended stay
•• Boat   ← Route

YELLOW
SEA

0   400   800 KILOMETERS
0   400   800 MILES

Sixteen Years in Siberia

Sixteen Years in Siberia

Memoirs of Rachel and Israel Rachlin

Translated from the Danish
and with Foreword by
Birgitte M. de Weille

The University of Alabama Press
Tuscaloosa and London

Library of Congress Cataloging-in-Publication Data

Rachlin, Rachel, 1908–
  Sixteen years in Siberia.

  Translation of: 16 år i Sibirien.
  Includes index.
  1. Rachlin, Rachel, 1908–   . 2. Rachlin, Israel, 1906–   . 3. Jews—
Soviet Union—Siberia—Biography. 4. Siberia—Biography. I. Rachlin,
Israel, 1906–   . II. Title.
DS135.R95A15813   1988   947′.004924022   86-25096
ISBN 0-8173-0357-X

British Library Cataloguing-in-Publication data available

Contents

v

Illustrations

Foreword

The historian Kliuchevsky writes that "the state swelled up, the people grew lean" to describe Stalinism, and indeed, thus did Stalin's Russia swallow up thousands of Lithuanians. But the phenomenon is not just a Stalinist one, and the day-to-day experience described in these memoirs are only meant to be a single, poignantly human lesson in how governments worldwide thoughtlessly manipulate the fates of human beings.

In April of 1939, Britain, France, and the Soviet Union began negotiations for a mutual alliance to halt the advance of Germany in Eastern Europe. Realizing that the British and French guarantees to Poland were meaningless as a deterrent without its active support to the east, the Soviet Union demanded in return the right to actively counter direct and indirect German aggression in the countries along its border. Although Britain and France were given the same rights in many Western nations, they feared that the Soviet Union's loose interpretation of "indirect aggression" would enable it to use the most feeble pretext to subjugate its neighbors. Negotiations dragged on without success.

As its distrust of Germany grew, the USSR changed its tactics and, on August 23, 1939, signed the Molotov-Ribbentrop Nonaggression Pact. Of practical importance was the "secret additional protocol," which declared that "on the occasion of the signature of the Nonaggression Pact between the German Reich and the USSR, the undersigned plenipotentiaries of each of the two parties discussed in strictly confidential conversations the question of the boundary of their respective spheres of influence in Eastern Europe." The document essentially stipulated the division of Poland and the Baltic areas.

What of Lithuania? Openly cynical, the two major powers made little effort to conceal that this small Baltic nation, coveted by the Soviet Union, had come to be a mere pawn during the course of their negotiations. From the sixteenth to the eighteenth centuries, Russia had sought to conquer Lithuania. Upon its success at the end of the eighteenth century, it started a campaign to denationalize the Lithuanian people, but its efforts were cut short by the independence of their country after World War I.

To realize its long-standing interest in and to secure its position in Lithuania, the Soviet Union was therefore quick to take advantage of the German agreement, without which it would not have dared to move against the Baltic States. On October 10, 1939, the USSR presented Lithuania with a list of the penalties it would incur by refusing to enter into a "mutual assistance" pact that would permit the Soviets to construct air bases and station soldiers in Lithuanian territory. Then, in late May of 1940, with Germany safely engaged in Western Europe, the Soviet Union launched its full-scale plan to incorporate Lithuania. It falsely accused the Lithuanian government of abducting Russian soldiers as well as entering into a secret military alliance with Latvia and Estonia against the USSR and, on June 14, presented the Lithuanian foreign minister with an ultimatum expiring nine hours later.

The Lithuanian government proved incapable of establishing, as demanded, a new regime deemed "acceptable" by Moscow, and the Soviets invaded the country by noon the next day. According to custom, a pretense of elections was made, while in reality the Soviet Union began a reign of terror to crush the people's spirit. Of "great political importance" were such measures as the mass deportation of "anti-Soviet elements," which had been planned even as the Mutual Assistance Pact with Lithuania was being signed, and on June 7, 1941, a week before the ultimatum, detailed step-by-step instructions (see Appendix to Foreword) were received in Lithuania. From June 14 to June 22 of that year, 34,260 Lithuanians, including many Jews, were silently and efficiently sent to Siberia.

*   *   *

It was June 14, 1941. Before they could answer the knock at their door, it was flung open, and three officers of the well-known Soviet security police stood before them. Minutes later, they found themselves perched on top of 220 pounds of luggage in the back of an open truck. Their five-year-old son was fetched from a nearby farm. They couldn't help smiling as their little boy marched toward them, his suitcase in hand, between the two big men with their loaded guns. They told him that they were going for a long pleasure ride, with the armed men protecting them against robbers along the way.

From June 1941 to July 1957, the Rachlin family lived in exile in Siberia . . .

Birgitte de Weille
McLean, Virginia

Sixteen Years
in Siberia

Introduction

Israel

Don't try to find the town of Kybartai on the map, for you won't find it, not even in a large atlas. You may, however, find the town of Virbalis, which is actually the same thing as Kybartai. In the latter half of the nineteenth century, a railroad was built to connect St. Petersburg with Western Europe. Virbalis was the village located closest to the point where the railroad would be crossing the border, and the frontier station was thus given the names *Virbalis* in Lithuanian, *Virballen* in German, and *Verzhbolovo* in Russian. Kybartai was merely a small collection of houses near the new station. In the course of time, Kybartai grew into a small town of around seven thousand inhabitants. It was located approximately a thousand feet from the Virbalis railroad station, and the distance to the German border on the other side was not much longer.

I was born in Kybartai on December 26, 1906. My early childhood memories are bright and happy. I grew up in a sheltered home, the object of my parents' constant attention and love. With his two brothers, my father carried on an export business, originally founded by his father. They bought horses and resold them to various countries for use as draft horses or for slaughtering. Their firm was well established, and horse dealing was profitable business at the time. My father was a well-known and highly respected man in the area and had been given the title of "merchant of the first guild," an honor rarely bestowed upon a man of Jewish background in czarist Russia.

The three of us often traveled to various European health resorts, where we would spend long periods of time. One of the first ones that I remember was a health resort called Cranz on the Baltic, approximately

1

Rachel and Israel Rachlin

thirty-one miles from Königsberg, the capital of former East Prussia. I was probably four years old, and we spent the entire summer in Cranz, from which time I remember long strolls along beautiful white beaches, handsome cane chairs lined up in straight rows, happy people in cafés, and shrill voices and laughter, which still resound in my ears. There was also a large park in the neighborhood where we would go for walks, often coming across a pair of storks sitting on the roof of a house. As soon as I caught sight of them, I would start reciting a nursery rhyme my mother had taught me. It ran like this:

Storch, Storch Bester   Stork, dear stork
Bring mir eine Schwester! Please bring me a sister!

The storks got to hear the nursery rhyme each time I passed the house, for I wanted very much a little sister, and my mother a daughter, but she was not able to have any more children. Many years later I learned that this was one of the reasons we traveled to the various European health resorts. However, neither the storks in Cranz nor our stays at the health resorts helped—I never got a little sister and remained an only child.

In 1913, my mother took me to Franzensbad, a health resort in Austria which is now located in Czechoslovakia. A few weeks after our return to Kybartai, I became ill. Our family physician, who was summoned immediately, realized right away that I was seriously ill and ordered me to be taken to Königsberg, where I was admitted to a private children's clinic under a professor by the name of Theodor.

The doctors soon found out that I had polio, and a long and exhausting stay at the clinic followed, involving intensive treatments and retraining of my muscles. After ten endless months, I had progressed sufficiently to be able to move around without a cane. Still, I was hardly capable of walking much on my own and was therefore given every other day a ride all around town in an open horse-drawn cab. The ride lasted for about an hour and provided a most welcome distraction from my otherwise rather dull and uneventful life at the clinic.

As a result of the disease, I developed myasthenia in both of my legs from the knees down, a handicap that was to last me for the rest of my life. No other muscles were affected. The doctors felt that I should spend some time at a health resort by the name of Wiesbaden in order to strengthen my leg muscles. My mother, who was very keen on health resorts, needed no persuasion, and we took off for Wiesbaden, where

2

we booked into the fashionable hotel of Schwarzer Bock, which offered various treatments on the premises.

Our stay in Wiesbaden was followed by after-treatments at a health resort by the name of Bad Kudowa. Here, we booked into the Fürstenhof Hotel and were shortly afterward joined by Uncle Eliyas's wife and their two children. My cousins were somewhat younger than I. Nevertheless, we were able to play together quite happily, and during this period of time my health improved to such an extent that I was from then on able to lead an almost entirely normal life.

Our peaceful and happy life, however, came to an abrupt end. On the morning of August 1, 1914, the porter at the hotel told us that Germany and Russia were now at war with one another and that we would no longer be able to stay at the hotel. As Russian citizens we had two possibilities. We could either leave Germany within twenty-four hours and travel to a third country, or we could remain in Germany and become civilian prisoners of war. My mother and my aunt decided to leave Germany and to go to Denmark, where my father had many business connections.

In Copenhagen lived a man by the name of Christian Westergaard, whose father, Peter Westergaard, had begun importing horses to Denmark from Russia in 1903. My grandfather was Peter Westergaard's supplier of horses, and my father and Christian Westergaard now carried on the business as the second generation of horse dealers.

The business flourished, for Russian ponies were in great demand in Denmark. The cost of two Russian ponies was nearly the same as that of one large Danish horse. Many smallholders, small businessmen, and artisans found it more practical having two small horses, which might be used both for work on the farm and for transport in general. Later on, when Denmark started importing Lithuanian ponies, these horses were given the name of cement horses, since Lithuania had committed itself to purchasing Danish cement in exchange for horses.

After a long and strenuous trip via Berlin, Warnemünde, and Gedser, we arrived in Copenhagen, a peaceful and beautiful city that came to play a very important part in my life.

My mother and aunt were busy making all the arrangements for our return to Russia. Most of the time we three children were left behind in the hotel with one of the chambermaids, but whenever my mother and my aunt had a free moment, they would take us sight-seeing. I vividly recall my first visit to a museum. It was an art museum, the Glyptothek, and it made a great impression on me. After approximately four weeks, all of the practical matters had been arranged and we were able to leave Copenhagen.

We traveled to Helsinki via Stockholm and Åbo, and from Helsinki we immediately proceeded to Petrograd, the new name for St. Petersburg. It was simply unacceptable that Russia's capital have a name containing the German word *burg*, and it had therefore been replaced by *grad*, the ancient Russian word for "town." In Petrograd, we were received by my father, and after a day of rest, we continued to the town of Penza, which was located about 435 miles to the southeast of Moscow. At the time, Penza had approximately seventy thousand inhabitants and served as the headquarters of the governor, a powerful person in the administration of czarist Russia. However, it was not the governor who was to play any role in my life during our stay in Penza. Irina Yakovlevna, my first teacher, and a girl by the name of Raya were to become much more important to me.

I had not been able to get any schooling at the clinic in Königsberg, nor during the subsequent period, and to make up for lost time, I now had to be privately tutored. I remember Irina Yakovlevna as a very competent teacher and an unusually friendly and fine person. I had been brought up speaking three languages, German, Russian, and Lithuanian, and spoke the first two quite fluently. Learning to read was no problem to me, and under the expert guidance of Irina Yakovlevna, I soon became familiar with the various subjects and enjoyed hearing about and learning all of the new and exciting things.

I met Raya and her elder sister when we moved into a room rented by their father, Mr. Novak, who was well-to-do and owned an estate in Penza. Raya and I soon became close friends, and even if she was three years older than I, we were entirely on the same wavelength and grew very fond of each other. In meeting Raya, my dream of a sister was fulfilled, and she regarded me as her little brother. Raya would read to me, and we always played together, indoors and outdoors, and went for rides in a sleigh. The horse pulling the sleigh was good-natured, and on occasion, I was allowed to hold the reins and go for rides without the coachman. I can still recall the happiness I felt in those moments and how Raya would laugh with excitement, anxiously pressing close to me when the horse would suddenly go too fast.

My mother was still keenly interested in spas, and in the spring of 1915, she decided that we should go to a health resort to strengthen my muscles. In the vicinity of the Ukrainian town of Kharkov was a health resort by the name of Slavyansk, which was famous for its mineral springs. I was very sorry to leave Penza, but since there was nothing to do about it, I sadly took leave of Raya.

Our stay in Slavyansk became brief and dramatic. The local doctor was of the opinion that my health could be vastly improved, and he prescribed mineral baths for me, the temperature of which was to be lowered by one degree every day. The doctor in Königsberg had told my mother that, on no account, was I to have cold baths. However, for some reason or other, she trusted the doctor in Slavyansk, and the result was that, after a few days of treatment, I had a relapse and became ill anew. I was taken to a clinic in Kharkov, where I remained for a whole year. I was fortunate, however, for the doctors managed to get me so well that my condition after the relapse was no worse than before. I was the only child in the entire clinic, and I remember the long stay at the clinic as an extremely sad and lonely period of my life.

At the time, we no longer had any permanent residence. Father was not able to get an apartment in Penza and traveled around a lot by himself. Expecting the war to be over soon, my parents decided to go to the Caucasus and remain there until peace was restored. The Caucasus had a mild and healthy climate and many tourist hotels and pensions where we could stay. We went to Kislovodsk and booked into the Grand Hotel, the best hotel in town.

When we had stayed at the hotel for about four weeks, my mother was suddenly informed that the Caucasus was located outside the area in which Jews were permitted to live. Being married to a merchant, she was exempt from these regulations, along with merchants, university graduates, and a few other privileged Jews and their wives. I had no right to remain, however, and we were thus forced to leave the area. The manager of the hotel wanted to help us and recommended a pension whose owner was on friendly terms with the local chief of police. For a small extra charge I was allowed to stay at the pension, and everything was in order.

I was again the only child around and had no other children with whom to play. I nevertheless enjoyed my stay in the beautiful surroundings. We went for many walks, admiring the mountains and the splendid views.

The repercussions of the February revolution in 1917 were felt even in Kislovodsk. New guests arrived at the pension—they were political prisoners who had been released and whom the new government had sent there to recover. The police force in Kislovodsk was dissolved, and its tasks were taken over by senior and junior students at the secondary school. I remember finding it very exciting to watch the young students in their secondary school uniforms patrolling the streets, red bands around their arms and holsters dangling at their sides.

On the first of May, I saw a huge demonstration in town, attended by many people from the mountains. They arrived in their picturesque national costumes on the backs of beautiful, fiery horses.

My uncle Eliyas had in the meantime moved to the town of Yekaterinoslav, and he now wrote us saying that we could have an apartment in the same building in which he and his family were staying. In June of 1917, we therefore moved to Yekaterinoslav, where, after three years without a home, we finally got a proper apartment and I got my own room.

Yekaterinoslav, which was later renamed Dnepropetrovsk, was a fairly large town with much industry. The town is located on the river Dnepr, and I remember it as a town of broad streets and large parks. The four years that we spent there were eventful and fairly dramatic. Seventeen different regimes replaced one another in rapid succession during our stay in the town. During the German occupation of the Ukraine, we lived for some time under German military rule. The town was controlled by several Ukrainian nationalist leaders, among them Petlyura and Skoropadskiy. For a short period of time, the town was the headquarters of the anarchist leader Makhno, and, finally, the town was alternately occupied by White and Red Forces. We suffered regardless of who ruled the town. The White Forces were often hostile to Jews and persecuted them, and the Red Forces were hostile to the well-to-do, and we could not expect anything good from either side. When they fought for the town, we invariably hoped that the fighting would go on for a long time, for while it went on, nobody had the time to come and rob us.

In December of 1919, just as we were beginning to celebrate my bar mitzvah, we were forced to take shelter in the basement of the building, because the fighting was going on very close to us, and the basement was the safest place in which to hide from stray bullets.

When one of the fighting sides had captured the town, the soldiers were often allowed to help themselves to the clothing of the inhabitants of the town, but they were allowed to do so only during the first three days after the capture. This probably provided an excellent incentive for the soldiers to fight, but it was hardly too pleasant for us who lived in the town. Fortunately, the soldiers were punished if they continued their looting after the lapse of the three-day period. One day, on my way home from school, I witnessed a soldier being punished in the middle of the street for having violated the regulations governing this rather special way of securing food supplies and clothing. He came out of a house, a bundle of clothing under his arm, and ran straight into a military patrol. After a short examination, the officer decided to punish the soldier on the spot: his pants were pulled down, and he received twenty-five lashes with a leather belt on his naked behind.

Civil war raged, the battles swayed to and fro around Yekaterinoslav, and during those years I witnessed many horrors. I saw people hanging from lampposts, and it was not unusual to see the dead bodies of people who had been shot lying abandoned in the streets.

The school which I attended was changed into a Soviet school after the Soviet takeover. The grades were called groups, for there could be no class division in a classless society, and we were all to be brought up in the new Soviet spirit. For example, we were told that we would always have to be alert and watchful, and if we noticed anything suspicious, even if it concerned the conduct of our parents, we should report it immediately to the school.

One day I became seriously wounded. It did not happen in street fighting, however, but in a fight for our daily bread ration. My mother had sent me out to buy bread, but when I reached the shop there was a long queue, with only ten people being admitted at a time. After having waited in the queue for a long time, I had finally reached the door and was thus in the group to be admitted next, when suddenly somebody shouted from within the shop that we might as well all go home, for there was no more bread left. The people who had been waiting became furious and broke into the shop. It did not take long for the pressure from the agitated crowd to crush a pane of glass in the door of the shop. I was standing right next to it, and a large piece of glass grazed my hand, cutting a deep wound in my thumb. I put my handkerchief over the bleeding wound, holding it tight with the other hand, while I did my best to get out of the witches' cauldron in which I had landed. With great difficulty I managed to elbow my way through the crowd and hurried to a camp hospital located close to the bakery. On my arrival, I was told that they were unable to treat me, as the camp hospital was for the military only. On my way out, however, I bumped into a nurse who felt sorry for me and took me with her into one of the treatment rooms. Although she was very nice and only meant well, she gave me a veritable military treatment. Before applying the bandage to my thumb, she poured a large amount of iodine onto the wound. My knees became wobbly, and I nearly fainted. I probably looked quite miserable, for the nurse dared not allow me to walk home alone, asking a soldier to accompany me. My mother took fright at seeing me with the large bandage and accompanied by a soldier. She soon calmed down when she heard what had happened, but she was sorry that my shopping trip had taken such a dramatic turn. A long, distinct scar on my thumb will forever remind me of Yekaterinoslav and my unfortunate shopping trip.

In 1921, the Soviet Union and Lithuania, which, in the meantime, had become an independent state like the other two Baltic States, entered into an agreement that allowed all those who had been living in Lithuanian territory to apply for Lithuanian citizenship and return to that country. My parents immediately decided to go back, but it took several months for all of the arrangements to be made. We sold all of our furniture, for we were only allowed to take soft things with us, and of these only a limited quantity. However, the trip home was free, on a train consisting of cattle wagons with space for twenty to twenty-four people in each wagon. Uncle Eliyas and his family traveled with us. We had to provide our own food on the way, and that was not easy, for famine prevailed in large parts of the country. Although the distance was not too long, the journey took two weeks because of lack of fuel for the locomotive and because of the chaotic conditions prevailing throughout the railroad system. The train would stop for long periods at a time, waiting either for fuel or for permission to proceed.

It was a difficult and strenuous journey, and although it was hard to tell what awaited us in Lithuania, we all looked forward to getting back. My father worried especially about the question of how to rebuild his business after all the things that had happened in the intervening years and without the necessary capital. As soon as we got into Latvia, we were met by people from the Red Cross who fed us and tended the sick. All the children were given hot chocolate and buns—things we had not seen for years. On reaching the Lithuanian border town of Obeliai, we were all delayed for several days in quarantine, while the Lithuanian authorities subjected us to thorough medical examinations and scrutinized our papers, asking us detailed questions such as where we originally came from in Lithuania and what our connection with Lithuania was. The Lithuanian authorities wanted to be certain of only admitting people who had the right to live in Lithuania, and they were probably also afraid that Soviet agents might infiltrate the country by pretending to be former citizens of Lithuania.

When we finally arrived at Kybartai, many of our friends and acquaintances were at the station to meet us. We were one of the last families in the town to come back after the war.

Many of the homes in Kybartai had not yet been rebuilt after the war, and it proved difficult finding an apartment. At first we had to move into a small two-bedroom apartment with Uncle Eliyas and his family. It took a whole year before we found another and better apartment for ourselves.

My father's worries about his business soon proved to be entirely unfounded. In a very short time he managed to rebuild his firm, and with the help of good friends, he began to carry on his import-export business anew. The economic recovery continued, and after some time we were again able to live under secure and orderly economic conditions.

Another major change was in store for me: I was to enter secondary school. As there was none in Kybartai, my parents decided to send me to a German school. After twelve months of preparation and tutoring, I was admitted as an *Untertertianer*, a student in his fourth year in the German secondary school, in the town of Stalupöhnen, which was located about seven miles from the border town of Eydtkuhnen.

The way to school was long and rather difficult. First, I had to cross the border and walk a little over a mile to Eydtkuhnen, where I had to take the train to Stalupöhnen, a distance of nearly seven miles farther. I would leave at 6:30 in the morning and would never get back until around four o'clock in the afternoon. Nor was it an easy transition changing from a Soviet school to a German secondary school, where they had entirely different ideals and objectives in their instruction. Many of the students at the secondary-school level were the sons of wealthy landowners and belonged to the Prussian nobility.

After finishing secondary school, I was to continue my studies at an institute of higher learning in Germany. I decided to study economics at the University of Leipzig.

I was to live alone for the first time in my life. My parents gave me 175 marks to cover my living expenditures during my studies, and my mother, who was an austere lady, pointed out to me that my allowance would never be raised and that I was not to expect any additional allowance to cover unforeseen expenditures. During my years of study, I never received more than the 175 marks per month.

In the summer of 1932, I passed my final exams and left Leipzig, where I probably spent the most carefree years of my entire life and where I made many good friends, male and female.

It was my dream to continue my studies and become a journalist, specializing in economics, but that dream was never to come true. My father became seriously ill and asked me to return home to work in his business. I could not refuse him and returned to Kybartai immediately. That is how Kybartai came to get its first and possibly only horse dealer with a university background.

My job was what would today be described as that of sales manager, and I was very much involved with the various state organizations and committees that supervised Lithuanian export firms. I often had to go abroad to deal with customers and thus traveled rather widely in Europe. Denmark was one of the countries with which we did a lot of business, and I therefore visited it several times a year.

I arrived in Copenhagen on a regular business trip in May of 1934. As usual, I took a room in the Terminus Hotel, which was located across from the central railroad station. As always, I immediately started contacting our various customers. A couple of days after my arrival, I met with a customer who introduced me to his son Georg, who was a couple of years my junior. Georg, who was studying law at the University of Copenhagen and spoke German fluently, suggested that we go out that evening together and enjoy ourselves. I readily accepted his offer, and when we met in the evening, he suggested that we go to Tivoli, which we did . . .

Rachel

My childhood and adolescence were not as stormy and not nearly as dramatic as Israel's. Fate willed it that I be born in England in the town of Liverpool, where my twin brother, Eyzik, and I were born in 1908. Nevertheless, I consider Copenhagen my native town, for we were only eight months old when we arrived.

I never knew my father—he died shortly after we were born, leaving my mother alone with two infants. My parents had come to England from Russia a couple of years before. My mother told me later on that they had been forced to leave because my father had been politically active and had been constantly persecuted and harassed by the czarist authorities. It may also well be that they left Russia on account of the pogroms that ravaged Russia during those years, forcing many Jews to emigrate to the United States and Europe.

After my father's death, my mother was unable to manage on her own in a foreign country and decided to go to Copenhagen, where she had a brother who promised to help her find work and a place to live, and with her two infants, she thus left for Denmark to start a new life.

Since my mother was a skilled dressmaker, it did not take her very long to find work. Still, it was not easy for her to manage as a single parent, for in those years there was no such thing as social welfare or unemployment benefits. In 1910, my mother remarried. By that marriage she had three children, so that, in the course of the years, our family grew to comprise seven members.

Some of my earliest childhood memories go back to our home on Ryesgade, where we lived for many years. We lived in straitened circumstances in a one-bedroom apartment on the fourth floor of a backyard tenement building, and our privy was down in the yard. Mother was not employed outside the home during those years but worked at home as a seamstress for various ladies' garment manufacturers, including Moresco, for which she worked for many years. However, they did not always have work for her, and when things became really difficult, she would gather together various things we could do without and ask us to take them down to the pawnbroker's office, which was located in the same tenement building. Although we were badly off, Mother always saw to it that our apartment was nice and clean and that we had all the things we needed.

Every morning my stepfather would go to the Hansen Bakery on Blegdamsvej and come back with a basket full of old bread. We children were always eager to find out what the basket contained, and we loved to munch on the bread.

One image that will always remain fixed in my memory is that of my mother working at her sewing machine from early morning till late in the evening. Sometimes she would sing some of her sad Yiddish songs, which we loved to hear. My mother was a talented storyteller, and she liked to talk about the happy days of her youth in the small town of Drissa in White Russia. The town was not far from Vitebsk, which is now world famous as the native town of Chagall. My mother is said to have been asked at a party once whether she knew Chagall. She answered quickly: "No, I did not, but I am certain that he knew me, for I was the prettiest girl in town."

Like everybody else, my brother Eyzik and I started school at the age of seven. We attended the Ryesgade School, where I remained for three years. One day I decided to go to the Jewish school, the Caroline School, located on Prinsesse Charlottesgade, to ask for admission; it was an idea that had occurred to me all of a sudden, but I was determined to change schools and was in fact admitted to the Caroline School.

I attracted quite a lot of attention when I arrived at the Caroline School, for I was wearing clogs: these were not considered proper, and none of the other girls wore them. One of the teachers told me that if I wanted to attend the school, I would have to exchange my clogs for a more proper pair of shoes. When I began at the Caroline School, my parents saw to it that I got a pair of real leather shoes, even though it was a heavy expense for them. I became very happy with that school and grew to like my teachers very much. They were excellent teachers and nice people, although they demanded a lot of us. The things I learned at the time I learned for life, and I remember the school and my teachers with much gratitude and happiness. I still recollect several of my teachers vividly. One of them was Mr. Sørensen. He taught us handwriting. He was a very good teacher, and all of his students learned to write beautifully. One day he was wearing a handsome suit, which he normally did not wear, and we girls naturally became curious and asked him why he was thus dressed. "I shall tell you why, my dear friends," he answered. "Today is December 21, which is the shortest day of the year, and my nice suit will not become as worn as it would on other days."

Hardworking and smart students got A's on their report cards, and I often managed to come home with those much-coveted A's. My school years were wonderful, and I recall them as carefree, happy, and bright.

I had many friends during my school years and often visited several of them after school. One was a girl by the name of Lise. Her parents were well-to-do, and she took piano lessons. I would occasionally accompany her home after school and would then sit for hours listening to her play the piano. I dreamed of one day getting the opportunity to play the piano myself, but that, of course, was an expense my parents could not afford, and my dream was never to come true.

When I finished school, I wanted to become a nurse. At the time, however, one had to be twenty-one to start the training. I was not able to wait such a long time, for I had to get a job and make money in order to help my parents make ends meet and earn my own pocket money. I therefore started working in an office. Both of my parents were quite strict, and I was not allowed to go out much until I reached the age of twenty. A trip to the movies was a major event. However, I had the opportunity to read a lot of books both in Danish and German, and in this way I learned much about the world outside Ryesgade and Copenhagen.

Introduction

The year 1930 saw an improvement in the financial circumstances of my parents, one of the reasons being that we children now had all reached the age where we were able to start helping them earn money. In that year we moved to a much better and bigger apartment on Amager. Though we had all become adults, none of us thought of moving away from home. We had a wonderful time together and felt no need to do so.

At the age of twenty-one, I went abroad for the first time. My mother's younger sister Sima and her husband lived in Berlin. They invited me to come and visit them, and I went. It was a wonderful experience for me. At the time it was still quite unusual for a young girl to travel abroad on her own, and I was very proud that I was able to do it. The German language presented no problem to me, and I met a lot of interesting people. Many people took me out, and I got to know Berlin as a wonderful city with a great many opportunities to offer its inhabitants. In the course of the next few years, I visited Berlin several times and gradually came to speak German fluently. I had made many friends in Berlin and enjoyed myself each time I visited the city. My good knowledge of German became useful to me in later years.

In May of 1934, my sister Lea told me that she was going to Tivoli to meet some of her friends. She asked me if I would like to come along, and although I did not feel much like going out, Lea managed to persuade me, and we left . . .

Israel

We met in Tivoli that night, for Georg and Lea knew each other and had arranged to meet. In this way I was introduced to Rachel, a beautiful, young woman who spoke excellent German. However, it was not merely her knowledge of German that impressed me, even though it meant that I no longer needed Georg as my guide: Rachel took over the role as my companion, not just in Tivoli but for the rest of my life. I believe that it is safe to say that it was love at first sight, and I was sad to leave Copenhagen a few days later to continue my business trip to Czechoslovakia. I did not get much out of that business trip, for I could only think of Rachel and only wanted to see her again as soon as possible.

As soon as I had finished my business in Prague, I returned to Lithuania but traveled via Copenhagen to see Rachel. We again spent some days together, and at my departure I suggested to Rachel that she come and visit us in Kybartai to see what life was like in a small Lithuanian border town. She declined since it was not proper—young women did not visit men in those days. Instead, we began writing each other frequently. I took every opportunity to get to Copenhagen and made quite a few trips to that city in the course of 1934. At the end of the year, we decided to get married the next spring.

In May of 1935, we were married in the synagogue of Copenhagen, and two days later we went on a honeymoon to the capitals of Europe, visiting Berlin, Brussels, and Paris. It might have been possible to spend one's honeymoon in a somewhat more serene atmosphere, but when one is young, newly married, and in love, I suppose that every place is right. This was the first of many trips that we were to take together in the years to come.

On our return to Kybartai, we moved into the house where I had been living with my mother since my father's death the previous year. Rachel and I got a couple of rooms to ourselves and shared the rest of the house with my mother. I had now become the head of the firm and was busy managing its daily operation. The business was doing well, and in 1936, I expanded it by becoming the joint owner of a flax-processing plant. This proved a good decision, for the business flourished. In 1936, Rachel gave birth to our first child, Schneur. We were happy and enjoyed life fully. The early years of our married life were marked by many trips and vacations abroad, the company of good friends from far and near, and domestic bliss. Unfortunately, this situation was not to last very long. Five years later, Lithuania became a Soviet republic like the two other Baltic States, and our lives changed drastically. All of our private property was immediately nationalized, and after a while I was given the job of economic planner at a factory. We were forced to move out of our house and were given a small apartment, where we remained until the next upheavals caught up with us.

Rachel

Although moving to Kybartai was a major change for me, I soon adjusted. Everybody was extremely kind and friendly to me and made every effort to make me feel at home. It had been a rather big transition for me to leave Copenhagen and settle down in the small border town, but the change from the modest circumstances I was used to in Copenhagen to the well-to-do home with entirely different habits and customs was an equally large transition. I was now the young mistress of the household, and it was somewhat difficult for me to get used to the idea of having a maid and a cook to attend to all of the domestic work.

I started helping Israel in his office, handling all of his correspondence with Denmark and otherwise trying to lend him a hand wherever possible. I often joined him on business trips, and we made several trips together to Denmark.

Around 1938, we really began to feel the unrest that was spreading all over Europe. Many Jewish emigrants started arriving in Lithuania from Germany, and a major relief effort was launched. We put up several of the refugees and listened with alarm to their disquieting reports on the developments in Germany.

I had close contact with my family in Denmark. We wrote and called one another often, and through *Politiken*, which I received daily, I was able to keep abreast of events in Denmark.

In July of 1939, we went to Scandinavia on vacation. We first went to Denmark, where we spent approximately one week with my family. From Denmark we went to Sweden, where we spent a lovely vacation in Rättvik in Dalarna. The situation in Europe did not look good at all, and we decided to remain in Sweden and await the outcome. We went to Göteborg, where we stayed with my sister Doba till early November. At the time, Israel felt that it would still be possible for us to go back to Lithuania. Israel's mother kept writing and calling him, asking him to return home to attend to the business. There was an unusually large amount of work to be done, the business was doing extremely well, and she was unable to cope with all of the work on her own. Having tried in vain to convince Israel that the best thing would be to remain in Sweden until the situation in the world had become more settled, I reluctantly agreed to go back to Lithuania with him, and on November 9, we boarded a ferry in Stockholm for Riga. During the entire voyage I felt extremely unhappy and could not help crying because I had the strong feeling that we were about to commit a fatal mistake. From Riga we took the train to Kybartai.

My forebodings proved correct. After a while the Soviet Union began to set up bases in Lithuanian territory. Lithuania soon became a Soviet republic, and then one dramatic event followed another in rapid succession. In September of 1940, Harrietta was born, one of the few happy events amid all of the misfortune which then befell us. We had been forced to move to a small apartment, and our only desire was to be left alone. They did not leave us alone for very long.

1

————•••————

Rachel · Israel

During the days following the Soviet occupation of Lithuania in 1940, we felt that we had been shut up in a small corner of the world and that powerful forces had been released over which we had not the least influence. We were but small, insignificant pawns, and around us war raged and the world was ablaze. In our situation there was nothing for us to do but to watch events and wait for them to catch up with us in one way or another.

Leaving Lithuania at the time was entirely out of the question. The Nazis were advancing on all of Europe. To the east was the enormous Soviet Union, which was as closed and inaccessible to us as the Europe that was ablaze. The Russians, moreover, had immediately and hermetically sealed off their country, and now only birds had the privilege of moving freely across the borders.

World events took their course, leaving behind a bloody trail of death and destruction. We had been cut off from the rest of the world and were no longer able to correspond with our relatives and friends in Denmark or other countries, and we would not have known anything about what was going on in the world if it had not been for the British Broadcasting Corporation.

Although the world was in disarray and pandemonium seemed to reign supreme, the BBC kept working without fail to provide us and millions of other people around the world with up-to-date news on the situation in our unsettled world. The BBC rescued us from isolation during that period, since we invariably listened to its newscast every night.

On June 13, 1941, we had, as usual, tuned in to the evening newscast. In his usual, matter-of-fact manner, the speaker announced that Germany was in the process of concentrating large forces along its borders to the east. We went to bed full of vague misgivings, not realizing exactly how the news of the German troop movements would affect our lives.

The next morning at around seven o'clock we were abruptly awakened by a hard knocking on our door. It was an ominous sound, and we opened the door reluctantly. Outside the door was Dina Bernike, the daughter of our close friends, a pretty, dark-haired girl of seventeen. Dina looked frightened out of her wits. She was red-eyed with weeping, and her hair was completely disheveled. She had been running and was breathing heavily.

"They have taken all of them," she said as soon as she got inside the door. She cried, and gasping for air, she told us in brief fragments that her parents had been picked up by the Russians and taken away on a truck. The only thing the Russians had told them was that they should take warm clothing along.

Dina asked in despair if we knew anything about it, whether it might mean that her parents were to be sent to Siberia. We knew just as little as she but had to admit that she probably assumed correctly.

Dina herself had not been taken along with her parents because she had been born in her mother's first marriage and therefore had a different last name than the rest of the family.

This is the way that long day began. But life had to go on despite the alarming news. Israel made himself ready to go to work. He had been working for some time at the "Labor" factory, which was then owned by the state like all other Lithuanian enterprises. The former owners were German, and like all other Germans, they had been repatriated to Germany after the Soviet occupation of Lithuania. The new management needed people with a good knowledge of Russian, and Israel had been given the position of economist at the factory.

However, before taking off for work, he wanted to check with our neighbors, the Telits, to see if they had heard anything.

He left the house, and a few minutes later there was another knock at the door. But before any of us managed to get to the door, it was opened from the outside, and three officers of the NKVD security police, wearing their well-known uniforms, entered. They were accompanied by a civilian. Later on, we discovered that the civilian was a member of the district committee of the Communist Party in the town of Vilkaviškis. From the very start he appeared particularly tense, and he was both aggressive and provocative in the way he spoke to us.

We immediately realized that it was now our turn, and that we would have to go through the same process that the Bernike family had gone through earlier in the morning.

When Israel returned from the Telits, he was ordered to stand facing the wall while one of the NKVD officers searched his body. Meanwhile, the rest of us had to stand with our hands up. Mrs. Telit had entered the house with Israel, but when she saw what was going on, she wanted to leave immediately. But she was ordered to remain where she was until all of us had left the house. The NKVD officers clearly were not interested in having too many people know about their action, since it might give rise to disturbances and panic or simply give people the chance to prepare some sort of organized resistance. The action had to be carried through in a discreet and smooth manner.

After a short while, the NKVD officers began a thorough search of the house. Everything was turned upside down, examined, and ransacked. Handles were removed from doors and drawers, pillows and cushions were felt and squeezed. Nothing was left to chance, and it soon became clear to us that the people searching our home were skilled and practiced.

It was the first time that our home had been subjected to a search; many such searches were to follow later on, but we never felt as humiliated and offended as we did during this first search. All of a sudden we had been deprived of control over our own affairs: our belongings no longer belonged to us, and we helplessly watched strange, unloving hands turn and examine every single object as though a bomb or at least some secret of vital importance to the state were hidden inside it.

It was not a question of the value of our things, for to us each individual object had its own significance and story—memories and experiences with which it was associated. They were all of them tangible remembrances of the life we had left behind, and which we later on were to recall with such great nostalgia and sadness.

And when the NKVD officers with their stern, arrogant faces touched these things, pushed them aside, or examined them from all angles, it felt as if we ourselves were being pawed over, body and soul.

However, the years and our experiences were to teach us that it would not do to be as sensitive as that and that one would have to dissociate oneself from such things in order to survive.

It was especially Israel's desk that attracted the attention of the NKVD officers. Everything was examined thoroughly, and each sheet of paper was read and thoroughly studied for a long time.

"Do you have any weapons?" one of them asked. That we did not have, but Israel told them that he had a Finnish sheath knife. He could not remember where he had put it, and it did not turn up during their search. Everything in our apartment was rummaged through, and while the search went on, we were not allowed to move.

When the three men had been busy for some time, Baba [Russian abbreviation of *Babushka*, "grandmother"] managed to sneak into the bedroom, where she had her jewelry. She wanted to rescue it.

The man who was in charge of the search feigned not to have seen it, but shortly afterward he dashed into the bedroom, taking Baba by complete surprise with her jewelry box in her hands. He tore the jewelry box from her, and shouting and abusing her, he demanded to know if she did not realize that she had violated their order not to move.

He threatened to arrest her, assuring her that they knew how to deal with "capitalist leftovers" of her kind.

Following that clash, the atmosphere became even more oppressed and tense. As a result of Baba's offense, she was only allowed to take a few of her personal belongings with her when, somewhat later on, we were told to pack our suitcases.

Several times the NKVD officer snatched Baba's things from her, saying, "You do not need that!"

Like the Bernikes, we were told to take warm clothing along. We were allowed to take 220 pounds with us—that was considered enough for three adults and two children.

Rachel

The children's clothes were the first things I started packing. The strange thing was that, for the last few weeks, I had had the idea that if we would have to flee from our home, I would put all of the children's clothes in a big eiderdown cover. For this reason, I somehow felt that I could cope with the situation, and I managed to get nearly all of the children's clothing into the eiderdown cover.

We had told the NKVD officers right away that our five-year-old son, Schneur, was not at home but at the farm of Israel's cousin. They promised to drive out there to pick him up when we were ready.

Before leaving the house, I asked Israel what we should do about our eight-month-old daughter Harrietta, for we were, of course, unable to take her cradle along with us. Israel answered briefly:

"Have you not seen the way Russian women swaddle their babies? You have to do the same thing."

A truck was waiting outside the house. A woman with a child was already sitting in the back. The moment for us to take leave of our home had come. We were unable to keep back our tears, but fortunately there was no time for great emotional outbursts. The NKVD officers were busy and hurried us up, shouting words which soon were to become so familiar to us: "Davay! Davay!" and "Bystrey!", which mean "Come now!" and "Hurry up!"

During the dramatic departure, I was mostly concerned with practical details—whether I had remembered the brush and the soap for Harrietta, whether I had taken Schneur's beloved toy horse, Israel's shaver, and all of the many other things I felt were essential. However, in the middle of it all, I was overcome by the thought of my family in Denmark, and I wondered what they might be doing at that moment, whether they were leading a peaceful life or whether the insane world in which we were living had also encroached upon their lives. Could they have been struck by similarly tragic events?

Naturally, I also wondered what might be ahead. When I arrived in Lithuania in 1935, I felt that I was far away from Denmark, but I now knew that I would be taken even farther away—where and for how long, probably nobody knew.

Rachel · Israel

Our suitcases and bundles were thrown into the back of an open truck, and we ourselves sat down on top of our things.

We had told them beforehand how to get to the farm, and with a jerk the truck began to move and drove off.

This is how our trip began. It was to last for the next sixteen years.

On our way to the farm we noticed people standing at their windows, concealed behind their curtains. The townspeople were frightened, for they realized that something unusual was going on. They had never before seen such a sight: trucks with suitcases and bundles of clothing and, on top of it all, men, women, and children guarded by armed NKVD officers. Many other families were picked up in the same way on that day. That June morning saw an unusually large number of military trucks in our otherwise quiet town.

Our family farm of approximately one hundred acres was run by Izi,

Israel's cousin. Izi was unmarried and had a housekeeper by the name of Manya. Schneur loved her dearly and always enjoyed staying with her on the farm. He loved the place with its many animals—horses, cows, ducks, and geese. There was always something at which to look and with which to occupy himself out on the farm.

The truck stopped approximately 350 feet from the farm. Two NKVD officers, both carrying guns, went into the farmhouse to pick up Schneur. He soon came out, carrying his small suitcase and escorted by the two armed men. Schneur did not appear to be too affected by the situation. Actually, he seems to have kept that coolness throughout his life.

However tragic our situation was, we could not help smiling when we saw our little son march along, his suitcase in hand, between those two big men with their loaded guns.

Izi did not turn up, and we realized that he, no doubt, was afraid that they would take him along as well. No one knew at the time that our tragedy was to become our salvation, whereas it was Izi who was heading for destruction. When Schneur reached us in the back of the truck, he found the whole thing very strange and asked us why we had to go on a truck, where we were going, and why the men carrying guns sat with us.

We told him that we were going for a long ride and that the men had come along to protect us against robbers. Being an innocent child, he readily accepted that explanation and found it exciting.

We went back the same way, drove through Kybartai for the last time and continued through the town of Virbalis to Vilkaviškis. We were taken directly to the railroad station, which was packed with people.

On the platform was a very long train, consisting of forty-two cattle wagons.

First, all of us were crossed off a list by a high-ranking NKVD officer, and then we were ordered to climb into one of the cattle wagons, which already seemed overcrowded. There were nine other families in the wagon—a total of twenty-three people. Including us, the last arrivals, the wagon, the area of which was approximately 225 square feet, now held twenty-eight people.

The four small flap windows at the top of the wagon admitted little light and were barred. On either side of the wagon was a sliding door—one had always been closed, and the other one was closed as soon as we were inside.

The wagons, which had been used for transport of cattle and horses in more peaceful times, had been quickly equipped with the bare necessities for the transportation of the two-legged creatures that had replaced the cattle. Shelves made of crude boards had been put up on each side of the wagon at intervals of sixty inches. These shelves were to be our beds for the next three weeks. We were fortunate when the shelves were distributed, for we were given the upper shelves where we got more fresh air from the barred windows.

All of the suitcases, boxes, and bundles were lying in a big heap in the middle of the wagon. It was impossible to avoid stepping on them, for there was hardly any space to move around in.

It was a warm, lovely summer day with a clear blue sky. What an enjoyable day it would have been if everything had been normal. But at that time we were unable to grasp the reality of our situation. People were sitting silently around the dark wagon, oppressed with despair and uncertainty about what was to come. The composition of our wagon was such that it was impossible to tell on what basis people had been selected for the deportation. It was a very mixed group, including a peasant, a policeman, and a chief pharmacist and their families.

There were also several women accompanied only by their children—immediately after arriving at the station of Vilkaviškis, their husbands had been gathered in separate groups and transferred to wagons that held only men. The wife of the mayor of Kybartai and her daughter and two nephews were also in our wagon. The mayor had been arrested a few weeks before the deportation took place.

The train remained at the platform in Vilkaviškis until June 16—it took time to gather all those who were to be included in the transport.

An elderly Jewish woman, Mrs. Bauer, who had come to Kybartai as a refugee from Germany, had been staying with us for several months prior to our deportation. She was waiting for a visa for Australia, where her children had been living for quite some time. She remained in our apartment after we had been picked up. We managed to arrange with her to send us some of our belongings once we had reached our destination.

But how naive we still were—five days after we had left Lithuanian territory, the war broke out between Germany and the Soviet Union, and on the same day, Kybartai became occupied by the Germans. Of course, we did not hear of this until much later.

The first night in the cattle wagon was long and dreadful. Harrietta was unable to fall asleep and cried most of the night on account of the heat and the suffocating air. The transition from our familiar surroundings to the filthy cattle wagon with people huddled together in the

22

small space was, indeed, an abrupt one. However, man's ability to adapt himself has been tested more severely before, and within a short time we got used to life in the cattle wagon. We were closely guarded all the time. We were not allowed to leave the wagon, and the sliding doors were not even allowed to stand slightly open. Apparently, our guards did not want others to see or get in touch with the passengers in the cattle wagons.

Our guards included many young soldiers from Armenia and other southern republics of the Soviet Union. Most of them spoke poor Russian. At one point, Israel asked one of them to open the sliding door a little for the sake of the children—it was extremely hot inside the wagon, and it was hard to breathe. The young soldier thrust his head inside the wagon and said angrily in broken Russian, "You do not want the Soviet power, but you will damned well feel it." And before he had even completed his sentence, he pulled the sliding door shut and locked it again.

Throughout the following years, these words and the soldier's brutal conduct haunted us as concrete evidence of what was happening to us. The small incident reflected all the senseless things that had already happened and heralded all the evil in the days that were before us.

What did that young soldier himself have in mind? What ideas did he have for justifying why old people, women, and small children are first forced to climb onto trucks and subsequently huddled together in cattle wagons? Did he at all reflect on what it meant, all of a sudden, to be torn away from one's peaceful everyday life and to be told that one will be deported to some distant place?

All Soviet military units have so-called *politruks*, political advisers who have been charged with the tasks of providing information on the most recent events and political developments and justifying the positions and courses of action taken by the party on specific issues.

Before the action against us and our fellow sufferers was started, the politruks might conceivably have told the soldiers that the threat posed by sections of the population opposed to the Soviet power or planning to overthrow the Soviet power had to be eliminated. Thus these hostile elements had to be deported so that they might learn to become good and loyal citizens who would support the Soviet power. The young soldier from Armenia apparently acted with this reason in mind.

The next day at the platform started in a dramatic manner. We shall never forget the events which took place when some NKVD officers with lists of names in their hands started going from one wagon to the next, calling out the names of different men. Those whose names were called out were placed in a row on the platform, while the officers continued calling out names. Many of the women cried in a heartrending manner, asking the officers to leave their men in the wagons.

Rachel

Naturally, I was terribly upset myself when I realized what was going on. One of the officers approached our wagon. With my heart in my mouth, I asked Israel what we should do if he was also removed from our wagon and separated from us. He tried to calm me, saying that it was not certain that all of the men would be separated from their wives. This, alas, was but poor consolation, since an increasing number of men were being lined up on the platform.

The sight of these pale and grave men, young and old, has burned itself into my memory forever. Nobody grasped what was about to happen. The idea occurred to me that they might have been lined up to be shot before our very eyes. The things that had already happened to us appeared so incongruous that we were preparing ourselves for the worst. The officer approached our wagon, stopped, looked at his list of names, and after a moment, which seemed an eternity, went on without summoning any men from our wagon. Everybody breathed a sigh of relief—the dark hand of fear had been withdrawn.

The men who had been separated from their families were placed in other wagons, which were attached to the back of the train.

Rachel · Israel

After a stop of forty-eight hours at the station of Vilkaviškis, our journey by train toward the unknown destination finally began.

The train traveled in the direction of Kaunas. The air was thick with all kinds of rumors, but nobody had any idea where we were going, nor what would happen to us. We all knew, however, that we had a long journey ahead of us, a journey which, in all likelihood, would end somewhere in Siberia.

The question that occupied our minds, and probably the minds of

24

most people on the train, was why we, of all people, had been selected for deportation.

Deportation as a means to enforce the policies of the government had long been a tradition in Russia. In czarist Russia, people were deported to remote regions of Siberia because of their political views, their religion, or their nationality. It was a convenient way of rendering one's opponents harmless without resorting to the more drastic means of imprisonment or penal settlement. Because of its vast and sparsely populated regions, Siberia provided a most suitable place of exile.

The deportations from the three Baltic States in 1941 were undertaken for political reasons.

Such a far-reaching decision had, of course, been made at the very top level, that is, by Stalin himself, and had been approved by the highest party bodies. Its implementation and the selection of the persons and families to be deported were left to local party organizations in cooperation with the NKVD.

It is difficult to see what a smallholder, a pharmacist, a businessman, and a policeman might have in common, for on the surface they seem completely dissimilar. Still, to the Soviet regime and its various authorities, they and thousands of other people were alike in that they all represented the nonsocialist society and were therefore not to be trusted. They were deemed unreliable social elements who could most safely be rendered harmless by being removed from their familiar surroundings and transported to an entirely different environment. Nevertheless, there was no consistency in the selection, for we were deported, while Israel's cousin Izi, who had more or less the same social status, was left alone. However, Israel's many travels abroad and many foreign contacts in connection with his position in the firm probably had a great deal to do with it. Philatelists and Esperantists were apprehended and deported on the basis of such considerations.

Our deportation had been carefully planned beforehand and was carried through swiftly with the precision of a military operation. From June 14 to June 16, somewhere between thirty and forty thousand people in Lithuania were picked up at their homes by NKVD officers, transported to railroad stations, and stowed away in cattle wagons, approximately thirty people to a wagon. Similar actions were carried out in Latvia and Estonia. As we ourselves had witnessed, some of the men were separated from their families and sent directly to Siberian labor camps; those who survived were not released until eight, ten, and, in a few cases, even fifteen years later.

The surveillance of the deportees had been left to special NKVD troops. The head of the convoy appointed some kind of representative in each wagon, whose job it was to see to it that the food for the people in his wagon was fetched and distributed. It was also the task of the representative to report any outbreaks of disease among the people in his wagon, and it was his duty as well to report to the NKVD if anybody escaped from the wagon.

It is not possible to give the exact figure of the number of people who were affected by Stalin's decision to deport all unreliable elements from the Baltic States. The Soviet Union has never published any official figures, and the Soviet archives, which contain the exact figures, are hermetically closed.

On the basis of our own experience and observations, we may, however, conclude that the deportations from Lithuania comprised people from all walks of life, irrespective of their social standing, economic situation, religion, or nationality. Just about anybody might be subject to deportation. The efficient manner in which the large-scale operation was carried through required the participation of a very large number of people at various levels of preparation and implementation. One might wonder why there had not been any leaks, but this operation was to us only the first of many examples of the efficient manner in which the Soviet machinery worked when it came to actions of this kind and, in particular, when such actions were classified as secret.

The train stopped for the first time in the town of Kaunas, fifty-six miles to the east of Kybartai. Rumors had apparently spread in Kaunas that our train was on its way, for quite a few people had already gathered at the station, awaiting its arrival. Relatives and friends of people on the train had arrived at the station to take leave of those who were to be deported. There were also quite a few of Israel's friends and acquaintances whom we managed to greet and exchange a few words with. As was the case with our relatives and friends in Kybartai, this was the last time that we were to see these people.

We were the doomed ones whose fate had now been sealed, and they were the free ones, but neither their facial expressions nor the things that they said revealed it. They, too, were doomed, doomed to uncertainty, for nobody knew when it would become his turn, nor what the Soviet regime planned to do with him.

Most of them died in German concentration camps, for the Nazi holocaust took a heavy toll among the Jewish populations of the Baltic

States. The extermination of Baltic Jews in ghettos and extermination camps was carried through with cruel precision and brutality. Others remaining behind were subsequently killed in the war against the Germans.

Our own fate was actually one of the paradoxes of history.

Only much later did we realize that our deportation actually was our salvation. If we had remained in Lithuania with Israel's relatives and all of the other Jews, we would hardly have been able to avoid sharing their fate. The wilds of Siberia and all of the ordeals we were to go through in the course of the following years were to save us from certain death. It is true that the object of our deportation was not to prevent us from falling into the hands of the Germans, but the course of history nevertheless caused this to become its paradoxical consequence.

In Kaunas, a couple of extra wagons were attached to our train, and after a wait of approximately two hours, we departed.

We reached Novo-Vileyka, the last stop in Lithuania, early in the morning of June 17. On the platform, people were waiting with bread and milk for the children on the train. During our brief stop at the station, we were allowed to talk to them. All of them were total strangers, Jews and Christians, yet they all tried to comfort us and to give us as much support as they possibly could. We should not be too sad, one Jewish couple told us. We ought to be happy that we were able to leave an area that was threatened by war. If they had to escape, they would have to do so by foot, and they were convinced that they would be forced to leave in a short time. The threat of war from Germany was a real one, and once the Germans had invaded the country, nobody would be safe anywhere.

We had sensed ourselves that the war was approaching our country. A few days before our deportation we had heard German aircraft, but they were so high up that we were unable to see them. The following day we learned that air combat had taken place between German and Soviet aircraft. Two Soviet pilots had been buried in Kaunas with full military honors. According to the official Soviet report, the two pilots had been killed in action.

After Novo-Vileyka, the journey continued into a country which none of us knew and where we were to spend the next long sixteen years. The atmosphere was oppressive and marked by the uncertainty of our fate. We gradually tried to adjust to the situation and to accept it. Polotsk, Yaroslavl, Kirov, Sverdlovsk, Tyumen, and Omsk were among the many

27

towns that we passed on our way east, farther and farther into the end-less Siberian wilderness.

As is the case in all other situations of life, our life under the un-familiar cramped conditions in the cattle wagon assumed the essence of a normal everyday life, with its own rhythm, rituals, and rules.

One of the major problems in the wagon was the lack of toilet facili-ties. The problem was solved in the simplest conceivable manner by making a hole in the floor through which, with the aid of some flexibility and acrobatic maneuvers, one was able to relieve oneself. The men had the advantage of being able to relieve themselves through the doorway and, therefore, did not have to use the hole in the floor every time. It was worse for the women, however. For one thing, they were shy, and, for another, it was not at all easy to squat over the hole in the shaking and jolting train. However, we all soon overcame our shyness and got used to not only the lack of toilet facilities but also the other inconve-niences of our cattle wagon.

It may sound strange, but after a while we came to rather like our wagon. However cramped and unreasonable our conditions seemed to be, after some time the wagon became our home or shelter, shielding us from the unknown world outside, and we got the feeling that it was better and safer to remain inside the wagon than to get out into the unknown world which surrounded us on all sides.

We passed through very desolate areas—endless steppes, fields, and forests—and there were no people, no animals, no houses in sight. It was all open and empty land—vast, uninhabited, and unknown.

In passing through swampy areas, we were often attacked by swarms of mosquitoes, which penetrated into our wagon and pestered us with their bites and their nerve-racking buzzing throughout the night.

Due to the war, the train proceeded very slowly, and our journey was to become even more prolonged. On June 22, Germany attacked the Soviet Union. At the time, we had already got quite a distance into the Soviet Union, and even if the war, for that reason, did not affect us directly, our train was often stopped, and we had to wait for hours be-fore continuing. We had to give way to approaching trains, which were on their way from the eastern parts of the Soviet Union to the front. The many trains we saw on the way were all full of soldiers and military equipment. Large sections of the Trans-Siberian Railroad were single-track, and we were always the ones who had to yield to military convoys.

We were not happy about those frequent and prolonged stops on our way, for they made our difficult journey even more unbearable. As soon as the train stopped, fresh air ceased to circulate, and the heat in the wagon became intolerable. Nevertheless, we were not allowed to leave the wagon. Often the occasion was taken to provide us with food, which consisted of hot soup and sometimes only salt herring and bread.

Rachel

Harrietta's normal feeding hours were completely disrupted. I had started weaning her some time before we were sent off on our journey. I had breast-fed her only in the morning and in the evening; but now that she was lying next to me all the time, she thought she was being breast-fed continuously and became confused. It at least solved the problem of feeding her for a while, and I was no longer as dependent upon the milk that we sometimes got on the way.

The schedule of our train—if indeed there was a schedule—could not be observed under the conditions now prevailing in the country, and as a consequence, we were often awakened in the middle of the night to be fed. We were fed at the stations where food had been arranged for us, regardless of the time of day.

When we stopped at one of the "feeding stations," a soldier came up to tell us that we could go and get our food. The food was collected in three buckets. The two men who were sent for the buckets were carefully watched by the accompanying soldiers.

Once the food had been brought into the wagon, each family was given its ration of bread and soup. It was extremely important to distribute the soup evenly. Israel, who had been appointed representative for our wagon, was in charge of the distribution and fulfilled this duty to everybody's satisfaction.

The atmosphere in our wagon was somber but, for the most part, peaceful and friendly. Although we were strangers, we all displayed a willingness to help each other. We were people from entirely different walks of life and would never have met under normal conditions. Now we were forced to stay together in this wagon, to adjust and together try to cope with the hardships of the journey. Of course, frictions and minor clashes were unavoidable with so many people packed together in such little space. Usually they soon dissolved, however, and the problems were solved without any major showdowns.

Rachel and Israel Rachlin

Israel

As representative for our wagon, it was my responsibility to make sure that nobody disappeared from it. Every single day, at the first stop of the train, a soldier came up to our wagon, asking for my report on the health and presence of each individual.

The reason why I had been appointed representative was probably that there were only four male grown-ups among the twenty-eight people in the wagon, and only Isaak April and I were able to speak Russian. That is why both he and I were given various so-called representative duties.

A couple of times the train stopped at a small river, and we were allowed to get out and wash ourselves a little. Each time we considered it a real privilege, feeling as refreshed and happy as the rest of the sweaty and tired passengers on the train. Rachel took the opportunity during those brief stops to wash some of Harrietta's diapers, which she still wore even if, at this point, she had more or less become toilet trained.

Our train kept traveling eastward until we reached Novosibirsk. Here we started going south, continuing till we reached the town of Biysk. Biysk is the terminus of the southbound branch of the Trans-Siberian Railroad. At Biysk, we were allowed to get out without being guarded for the first time, but, as usual, under the accompaniment of the well-known shouts of "Bystrey! Bystrey!" We were told to gather all of our things together, and everything was taken to the railroad station. It was a strange feeling leaving our wagon, which had been our home for as long as three weeks.

Orders were given for the passengers of each wagon to stay together in their groups and not to mix with any of the others, because the passengers of the various wagons had been entered on separate lists, and "the contents" of each individual wagon had to arrive intact for distribution among the various working places awaiting our arrival.

After three strenuous weeks and thousands of miles covered at the steady beat of the wheels of the train, we had reached our first stop on our journey toward the unknown destination.

2

Rachel · Israel

It felt rather strange having firm ground under our feet again after the long stay in the cattle wagon, and we almost felt like sailors going ashore after a long voyage. As soon as we had left the wagon, several local NKVD officers appeared and began a thorough search of all of our luggage. They looked especially for valuables, our papers, and Lithuanian coins.

Nobody was allowed to be in possession of his birth certificate, degree certificates, or other personal papers. The NKVD officers were extremely thorough and efficient in their search through our many belongings. Many valuables were confiscated that day. The search lasted for several hours. Darkness fell, and it started raining, but the NKVD officers kept searching our things, and we were forced to spend the night in empty storehouses at the station.

Very early the next morning, representatives of various enterprises in the district started arriving at the station. They had come for labor and were able to pick and choose from among us to cover their needs as satisfactorily as possible.

We were lined up, each wagon separately, so that they could have a really good look at us and decide whether we would be of any use to them. It was humiliating and degrading to be examined and evaluated like a herd of cattle.

Naturally, they were primarily interested in able-bodied men and women, preferably in good health. The whole situation seemed like a slave market, and after all, that is what it probably was. It was a strange power that these people held as they walked back and forth, viewing the displayed goods with expert eyes and, with a nod or a movement of the hand, deciding where people would go and what their lives would be like in the future. As soon as they had decided whom they wanted to take along, a truck or a horse-drawn carriage arrived to take the selected workers and their families to their destinations.

Nobody wanted our wagon, and, of course, it was not for us to decide where we would be going. After a while, most of our fellow travelers had left, and the passengers of our wagon numbered among the few remaining. All of us were still standing the way we had been lined up when the selection started. It was a most unpleasant situation.

Israel

I decided to take action. We knew that the commander who had been in charge of the surveillance of our train during the entire journey was extremely fond of liquor. On the way we had often seen him get off the train even before it came to a standstill and run into the station restaurant to quench his thirst with a glass of vodka. Each time the liquor caused an obvious and enormous improvement of his spirits.

I managed to speak to the commander alone, thanking him for the protection he and his people had given us during the journey and for getting us all safely to Biysk. He was clearly flattered at my words. I then asked him whether he would like to have a drink with us to celebrate the conclusion of our journey.

The commander hesitated a moment, but his thirst decided the matter for him.

"Why not?" he said. "But it is still too light—let us wait till the evening."

We agreed on the time, and that evening I took my good friend Isaak April along to our small party. We brought a bottle of cognac and a bottle of red wine.

The commander had taken his aide-de-camp with him. We found a warehouse where we would be left in peace, and having sat down, we started drinking. It was not long before both bottles were empty, and it bothered neither the commander nor his aide that we had merely sipped from our glasses each time they had emptied theirs.

When their spirits had risen sufficiently, I approached the commander, asking him point-blank: "I am sure you are aware of the kind of people we have got in our wagon. Can't you see to it that we all get to a place where they can use all of us, preferably not too far from Biysk?"

The commander listened attentively, and when we broke up, he promised to do his best to help us.

On our way out of the warehouse, I asked him what would happen to the men who had been separated from their families. He told us that all of them would be tried and given long sentences in special labor camps. It later on turned out that he was entirely right.

Rachel · Israel

Again we had to spend the night in a warehouse, but the next morning saw a change in our situation. We were told to get into two trucks, which took us to a state-owned farm, a so-called *sovkhoz*, located four and a half miles from Biysk. We drove through beautiful countryside with vast fields full of sunflowers. It was a beautiful sight that made a deep impression on us, and this, combined with the friendly countryside, cheered us up right away.

The sovkhoz to which we were sent may probably be best compared to a village. It consisted of administrative buildings, a school, a nursery, and an infant day-care center. It also had a small hospital and club facilities where people could spend their spare time. All of these buildings were situated in the center, with small single-family houses and log houses on the outskirts. People in top positions lived in the single-family houses, while the rest lived in log houses.

The official name of the sovkhoz was Biyskiy Zernosovkhoz imeni pervogo Maya, which in English means "Biysk State-Owned Grain Farm in Commemoration of May 1." With its sixty-two thousand acres, it was one of the largest farms in the Altay district. In addition to the main farm, the sovkhoz comprised two minor farms which were located several miles away.

As it turned out, our bottle of cognac had been a good investment.

At the sovkhoz, our new life in Siberia started. All of us were put up in the school, which was empty during the summer holidays. We were placed in two large rooms, where we were to spend only the next couple of days at first, but eventually an entire month. Since there were no beds, we had to sleep on the floor. That was no major transition, however, for after three weeks on the train, we were not accustomed to too much comfort.

The first two days we were allowed to relax and to spend the time arranging our living quarters and getting used to the new environment. We were given free food in the canteen of the sovkhoz.

The first thing we did after our arrival was to visit the *banya* (bathhouse) of the sovkhoz. We were very happy for that bath, which was badly needed after the long journey with all its hardships.

We spent the first two days walking around the sovkhoz, talking to people and hearing about their lives and work there. The whole thing was so new and unfamiliar.

In the evening, we were all summoned to an important meeting where we were told about the structure and working conditions of the sovkhoz. Everybody would receive the same pay as the sovkhoz's own people, we were told, and everybody who was capable of working was obligated to do so. On the third day we were to report at 7:00 A.M. to be assigned our work. It was the deputy manager of the sovkhoz who told us all of this. In addition to him, there was a man from the local NKVD who told us about the administrative rules and regulations that applied to people like us; for the first time, we heard the word *spetspereselentsy*, that is, "special deportees." That description was to stick to us throughout all of our stay in Siberia. The NKVD officer told us that (a) we were not permitted to leave the sovkhoz without special permission, (b) we were to appear twice a month at the local NKVD office for registration, and (c) we were obligated to perform the work to which we had been assigned by the sovkhoz.

Violation of any of these regulations might lead to a trial and a sentence of up to three months' imprisonment.

Israel and Isaak took turns interpreting during the meeting. At the end of the meeting, everybody had to sign a document confirming that he had been informed of the regulations and would observe them. Following this introduction and the two days of rest, we had to start working.

Rachel

Carrying Harrietta, I walked around the sovkhoz to get a good look at it and eventually decided to enter a house. I shall never forget the sight that I encountered.

In a small room I saw a family, or rather a mother with her seven children, seated around a table.

Her husband was at the front, she told me.

On the table was a big bowl of boiled, unpeeled potatoes. In front of each child was a mug, which I believed to contain milk; as I looked closer, I realized that it was water.

Next to each mug was a large chunk of bread and a bit of salt, in which the children dipped their bread and potatoes.

I clearly remember my surprise at the healthy appearance of the children, secretly wondering whether we would have to eat like them and what our children would look like if given such a diet.

Israel

Along with some other men, I was ordered to dig a deep pit. The pit was to be used for storage of ensiled fodder. However much I wanted to carry on in order not to fail the rest of the gang, I simply did not have the strength for the hard physical work. After a day of digging in the pit I had to give up and went to the doctor, asking to be excused from the job. The local doctor could not do anything for me and referred me to a committee of medical experts who handled such matters in Biysk. I arrived at Biysk, was given a thorough medical examination, and finally received a certificate to the effect that I was physically handicapped as a result of polio and was therefore exempt from performing any kind of physical work. When I got back to the sovkhoz and showed it to the manager, he asked me what kind of education I had had. I told him that I was an economist and had graduated from Leipzig, and before I had completed the sentence, he said, "Then I have got just the right kind of job for you. You will be the bookkeeper of the central repair shop."

Rachel · Israel

Rachel was permitted to remain at home with the children, for there was no space for Harrietta at the infant day-care center. Baba, however, was sent to an orchard with some other women. We remained in the schoolhouse for about four weeks, whereupon we moved into one of the rooms of a fairly large log house, which had recently been restored. We were to stay in that log house with all the other passengers from our wagon. Israel's position as bookkeeper proved to give him a higher status—he was a salaried employee—and we were therefore the first ones to be moved into the log house.

The room assigned to us was large—approximately 270 square feet—and since the log house had been wired for electricity, we were able to use the electric hot plate which Mrs. Bauer had brought us at the station of Vilkaviškis. It felt good after two months to be finally alone in our own room and to be able to shut the door behind us. We were actually happy to move into our first Siberian home.

We had no problems deciding on furniture, for we were given four beds, one table, and four stools, and that was all there was room for, as the stove took up a fair amount of space.

Baba and Israel were the ones working outside the home, and Rachel, consequently, had to do the housework. The cooking did not take long, for the few articles of food that were available did not allow for any major culinary artistry. There were, however, many additional duties to which we were introduced. Wood had to be cut and brought in for the stove, water had to be fetched from a well, and the dirty water had to be carried out again, as there was no drainage in the house. Since the floor was not varnished, it had to be washed and scrubbed every day. A girl from Copenhagen generally would not be familiar with such chores, but Rachel learned how to do not only these but, in time, many others.

After some time, we became very friendly with our Russian neighbors. They were extremely helpful and always gave us their advice in situations with which we were unfamiliar. They helped us cope with the many difficulties that arose when we first started adjusting to our new life. Our neighbors were ordinary, hardworking people for whom our arrival provided an exciting and welcome change in their otherwise rather dull and uneventful everyday lives. They were aflame with curiosity concerning our family and our life, and they often visited us, asking us where we came from, what our life had been like, which countries we had visited, and all kinds of other questions. The women, in particular, were very impressed with our clothing. They wanted us to sell some of it to them, for they had never seen anything like it in their lives. They could not understand that Rachel was able to wash the children's clothing as much as she did without the colors fading. Indeed, it was a real mystery.

One day one of the neighbors who had not been to see us before entered our room, and after having looked around, she exclaimed, "You certainly have got a lot of beds in here—it looks like some kind of hospital." At first, we did not understand her surprise, but later on we realized that the local people were not used to seeing such a large number of beds in one room. In visiting our neighbors we would invariably see only one bed with a large pile of pillows and, on top of the pillows and the bed itself, a large white cover of lace material. The parents slept in the bed, while the rest of the family slept on the floor. They made up their beds with whatever they had by way of under-covers, mattresses, and blankets and prepared themselves for the night as best they could. We thus encountered many new things.

Israel

There were forty employees at the repair shop where I started work-ing as an accountant. The administrative staff consisted of four men: the manager (Yermolayev), the engineer (Vasil'yev), a mechanic, and my-self. The workshop was to handle the maintenance and repairs of all of the machinery and tools of the sovkhoz and was equipped with fairly modern, partly foreign machinery.

I had to myself a small room that had been set up as a bookkeeper's office. The task of bookkeeping was quite demanding for one person. All of the work at the repair shop was performed as piecework, and for every single spare part or piece of metal ordered, an order form had to be filled in. As a result, a huge pile of vouchers had to be processed, prepared, signed, and handled.

Yermolayev, the manager, was very surprised when one day he dis-covered that I was not familiar with the abacus, which was used for all calculations within the bookkeeping departments of all Soviet enter-prises and shops.

He stood watching me for a while, then said:

"It is beyond me—you are such a well-educated man, and you can-not even use an abacus."

It did not take me long to become entirely familiar with this excellent calculating instrument. I brought the abacus home after work and prac-ticed various calculations on it. Gradually, I became as efficient at using the abacus as all of the others who used it.

My relations with the other employees in the repair shop were good and, indeed, in some cases even friendly. Yermolayev, the manager, was a man of around forty. He was not particularly tall but stocky and extremely strong. He told me that he had had only four years of school-ing and that he had been apprenticed to a blacksmith.

"I am indebted to the Soviet power for having got as far in life as I have," he said with pride.

All skilled laborers at the repair shop had been exempt from military duty because the workplace had been declared part of the war industry. Yermolayev, too, had become exempt, which he was very sorry about, for he wanted very much to go to the front and help fight the "Fritzes," as he called the German soldiers.

In a way, the relationship I gradually developed with Yermolayev became typical of my relations with most of my subsequent superiors and the many other Russians with whom I worked.

In official Soviet quarters, we, the special deportees, were regarded as unreliable elements. Having contact with us might, under certain circumstances, cause a lot of trouble for the ordinary people who surrounded us. However, as in many other situations, it turned out that normal human emotions and relations were stronger than the orders and restrictions laid down by the party. Yermolayev often asked me to stay on after work. When all of the others had left, we went into a small clubroom where a big map was hanging on the wall. Yermolayev asked me to show him the front lines and the focal points of the war and to tell him about geographical conditions which might affect the course of the war.

One day he asked me to show him where Pearl Harbor was. This was after the Japanese attack of December 7, 1941, on the American naval base and after the reports in the Soviet press on the event. Yermolayev's knowledge of geography was rather limited, but he did not attempt to conceal his lack of knowledge from me and was extremely anxious to hear about and learn of events in the outside world.

However, I was soon to realize that his human qualities far exceeded those of many people more knowledgeable than he.

The Altay district is known for its violent winter storms (*buran*). One night when one of these snowstorms raged and nobody dared venture outside, there was a sudden knock at the door. I went to the door to open it and was very surprised to find Yermolayev, completely covered with snow, standing outside the door with a big rucksack on his back. I asked him to come inside, and he said that he was a Home Guard officer and was on a maneuver with the Home Guard.

Upon passing our log house, he had seen the light in our windows and had felt like coming inside for a chat with me.

I asked him why he had chosen such a horrible night for the maneuver. He answered that his men had to get used to being out-of-doors and marching in all kinds of weather.

I offered him a glass of vodka, and he did not refuse it.

Several glasses followed the first one, and it did not take long for the bottle to become empty. Yermolayev still did not want to go home. It was late, and Rachel and Baba wanted to go to bed—the children had been tucked in a long time ago. Yermolayev, however, did not look as if he was about to leave. When somewhat later he realized that his presence prevented Rachel and Baba from going to bed, he considerately suggested, "I shall now sit with my back to your women, so they do not feel embarrassed if they want to go to bed, and I guarantee you that I shall not cheat."

When "my women" had gone to bed and everything was quiet around us, Yermolayev went to his rucksack, from which he took a large bag of flour. He approached me, saying in a low voice, "It is for you, but I did not want anybody to know about it."

The workers at the sovkhoz were able to buy chaff for fodder for their chickens and pigs. It was cheap and excellent as fodder, so practically everybody took advantage of the offer. The repair shop was the only one in the area that was able to repair machinery, engines, and tractors. Not far from the sovkhoz was a mill that also used the repair shop when its machinery had to be repaired. The manager of the mill, therefore, had many reasons for being on friendly terms with the manager of the repair shop, who would come to his rescue in a critical situation. That is why Yermolayev received very special treatment at the mill. When he arrived at the mill with 220 pounds of chaff, he got 220 pounds of the best flour in exchange, according to the well-known and widely accepted principle that "one good turn deserves another." This principle probably applies in all countries, though it is hardly adhered to as much as in the Soviet Union, where it is more or less a necessity for making ends meet.

The blizzard had enabled Yermolayev to get to our house unnoticed and to bring us the bag with the valuable contents. Should he have been unlucky and somebody have taken an interest in what he was doing out-of-doors in such horrible weather, he would have been able to tell them that he was on a nightly maneuver with full marching equipment.

To be caught contacting us and even providing us with such a desired and scarce article as flour would have had very serious consequences for him, for he was a party member and had an important position of responsibility in the sovkhoz. Socializing with unreliable social elements such as us would not have promoted his career. Nevertheless, his simple but courageous act proved that, however powerful the party and the state may seem to be, they cannot crush man's emotions and sympathies, which transcend party politics and ideology and the various orders and directives of the authorities.

It was, of course, entirely impossible to purchase flour anywhere at the time, and Yermolayev's present meant that we would be able to add some variety to our otherwise uniform and modest meals. Still more important, however, was the feeling that in this distant corner of Siberia we had found our first Russian friend.

Our life at the sovkhoz gradually adjusted itself to a daily routine. I was satisfied with my work even if we only managed to live for a week on my monthly salary. The remainder of the month we had to live on the money we received from selling children's clothing we no longer needed, as well as other things from the modest wardrobe that we had hurriedly packed into our suitcases in Lithuania. In this manner, we got many gallons of milk, many pounds of butter and potatoes, and many other things.

It was not possible to buy clothing in the local shops—they were empty. The only place where we were able to get any clothing, shoes, and other articles for everyday use was the flea market. Here we were able to buy and sell everything under the sun, and crowds of people came from far and near every single Sunday to strike a bargain.

It goes without saying that our housing conditions and life in general at the sovkhoz were very different from what we were used to in Lithuania. Our home and our life in Lithuania seemed so distant and dreamlike after everything that we had already been through. Nor could we succumb to daydreaming and wishful thinking—the situation demanded that we concentrate on the present in order to cope and survive.

Despite all of the misery and poverty, we soon came to like our life at the sovkhoz; in fact, compared to the three weeks of nightmare on the train, it seemed like sheer luxury.

Altayskiy Kray had a good and healthy climate, and the change of climate actually proved to have a good effect on many of the deportees. Baba had for many years suffered from an allergy, which doctors had diagnosed as a particularly stubborn strain of nettle rash. She had consulted numerous specialists in various countries and had tried all kinds of remedies and diets, but nothing helped. However, after our arrival in Altayskiy Kray her allergy disappeared entirely after some time, and she never noticed it again.

The Altay area was located at a rather high altitude in a beautiful and fertile region. The surroundings did not at all resemble the cold, dark and inhospitable Siberia of which Rachel had heard. She kept saying, "This cannot be the real Siberia—everything is so lush and rich, and already in February the sun starts giving off such a beautiful warmth."

Unfortunately, Rachel's astonishment turned out to be justified: the real Siberia was still in store for her. Siberia is a vast area, and the climate differs widely from place to place. In the coming years, we were to become acquainted with some of the most inhospitable regions of its wide expanse.

3

_____

Rachel · Israel

After the fruit harvest had ended, there was no more work for Baba in the orchard, and she was unable to do any heavier physical work. She soon adjusted to the new situation and attended to shopping and exchanging goods. In the market square at Biysk, we were often able to exchange pieces of clothing or shoes for food. Biysk was approximately four and a half miles away, and Baba sometimes went by foot to the market.

One day she returned from one of her shopping trips radiant, and we were eager to hear about the bargains she had made. She proudly showed us a bag containing several pounds of unroasted coffee beans. She told us that she had entered a shop, in the dark corner of which she had caught sight of a large bag of unroasted coffee beans. It was a mystery how such a bag had ended up in Biysk, where absolutely nobody drank coffee. She asked the shop assistant what it was. He did not really know, but he could not recommend it, for some of his customers had bought two pounds of the beans a couple of days earlier and had afterward told him that the beans were inedible and did not turn into porridge, though they had boiled them for several hours. The shop assistant was speechless when, despite his warning, Baba bought several pounds of the inedible beans.

It was hard to say where the coffee beans had come from or for how long they had been left standing in the corner of the shop in Biysk, but at least they were now appreciated. We and many of our friends from Lithuania enjoyed the coffee beans a lot. We roasted them in an ordinary frying pan, and since we did not have a coffee grinder, we placed the roasted beans in a towel, crushing them with a hammer. This was a primitive but effective method, and the resulting coffee was quite excellent, although it did not compare with the coffee we were used to from Denmark and Lithuania. However, as always, it was a question of adjusting to circumstances. Many years were to pass before we got coffee again.

Many of the women at the sovkhoz were illiterate and were only able to write their names and this with difficulty. When they discovered that Baba was able to both read and write, they came to her with their letters, asking her to read them and to write the answers. Most of the letters were from their husbands and sons at the front. They were very grateful to Baba and wanted to pay her for her help, but she naturally refused to accept any payment. One of the women was very sorry that there was nothing she could do in return, and so she offered Baba to help her get rid of her lice.

It was a great honor, for it was a custom among the women to help one another with the delousing as a sign of friendship and respect. Baba thanked her very much for the offer, saying that it would have to wait until another time.

Rachel

The first time I saw it, I did not know what was going on. We were in a bathhouse for women, and in a corner on a bench I caught sight of two women deeply absorbed in a very strange task. They took turns examining each other's hair, a comb in one hand and a broad knife in the other. They were in a state of deep concentration and did not exchange a word. After having watched them at a distance for some time, I realized what they were doing. They were delousing each other—the fine-toothed comb was used to find the lice, and once a louse had been found, it was lifted on to the blade of the knife and crushed with a nail. Later on, I often watched similar scenes—it was a widely used form of personal hygiene.

Rachel · Israel

Everyday life was difficult and strenuous. The most commonplace household items to which we had never before paid a second thought— water, firewood, and ordinary kitchen utensils—were not readily available but had to be found, transported, and arranged. Nothing was taken

43

care of by itself. The housework and the children gave Rachel more than enough to do; she nevertheless found time in the evening to read Russian, and after some time, she started reading Russian newspapers.

It was not easy for us to adjust to the new conditions. We had been transplanted to a completely strange place and were living among people who were often friendly to us but with whom we had nothing in common. We did not think and feel like the Russians, and their mentality was strange to us, even after we had lived among them and gradually become accustomed to the idea of having to remain with them.

In time, the idea of our deportation became less painful to us, especially as we received an increasing number of reports on the actions of war and the horrors committed under the German occupation. We understood that the deportation had protected us from the atrocities of the Nazis and probably certain death in one of the German ghettos, where most of the remaining Jews in the three Baltic States had perished.

However, not everybody felt the same relief at being so far from the front. Several of the Lithuanians said that they would have preferred a German occupation to their deportation to Siberia. Only much later were we to learn that many Lithuanians had welcomed the German occupation troops because they drove away the Soviet forces and thus the Soviet system which had been forced upon Lithuania.

March was the harbinger of spring in Altayskiy Kray and our sovkhoz, but with the coming of spring an event occurred which caused a rapid deterioration of our life at the sovkhoz.

A politruk arrived at our sovkhoz to ensure that Soviet policies were being enforced and to keep an eye on the deportees and their dealings with the local population. *Politruk* means "political guide." A party official is appointed to that position, and his task is to head the party organization and also to watch over and guide the rest of the population—those without party affiliation, as they are known in Soviet terminology.

The politruk at our sovkhoz turned out to be a real *apparatchik* (bureaucrat). One of the first tasks he set for himself was finding out who we, the special deportees, were and what we had done prior to our deportation. This was no particularly difficult task, since all he had to do was approach the NKVD commander, who was able to provide him with all the information he desired. The commander had a file with folders on all of the families, and all of the necessary information could be easily and efficiently procured without the use of computers or central registration departments. These files followed us everywhere. The politruk considered it his task to remove all of the deportees from clerical jobs and to transfer them to jobs consisting of purely physical work. He sent a girl off to a crash course in bookkeeping, and when she returned after six weeks, Israel was immediately fired and told to start doing physical work.

Israel went to see the manager of the sovkhoz, Dmitriy Syelukyanskiy, and told him that he did not intend to refuse to do physical work but that he simply was unable to do it on account of his weak legs. The manager answered without hesitation: "You need not be nervous. I have been in the banya with you several times and have seen your poor legs. Don't worry, I shall find you a job which you will have no difficulty performing."

As it turned out, he kept his word, assigning Israel to a job he was able to do. The politruk had also seen to it that Rachel would no longer be able to stay at home, since Baba, in his opinion, could easily manage the housework alone. A team was composed of the two of us.

Our job was to dismantle old, tumbledown huts—built of what the local population called *saman*, that is, blocks of unburned clay mixed with manure and pieces of straw. It was a building material which had been used for many years in that part of Siberia. During our work, we had to be careful not to break the blocks, since they were to be used again. It was a rather difficult task, for many of the blocks had become quite fragile and would crumble into small pieces and dust if grabbed too firmly.

However, we managed the job to everybody's satisfaction and also earned a fair amount of money. We were free and more or less able to determine our pace of work, since there was nobody to keep an eye on us.

Sometime in April it became time for planting potatoes. Like everybody else at the sovkhoz, we were given a plot of forty-three hundred square feet, but we were too poor to purchase seed potatoes. Once more, Syelukyanskiy, the manager of the sovkhoz, came to our rescue. When he heard about our problem, he allowed us to obtain potato peels from the canteen. The people who peeled the potatoes were told to make the peels a bit thicker than usual. Syelukyanskiy told us to use only the peels which had at least three eyes on them. That meant that there would have to be at least three buds which would start sprouting after the peel had been planted in the soil.

We listened to his directions with incredulous expressions on our faces, but since we had no choice, we did as we were told. We were a little worried that we were being ridiculed and remained very skeptical until, some weeks later, we saw small green potato plants starting to appear in our potato field. In time, they developed into big, strong plants, and we even managed to taste new potatoes from our own plot. We felt that we had never tasted such delicious potatoes and looked forward to the actual crop. We only had the joy of expectation, however, for we were never to harvest our potatoes.

One day in late June of 1942, one of the usual, anonymous NKVD officers turned up and told us with a deadpan expression on his face that we had to pack our things and make ourselves ready for another journey. He did not say where we were going, for how long we would be on the way, or why, indeed, we were being moved again. And we asked no questions. We had already found out that it was no use asking questions of the NKVD people. We simply had to answer their questions and obey their orders. It no longer occurred to anybody to protest or to ask for a postponement. We packed our things and prepared ourselves for our departure.

We took leave of our Russian neighbors and friends. In the course of the past year, we had developed close and warm relationships with many of them. And several of them cried when we took leave of them, for they apparently realized that the experiences awaiting us were much worse than those we had hitherto undergone. It would be an exaggeration to say that we had already become used to the local climate, but we had gradually started adjusting to the new environment. That is why it hurt us to be uprooted anew, even if we did not have much to leave behind or to lose.

We lived with the constant feeling that each change was for the worse, because we could not imagine that anybody would want to make life easier for us. In our situation, one could only expect the worst from new changes.

4

Rachel · Israel

The very next day we packed up and were transported to Biysk, where we were put up in a schoolhouse. Here we stayed for a few days and gradually encountered all of the people with whom we had been deported from Lithuania. Like us, they had been brought to Biysk from the state-owned farms in the area where they had been living and working during the past year.

Rachel

We spent the day at the school selecting from among our belongings the last things which we could do without and selling them to the local population. The school looked like a regular market, for the news quickly spread through the town that the deportees were being rounded up for another trip, and everybody then knew immediately that he had the possibility of buying things that were not available in the usually empty shops.

I had a very beautiful, handmade silk nightgown, which Israel had once bought for me in Riga. When one of the Russian women caught sight of it, she became frantic with eagerness and immediately offered me two thousand rubles for it. That was quite a lot of money at the time, and we immediately accepted her offer. I was well aware that silk nightgowns with fine embroidery were not exactly the kind of clothing I would most need in the future; thus, I felt no sorrow in parting with a cherished article, which once, in the very distant past it seemed, had given me the simple joy a woman feels at this kind of attention from her husband.

With the money we bought food. We bought everything that we could get hold of, for it was not hard to figure out that we would need all of it for the impending trip. We bought sugar, flour, grits, melted butter in bottles, and several bottles of vodka, which we knew would always be good for bartering. We were quite satisfied with the deal we had made, and it turned out that the Russian woman who had purchased the nightgown also felt that she had made an extremely good deal.

The next day we met her by accident in the street, and to our surprise, we saw that she was wearing the nightgown, showing off the new acquisition for her wardrobe with obvious joy and pride. Later on we learned that it was not at all unusual for Russian women to use such nice nightgowns for going out, not merely for a lack of better clothes, but simply because they felt that it was a pity to use such beautiful pieces of clothing merely for sleeping in during the night.

Rachel · Israel

After having spent two days in the school, we were taken to the railroad station by truck and horse-drawn carriage. Some NKVD officers were walking around with lists of names and placing people in the well-known cattle wagons, and even more people were huddled together in one wagon than when we were deported from Lithuania. Now it all began again from the very start—strict surveillance, unfriendly soldiers who always shouted at us and hurried us on, the two daily food rations distributed at arbitrary places and times. It was just as it had been twelve months ago, and as before we did not have any idea where we were going or what would happen to us.

It was no use asking the people in charge of the convoy where we were going. They were silent, unresponsive, and apparently entirely unaffected by the situation. Although the deportation meant humiliation and hardship for us, it was simply routine work for them.

Despair slowly spread within the wagon, and the mystery of our destination especially bothered all of us. Though we could guess that we were to be sent farther north in Siberia, none of us knew exactly what awaited us.

We arrived in the town of Novosibirsk and went from there east on the Trans-Siberian Railroad toward the town of Cheremkhovo. The journey was only interrupted once when we stopped at Krasnoyarsk and were taken to an enormous bath in the town's transit prison, which had been set up for the use of convoys of prisoners. Hundreds of thousands of people had in the preceding years been transported via the same route and in the same way as we were—the world still had no knowledge of the extent of Stalin's purges among his opponents, his real enemies and those he imagined to have, while the entire route through Siberia was strewn with the sufferings of innocent people and their tortured thoughts about an uncertain future. It was, of course, little comfort to us to know that we were neither the first nor the last to take that route.

We were given a much-needed but short bath while our clothes were taken for delousing to special delousing ovens. Everything took place in an extreme hurry while the guards kept shouting: "Davay! Davay!" Again we felt like a herd of cattle, helplessly driven along at the mercy of our guards' whims.

Rachel

I felt sick at heart looking out through the small, barred windows of the wagon and seeing the strange, unknown country pass by my eyes. What were we doing here? What had we done to be treated in this way? Why were we not allowed to live our lives the way we wanted to? Although I always tried to suppress the memories of our previously peaceful and carefree life, these questions sometimes overwhelmed me. The memories gushed forth, and my thoughts went back to our home, which we had left so precipitately, and to my family in Denmark, where nobody had any idea of our fate. It was a fantastic, incomprehensible idea that they might still be living an undisturbed life, preoccupied with the usual problems and joys of everyday life. Or had the war touched their lives as well? I had no way of knowing, and it would be long before I would.

I could not help feeling a pang of jealousy when the train passed inhabited areas where people were walking around freely, leading normal lives. The houses often looked wretched and poor, but they nevertheless proved that there were still people leading entirely ordinary lives. How much I would have liked for us to have been allowed to remain in one of those peaceful places, living safely and quietly without fear of being uprooted from one day to the next and sent off God knows where.

Actually I seldom had occasion to lapse into such thoughts and memories, for there was always enough to do. My most important task was to see to it that the children did not suffer any harm. Schneur was six years old, and Harrietta was a little under two. I had to breast-feed her, and that was not always too easy in the uncomfortable, cramped cattle wagon, with strange people surrounding us on all sides.

Rachel · Israel

We arrived at Cheremkhovo at around ten o'clock in the morning in pouring rain. It seemed almost like a tropical storm—the rain was coming down in buckets. Nobody felt like going outside in this weather, but it was not long before we were ordered to leave the wagons.

Beforehand we had witnessed a clash between the stationmaster and the head of our convoy, Yakusyev, the NKVD officer. It was Yakusyev's responsibility to see to it that the convoy of the deportees proceeded according to schedule. The stationmaster had been ordered to send the train back at once and insisted that we leave the wagons right away. Yakusyev, however, wanted us to remain in the wagons until we were collected. For one thing, it was easier keeping an eye on us while we remained within the wagons, and, for another, Yakusyev did not want to risk any outbreaks of illness among the deportees as a result of ordering us outside in the cold, torrential rain. He had to see to it that the deportees reached their destinations in reasonably good health. Nobody was to be left behind along the way on account of illness, and it would be an additional burden for the convoy if there were sick passengers. The dispute ended in favor of the stationmaster, and Yakusyev ordered the wagons to be emptied.

We reluctantly left the stifling, filthy cattle wagon, which we had previously been longing to leave. It now protected us against the merciless rain, which seemed a forewarning of what was in store for us. However, there was nothing that we could do about it, and gradually the train was emptied. As soon as everybody was out, the train left.

We had been discharged on a sidetrack far from the station building. There were only fields around us and nowhere for us to seek shelter. Our luggage had been piled up at random, and we remained standing next to it in small groups in the pouring rain. Being soft and made of clay, the ground soon changed into one big puddle of mud, into which we kept sinking. There were one thousand people standing in the constant downpour along the railroad track, surrounded by naked fields on all sides. Tired, cold, and wet to the skin, we waited for more than two hours to be taken further on our trip.

At long last, some horse-drawn carriages came for us. As usual, we were among the last to leave, this time because our cattle wagon had been in the rear of the train. When our luggage had been loaded into the back of the carriage, the horse began to slowly pull the carriage along; the Russian driver walked next to it, the long reins in his hands, while we plodded along behind through the sodden field.

We were again put up in a school and placed in an empty classroom with several other families. It was hard to tell at how many schools we stayed in the course of our numerous transfers, but it gradually dawned upon us that the convoys of deportees ran on a schedule adapted to the school holidays—school buildings would stand empty and, without further preparations, could be used to provide shelter for the many people who were sent from one end of the country to the other.

As soon as we got inside, we changed into dry clothes and had a glass of vodka to warm up. Soon afterward we all lay down, and after the exhaustion of that long day, we were able to fall asleep immediately.

In the course of the night we were suddenly awakened. One of the families in the classroom was carrying its luggage out, apparently to move it into another room. We were too tired and sleepy to pay any attention to them. Not until the next morning did we discover that a bag of sixty-six pounds of flour, which we had taken along with us with great difficulty, had disappeared. The people who had moved their things out in the night had probably taken the bag along with them, knowing just as well as we did that it would be impossible for us to trace such a bag of flour among a thousand people. We did not know them and could thus do nothing. We had not been alert enough, and our sole comfort was the hope that the loss of the precious bag of flour would teach us a lesson.

The next morning we were awakened very early. The fatigue from the hardships of the previous day was still in our bodies. Despair slowly overcame us. We walked along, our sole concern being to remain alive until we arrived at our unknown destination.

From Cheremkhovo we were to go by boat on the Angara River to the town of Zayarsk. The boat was a paddle steamer with two large barges in tow for the transportation of the thousand people. We got into the rearmost barge. On the way up the river, the front barge was grazed in the middle of the night by a steamer approaching from the opposite direction, and our barge gave a jolt. For a few minutes, panic threatened to break out among people, with some already jumping overboard with fright from the lower deck. Luckily, no damage had been done to our barge or the barge in the front. People calmed down again, and the voyage continued toward Zayarsk.

A rumor, which nobody was able to trace, spread like wildfire among the deportees. The rumor had it that we were all on our way to the port of Tiksi on the Arctic Ocean, from where we would be taken by boat to the United States. It was soon suspected that it must have been the NKVD officers themselves who had fabricated the rumor to ease the work of the convoy and make the deportees more eager to leave. Depression and despair had begun to mark people, and several young people had attempted to flee en route. It was therefore in the interest of the NKVD to entice the deportees with the prospect of an early and happy ending to their sufferings.

There were, of course, no official announcements, but till the very end there were people who stubbornly believed the rumor to be true. It was rumored that the American government had demanded that the deportees from Lithuania be sent to the United States, where three million Lithuanian immigrants were conducting a campaign for the release of their countrymen. Whether one believed in the rumor or not, hope began to grow in most of us. In a situation such as ours, one readily pins one's faith on even the most slender hope of rescue. Circumstances made us susceptible to the belief in miracles. In a way, we were in the same situation as the German Jews who, on their way to the gas chambers, believed in assurances that they were merely being taken to a safer, more secure place.

After two days of sailing, we arrived at Zayarsk, from where we were to be sent on to the Lena River, 186 miles to the northeast. We had to remain in Zayarsk for three days, since they had only about twenty trucks for the transport of all the people. Even though the trucks drove back and forth constantly, it took three days for all of us to be transferred. Since there was no school in which to stay in Zayarsk, we were all forced to remain in the street and spend the night in the open next to our luggage, which nobody dared leave for fear that it be stolen.

Israel

I succeeded in finding a small outhouse in which Rachel and the children could sleep. The shed was in the center of town and belonged to a

Russian family who received Rachel and the children with the usual Russian hospitality and without thought to the consequences of giving shelter to special deportees.

My mother and I had to remain in the street, and we arranged ourselves as best we could next to our luggage. Under these wretched circumstances, various illnesses started breaking out among the people. Malaria, diarrhea, and pneumonia were among the most common. My mother also contracted diarrhea, and for two days she lay weak and helpless on an uncomfortable bed of various bundles of clothing in the street. I managed with great difficulty to obtain some medicine for her, and she had more or less recovered when, on the third day, we were taken by truck to the town of Osetrovo on the Lena River.

Rachel · Israel

In Osetrovo we boarded a huge paddle steamer, which would take us farther north toward the town of Yakutsk. Compared with the hardships of the preceding days, the voyage up the Lena River was rather pleasant and comfortable. Even if we were crammed together with several other families in one of the saloons of the steamer, we felt as if we were traveling first class after the days in the cattle wagon, in the dumb barges, and in Zayarsk.

We sailed for eight days and nights and managed to pick up anew. The encounter with the magnificent Siberian scenery in this part of the country was a very special experience—the river with its fantastic rock formations, the endless, bluish forests, and the immense plains made a deep, though intimidating, impression on us in all of their untamed wilderness and the serene, almost impregnable calmness with which they were permeated. We had never before seen such virgin and untouched scenery.

The steamer put in at various ports on the way to take fuel on board, and each time we had the opportunity to go ashore and do some shopping. In this way we were able to supplement our food supplies. Altogether, our situation seemed to improve during this part of our trip, and everybody on board became appreciably more cheerful.

We arrived in Yakutsk in early August and had to remain on board for several days until another steamer came to take us even farther north up the Lena River.

Rachel and Israel Rachlin

Israel

While the boat lay alongside the quay, several men went into town. Permission had been easily granted, for their families remained on board as hostages of the NKVD officers.

Afterward I learned that they had gone to the local authorities in Yakutsk to apply for work, hoping to avoid being sent even farther north. Strangely enough, they all succeeded in finding work and obtaining permission to remain in the town with their families. This unexpectedly accommodating attitude on the part of the authorities was due partly to the fact that all of the men who had gone into town spoke fluent Russian and partly to the fact that the war had left the entire country with a severe labor shortage. Nobody had as yet any idea of how fortunate these men and their families were.

I could have gone to town with them and undoubtedly would have found a job in the same manner. But I dared not leave Rachel, my mother, and the children, for nobody knew when we would be leaving, and I was afraid that they might have left when I returned. I dared not take that risk, but later on I was to bitterly regret my caution. However, it is no use being wise after the event. Who could know what might happen and what would occur later on?

The incident, however, clearly shows how fortuitous everything was under the system in which we found ourselves, and how accidental occurrences decided the fates of human beings.

By that time, our last hope that we would be sent to the United States had failed us. If that had been the case, they would not have allowed anybody to remain in Yakutsk.

Rachel · Israel

From Yakutsk our voyage continued in two barges that were pulled along by a tugboat. We went farther and farther north, and the scenery changed rapidly as we left Yakutsk farther and farther behind. There were no longer any fields to be seen along the river—only forests and rocks. The forests gradually became increasingly sparser, and the vegetation increasingly lower and poorer. We had arrived in the tundra. The scenery now appeared gloomy and inhospitable, and the temperature had already dropped appreciably, even though it was still August.

54

Rachel

There is one experience from this part of our trip which has forever burnt itself into my memory. One day several of us were standing on the deck of the barge. The sun was low in the sky, shedding a dim, reddish-golden light over the gray, desolate landscape with its solitary, miserable, and stunted trees. It was a sad and depressing sight, and I became even more desolate when I realized that several of the slopes facing north were still covered with snow from the previous winter. It had not been possible for it to melt during the brief, cold summer. We felt as if we were at the end of the world.

While we stood watching the depressing landscape, somebody suddenly started singing:

Kol od balevav penima
nefesh yehudi homiya . . .

The words mean: "As long as the Jewish heart beats in our chests, there is still hope for us."

It was some of the young Jewish men and women on board who had struck up the *Hatikvah*, which means "the Hope" and which has now become the national anthem of the state of Israel. The song expresses the wish of the Jews over the last thousand years to become a free people in their own country and their unquenchable longing for Jerusalem and the land of Zion.

The young people had started singing the song quite spontaneously, and I believe that we were seized with the same indescribable feeling of brotherhood and united strength. An increasing number joined in singing the song about the sunny promised land, while the barge gently rocked in the waves, taking us through the arid, hostile landscape on the way to the Arctic Ocean.

The atmosphere had been marked by helplessness and despair, but the song gave us hope. Neither the NKVD people nor the non-Jewish Lithuanians knew what kind of song it was, nor did they comprehend that our singing it was a protest. The song was entirely our own. They could take everything from us, but the ideas and feelings aroused in us by the Hatikvah belonged to us, and no power in the world could take them from us.

Many were singing with tears in their eyes. The hopes and feelings we expressed in our singing united us with the numerous generations of

55

Jews who, in the course of time, have found themselves in similar situations. Many of these young women and men were to see their dreams come true many years later. In the late sixties and early seventies, many of them were permitted to leave the Soviet Union to go to Israel, where they still live today.

We remained standing on the deck for a long time, and the singing kept echoing within us a long time after it had ended. Here we were, a varied group of people, each member with his own background and different views of the world and our fate. But despite all the differences, I believe that during those minutes we felt that the singing united us through invisible ties with the long history of our people. Our fate was only a tiny section, but a few lines, of the many chapters of our people's history.

Rachel · Israel

On the way, the barge stopped several times, and an increasing number of families were ordered to get off at small villages and settlements along the river. It seemed as if our guards were allowed to do as they chose with us, entirely at their own discretion—nobody asked us our opinion, and there was not much we could do, confronted as we were with the superior power of the Soviet Union. Naturally, we tried to figure out the basis on which people were selected, and why they were ordered to get off at the various places. But, as usual, it was quite impossible to find credible explanations or a logical pattern in the decisions and actions of the NKVD people.

The landscape became increasingly rugged and gloomy; thus it was easy to believe that those of us remaining on board the barge were to be punished even more severely, for crimes that none of us had committed, by being banished to even more dreadful regions. After Yakutsk, we were not guarded as closely: there simply was no risk that any of us might get the idea of fleeing into this desolate wilderness.

On August 16, eight days after we had passed Yakutsk, we arrived at Bykov Mys, a small tongue of land in the Arctic Ocean at the mouth of the Lena. About four hundred people were ordered to get off here, including us. The sight we encountered upon our arrival at Bykov Mys was a landscape that, if possible, appeared even more depressing and desolate than any of the other places through which we had passed on the way. No houses or harbor were to be seen anywhere. The flat-bottomed barges were pulled practically all the way up to the shore. A makeshift gangway had been hurriedly constructed, and people started disembarking.

Behind the shore loomed a steep slope of eternal ice covered with a thin layer of soil. Dirty gray, brown, and black colors met our eyes everywhere. There were no trees, bushes, vegetation, or living creatures to be seen anywhere. It rained. This was our destination, which we had reached after twenty-four days of traveling. Once more we were among the last ones to disembark, and later we discovered that we had been robbed again. A man from the barge had helped us carry our luggage ashore and had apparently seized the opportunity to steal a sack containing some of our most valuable belongings: warm coats, boots, woolen underwear, and other pieces of clothing that we were to need so badly here in Bykov Mys. We only discovered the theft when we were ashore and the barge was already on its way back to the waiting steamer. There was nothing that we could do.

We remained standing on the shore in small groups. Nobody knew where we would go, where we would live, or what we would do in this godforsaken wilderness. We all felt lost and lonely. The steamer pulling its two barges continued its voyage. We followed it with our eyes. Many of our friends had remained on board and were to be transported even farther away. We waved at them for a long time from the bank of the river.

5

Rachel · Israel

We remained standing on the bank of the river with our luggage spread all around us. We looked in every direction but were unable to discern any houses or other buildings which might indicate that the place was inhabited. After a while, some men arrived and approached us. Among them was the NKVD commander, Kuriganov. He was a Buryat, a member of one of the many Mongolian minorities living in Siberia. He looked stern and spoke with a hoarse, husky voice, which testified to a huge consumption of alcohol.

Farther down the bank was a large barge we believed to have run aground. Kuriganov pointed to it, saying that this was where we would be staying. However, before being allowed to enter the "hotel," we had to go to the bathhouse. We were taken there in a long line and had to walk along a crooked path over a steep slope. When we reached the bathhouse and saw what kind of building it was, we immediately realized that if we did not already have lice, we would most certainly get them there.

A small chat with the supervisor of the bathhouse and a ten-ruble note, which discreetly changed owners, saw to it that a certificate was issued to the effect that the Rachlin family, consisting of three adults and two children, had undergone the hygienic cleansing process. We were now allowed to board the thousand-ton barge, which was to become our home as well as the home of six hundred other people for an unknown period of time. Among the other residents were approximately 170 Lithuanian Jews, while the rest were Germans from the Leningrad region, Karelians from the Soviet-Finnish border area, and other Lithuanians.

We were assigned the broad upper bunk of a bunk bed in a large dormitory. This was where all five of us would be staying and sleeping, and below us was another family. The place was swarming with people, and it felt like an ants' nest, with sick, dirty, and exhausted people packed together in a dark and stuffy room. It seemed the forecourt of hell, and the problem of surviving in this place filled us with horror. In the village we had seen one of the well-known political slogans written in graffiti on the wall of one of the houses: "The welfare of the people is the party's most important task!" It clearly was not the task of the party to see to it that the deportees would be given tolerable living conditions.

On board the barge were two so-called stoves, which were to be used by six hundred people. In reality, they were iron barrels that had been converted into wood-burning stoves, on which we were able to cook a little for the children and make tea for ourselves. It was not possible to prepare any major meal, for there was always a long queue, and we had to hurry, for if we took too long cooking, people would immediately start complaining.

In that way, our housing problem was solved for the next few weeks, and it was now a question of finding work.

The question that occupied the minds of all of us was why the authorities had decided to send us up here. Had they found that Altayskiy Kray was far too pleasant for people such as us? Or did they feel more secure having us here at the Arctic Ocean, completely cut off from the rest of the world? Or did they simply need labor? There hardly was any unequivocal answer to these questions, and all of the motives mentioned probably played a role in the authorities' decisions with regard to the special deportees.

To us, the deportation to Bykov Mys felt like an additional punishment. People working in the Arctic regions of the Soviet Union were hired from all over the country. In most cases it was a question of hard and demanding work, and not just anybody was given such a job. First, the applicant had to undergo many medical tests to find out whether he would be suited for work in the Arctic region, and only the strongest and healthiest applicants could hope for a contract. On the other hand, there were many benefits in the form of higher salaries, longer vacations, and free trips to the southern parts of the Soviet Union. In addition, men working on contract in the Arctic regions were exempt from military duty.

However, the same criteria for selection did not apply to the deportees, and no attention was paid to age, state of health, or sex. We had no rights whatsoever and were unable to appeal the decisions of the authorities.

One might wonder why this enormous operation, involving convoys, organization, and planning, had been started merely to take physically weak men, women, and children to a region with the worst possible climatic conditions. Quite a lot of resources and time had been allocated to this task.

One should not try to search for logical answers when it comes to the decisions and actions of the Soviet authorities, but the most reasonable explanation was that our labor was needed to catch and process the fish abounding in the region of the Lena delta. There were large quantities of various kinds of salmon, as well as sturgeon and many other kinds of fish. Food was in short supply all over the Soviet Union. It is true that this condition had existed for years, but the problem had now become acute because of the war, and it had become necessary to take steps throughout the country to provide food for the population. Fish played an important role in the efforts to solve the food shortage.

We were now to participate in catching, processing, and shipping these huge supplies of fish. It was soon discovered that the labor force we represented fell far short of their needs. Very few of the men were able to perform hard physical work under the unusually taxing climatic conditions. It was not long before disease broke out among the deportees, and many succumbed after a very short time. Funerals became the most common occasion for people to get together. The simple coffins of rough boards were lowered into narrow graves in the stony ground, which remained frozen throughout the year.

Only about ten percent of our group worked as fishermen; another fifteen percent was occupied in salting and packing the fish into huge wooden barrels. Some of the women were occupied in making and repairing fishnets.

It all seemed completely absurd. In Altayskiy Kray, where most of us had been working in agriculture, everybody had been satisfied with our work, which represented a much larger contribution than our work as fishermen. They needed us just as much in agriculture as in the Arctic fishing industry, but instead of getting actual benefit from our contribution, they chose to send us several thousand miles north, where our labor was of no major value. The Ministry of Fisheries in Moscow had probably decided to increase the volume of fish caught. Due to the shortage of labor, it had then approached the NKVD to find out whether that organization could provide it with a labor force from some of its many reserves of labor existing for various reasons throughout the country. In this case, the deportees must have presented the ideal solution to the problem. The NKVD was able to move us to any part of the Soviet Union without consulting either us or our employers.

This was probably how it came about that we were transformed from a group of people who had made a good and effective contribution in Altayskiy Kray into a bunch of sick and exhausted people bound to be a burden to society. We shall never learn whether those who were responsible for our transfer were satisfied with the result and had achieved what they wanted. To us, the transfer seemed not only a great mistake but also a tragedy.

We came to live under the most primitive conditions conceivable. Bykov Mys is a narrow isthmus, consisting mainly of eternal ice covered with a thin layer of soil. The environment itself had a depressing effect on us—we saw no birds, no animals, and hardly any vegetation—everywhere we saw only tundra covered with reindeer moss and other lichens. Seventy-two days a year are polar nights, when everything is swathed in total darkness. This phenomenon had a particularly strong effect on us, since we were not used to it. The closest town, the port of Tiksi at the mouth of the Lena, was twenty-five miles away, and there a hospital and a school were located. Several times in the winter, we experienced the much dreaded *purga*, the Arctic snowstorm that causes the horizon to be completely blotted out and makes it highly dangerous to venture outside. When the purga raged, we were completely isolated from everything and everybody.

The food situation was not as bad as one might have feared, even if our diet was very monotonous and did not contain any vitamins. During the entire period that we stayed in Bykov Mys, we did not eat any potatoes, onions, or any other vegetables. Most of the people were in poor health and many contracted scurvy. Our uncertainty as to how long we would have to remain in Bykov Mys was one of the major reasons for our despondency and despair. There was nothing much on which to pin our hopes, and in our darkest moments we were seized with the fear that we would never escape from the area. The friendships and the spirit of solidarity that developed among the deportees formed the only bright spot in our otherwise dismal situation. We not only shared the same fate but also our difficulties and our few joys.

At the northernmost point of the isthmus, the northern part of which faced the Arctic Ocean while the other side formed a bay, were the state-owned fish storehouses and part of the fish-processing plant.

Here the catches of the collectives and of the state-employed fish-ermen were processed. The fish were usually cured and placed in large wooden barrels, which were stored until they were sent south when the river became open for navigation—usually during the first week of July.

The offices, the factory, and some of the workshops where the nets were produced and repaired were located high up on a hill. It was here that the women and the men who were too weak to work in the fishing industry had to work.

The place had one advantage granted by nature and the climate— the frozen and cured fish could be kept in natural cold-storage rooms, which were cut into the eternal ice; unlike goods stored in modern freezers, the fish were not subject to the risk of loss due to power failure.

Israel

The manager of Rybzavod, the fish-processing plant, was Akim An-dreyevich Semikin—a handsome and sympathetic man of about forty. I found it easy to get on speaking terms with him when I met him during my search for work. After a brief chat he offered me the position of economist at Rybzavod. This was the best job I would be able to obtain, and I immediately accepted his offer. The local school had only four grades, and they did not need a foreign language teacher.

When I asked Akim Andreyevich Semikin where we were to stay, he answered, "You have to build yourself a yurt." A yurt was the type of mud hut in which most of the local people lived. When I told him that I had never used a carpenter's ax and did not know anything about car-pentry, he advised me to join forces with some other men in building a yurt. He would see to it that we got all the necessary building materials from Rybzavod.

I had no choice and started on the project. I found six other men who were in the same situation and who were interested in building a yurt. None of us had previously participated in the construction of a house, but driven by necessity and the desire to provide our wives, mothers, and children with a roof over their heads, we started on the construc-tion, filled with optimism and indomitable energy. The yurt was to be ready before winter really set in—already in early September it had started snowing, although the snow did not yet remain on the ground for any length of time. Soon, however, the waters around us would become icebound and cut us off in all directions. It would then become important to have a place in which to keep warm and survive the hardships of the coming months.

Rachel · Israel

One day we were both asked to appear before the ever-present NKVD, where a man wearing the uniform of an officer told us with a frozen, emotionless expression that we would have to remain in Bykov Mys for the rest of our lives. We both became paralyzed with terror when we realized what the NKVD officer with the wooden face had just told us. However, we had by then become sufficiently experienced to refrain from asking any questions and thus giving the NKVD officer an opportunity to humiliate and torture us even further. After having informed us of the conditions for our stay in Bykov Mys, the officer pushed a statement across his desk toward us, asking us to sign it. The statement was to the effect that we were aware of the fact that we would not be permitted to leave the place without a permit.

This was actually an entirely superfluous statement, but none of the bureaucratic regulations were to be neglected, not even up here on the other side of the Arctic Circle, where no human beings could survive fleeing into the tundra and the wilderness. In the winter, it would be tantamount to committing suicide. We signed the statement and returned to the barge, filled with the gloomiest thoughts and feelings.

We lived on the barge for three weeks—probably the worst three weeks of our entire deportation. We had to live in an intolerable stench, in the most horrible sanitary conditions, and we were constantly pushed by the hundreds of other people staying with us on the barge.

We had several nightmarish experiences while we were on board the barge, as when a storm broke one night, threatening to detach the barge from its moorings. A handful of men worked for several hours with ropes and moorings to ensure that the barge would not float into the river. Rainwater and heavy waves washing over the deck penetrated into our sleeping quarters, and we all became drenched to the skin. Later on, when all of the wet clothing had to be dried, the atmosphere among the many people on board the barge was charged with a mixture of despair and aggression. Everybody wanted to leave the barge, but there was nowhere to go.

After three weeks of suffering, Israel finally managed to obtain shelter with a Russian fisherman and his family. Their name was Zemlyakov, and they showed us the same hospitality and human warmth that we had already encountered among several of their countrymen. Our yurt was not yet ready, and the Zemlyakov family offered us shelter until we would be able to move into our own yurt. Nowhere did the saying "Where there is a will, there is a way" apply better than here. Zemlyakov's small hut was probably not much larger than eighty square feet, and the family consisted of two adults and two children. They now had to share their modest space with an additional five people, but that did not seem to bother them, and we were delighted. There was nowhere for us to sleep but on the floor, but we were so happy and grateful at being able to leave the barge with its stench, heat, and tense atmosphere that we did not for once consider that our sleeping quarters were probably not the most comfortable in the world. The Zemlyakovs were kind and friendly toward us and helped us as much as they could during the couple of weeks that we stayed with them.

We all worked very hard to get our yurt completed, but the work took longer than we had expected. The delay was primarily due to difficulties in obtaining the necessary building materials, such as bricks for the stove and the chimney, glass for the windows, and many other things one could not simply pick up at the hardware store around the corner. Bykov Mys was like an island cut off from the rest of the world. Practically everything the local inhabitants needed in the course of the year had to be transported via the Lena River for a distance of one thousand miles or more while the river was navigable—a period of about two months a year. During the nine to ten months of winter, Bykov Mys was entirely isolated, and the supplies reaching us were extremely limited. The closest place with connection to the outside world was Tiksi, where an airplane arrived once a week with mail and a few passengers. During the winter, all transport covering the twenty-five miles to Tiksi took place by dog sledge. When a purga broke, there was no way of maintaining contact with the outside world. Nobody dared go anywhere, by foot or by dog sledge. The dangerous thing about these snowstorms was the strong wind whirling huge masses of snow around and preventing one from seeing or finding one's bearings on the basis of the direction of the wind. People would sometimes step a few steps away from their homes and lose their bearings in the snowstorm. Thus, when we had to go outside for firewood, we usually tied a rope around the waist, enabling us to find our way back or literally be pulled back into the house. The native Yakuts were able to predict the arrival of a purga several days ahead of time.

The yurt was built of larch wood, which we got from Rybzavod. The logs were approximately twenty-one feet long and were transported to Bykov Mys by way of rafts pulled up the river by a tugboat. We had to see to it ourselves that the logs were pulled ashore by means of long boathooks, and this often took place in a rather hazardous manner, because the inexperienced men of our group had to wade into the water and balance on the rafts like professional lumberjacks who jump around on rafts like acrobats. Many unfortunate people fell into the water quite a few times before managing to get all the timber that was needed.

The yurt had a floor space of about 750 square feet. The foundations consisted of entire logs, and the walls were constructed of the same kind of logs, which were simply cut over in the center and then split into two parts. Our only tools were saws and axes, and it was a difficult and strenuous job splitting those huge logs with these tools. However, the idea that we were constructing the yurt in order for our families to survive gave us additional strength, and we toiled long and hard to complete our structure. When we had completed the carpentry, we cut large pieces of peat and placed them around the entire yurt as some kind of external wall. Inside the yurt, the walls were covered with rough boards.

The yurt was divided into three rooms, each with a small stove and a tiny window. We were given the room in the center, because Schneur and Harrietta were the youngest among the children, and the room in the center was, of course, the warmest room. At long last, we were able to move in and have our housewarming party with the other people who had been building their own homes. We were never as proud and at the same time as relieved as we were at that housewarming party.

The furniture of our new home was extremely modest—it consisted of a wide bunk for us and the children, a narrow bunk for Baba, a table standing under the small window between the bunks, and two stools. We had designed and constructed the furniture ourselves. We shared the room with a Polish family of three people—an elderly woman and her adult daughter and son. The two other rooms were occupied by eight and ten people, respectively, and our yurt thus held a total of twenty-six people.

6

Rachel · Israel

After we had moved in, ordinary everyday life in Bykov Mys was able to begin. Israel attended to his job at the office at Rybzavod, while Rachel and Baba looked after the house and the children. It was not easy getting into a normal everyday rhythm, given the conditions. It is true that we had solved the problems of housing and work, but what would happen later on? How were we to manage under these inhuman conditions? Our sole consolation was that we were not alone but with many people in exactly the same situation, and everybody on the whole was helpful and cooperative. We often got together in each other's homes—none of us had anything special to serve, but we always had a cup of tea to offer, and that was enough to create a cozy atmosphere and start us talking and telling stories about everything under the sun.

Far away from us, the war raged with bitter fights on all fronts. But the reports we received on the progress of the war were very few. Rybzavod had a small radio station, which constituted our only connection with the world outside our small isolated society. Every evening at seven o'clock, two young people from our group went up to the radio station where they were permitted to join the others in listening to the news from Moscow. And every evening we sat anxiously in the yurt, awaiting their return with the latest news on the progress of the war.

Many months, however, went by without any encouraging news. Only in February of 1943 did our young news reporters return with welcome news: the German Army, which had been besieging Stalingrad for months, had capitulated. Although the victory of the Red Army, which heralded one of the turning points of the war, would probably not have any direct influence on our situation, the news generated joy and optimism among us in our otherwise sad and gloomy lives. In spite of everything, the faint hope arose among us that the conclusion of the war might bring about a change in our situation.

The polar night descended upon us and lasted for more than two months. For seventy-two days, the sun did not appear on the horizon, and people suffered physically and psychologically. The Polish woman with whom we shared our room in the yurt succumbed. We could hear her groans and coughing on the other side of the thin partition wall. She died after a long illness. After some time her daughter also became ill and was taken by dog sledge to the hospital in Tiksi, where she died a few days later.

We always had the feeling that gradually all of us would perish and that nobody would ever realize our fate.

In compensation for the missed sunlight, we often witnessed northern lights, a breathtaking natural phenomenon in light and color. Everybody left his yurt to watch the mysterious game of nature.

We were, of course, unable to take the northern lights with us into our dark yurts. Here we had to make do with the very primitive lighting of lamps, which we had made ourselves from small cans filled with wicks and kerosene. Our lamps smoked and stank but did provide us with some light. Only the office buildings, the fish-processing plant, and the workshops were provided with electric lighting.

The stove in our room gave off a good deal of heat, and it turned out that we had done a good job in our construction of the yurt—it was well insulated and retained the heat. However, obtaining firewood was a major problem. We were allocated a certain amount of firewood from Rybzavod, but it was soon used up, and we then had to obtain firewood ourselves for the remainder of the winter. When lucky, we found some driftwood, which we sawed up into firewood. Otherwise, we were compelled to hunt for firewood at the various building sites. That method was perhaps not entirely legal, but the watchmen usually closed their eyes, for they were, of course, in the same situation themselves. It was not otherwise possible to procure firewood in the Arctic region, where no suitable trees grew.

Our water supply, however, was never lacking, for we had only to go down to the river; of course, it was somewhat more complicated in the winter, when we had to go onto the ice quite far in order to cut a hole in it.

Rachel

I was usually the one who had to fetch water, for there was nobody else to do it after Israel had gone to work. We always went as a group of women to collect water. It had become quite a ritual for us to set off with ice axes and buckets in our hands. I recall several silent nights with the moon and stars shining in the dark sky. The air was pure and fresh, and it was a relief to get outside after having been confined inside the yurt. The scenery all around us—with the landscape of ice and moonshine—was beautiful and captivating, and if we had experienced it under normal conditions, we would have enjoyed it. But given our situation, we did not feel inclined to dwell upon experiences of natural phenomena on the shores of the Arctic Ocean—our everyday life provided far too many sorrows and worries for such pursuits.

It was Baba and I who together were in charge of the shopping. The only shop was located about a third of a mile from our yurt at the top of the hill. Here we went shopping practically every day and got our supplies of bread and other foods: sugar, flour, egg powder, and milk powder. Everything was rationed, and most of the goods had been shipped to Tiksi from the United States.

We were able to buy unlimited quantities of fish. It was frozen but usually of fine quality. We ate fish in some form or other every single day. There were various kinds, and Baba and I tried moreover to vary the preparation as much as possible so that our diet would not become too monotonous. Schneur and the other boys tried to smoke fish in the chimney, and sometimes they managed to obtain quite good results, and their smoked fish would be delicious—one particular kind of large, fat herring lent itself especially well to this kind of smoking. Among the fish we were able to purchase were various kinds of salmon and, from time to time, sturgeon. The sturgeon was so fatty that when we fried it in the pan, we ended up with several glasses of oil to use for other purposes in the household. The major problem with our diet was the lack of vegetables—not even potatoes were available here, and as a result, people soon developed vitamin deficiency problems. By spring, many of the deportees had contracted scurvy.

Israel

We had great difficulty making ends meet. We were only able to manage for about two weeks on the salary I received at Rybzavod. As neither Baba nor Rachel worked outside the home, it was not easy.

However, once more we were rescued by means of the modest remnants left in our suitcases. We naturally did not have unlimited amounts of clothing and other things we were able to sell, for the NKVD had carefully checked the quantity and weight of our luggage when we were deported from Lithuania. Still, we were able to sell a few things in Bykov Mys. It was difficult to find buyers, and we had to seek them among the fishermen. Some of them had had luck with their catches and made a lot of money to spend on the purchase of goods not available in the shops.

Sometimes they even came into our yurt, asking for some of the things for which they were looking. One day we received a visit from a tall fisherman who asked for a suit. Fortunately, he was able to fit into one of my suits, and we then made a deal: the fisherman paid for the suit with one hundred pounds of American flour and two cans of American canned meat. It was difficult to determine which of us was most satisfied with the deal.

The next thing to be sold from our suitcases was a travel alarm clock, which was sold to another fisherman. Originally, he wanted a wristwatch, but when he saw the alarm clock and we showed him how to work the alarm, he became so enthusiastic that he bought it immediately. He put the alarm clock in his pocket, and afterward he let the alarm ring to the great surprise of all of his friends and to his own great amusement.

My work as economist and bookkeeper at Rybzavod introduced me to fields and methods with which I had not previously been too familiar. Like all other enterprises in the Soviet Union, Rybzavod had a plan that had been prepared by the Ministry of Fisheries in Moscow, and it was the task and responsibility of the manager to see to it that the plan was fulfilled. The plan for Rybzavod stipulated that twenty thousand tons of fish were to be caught on an annual basis. Rybzavod received its supplies of fish from a large number of small fishing hamlets scattered throughout the vast Lena delta, which covered an area of 250 miles. These catches were taken to Bykov Mys and formed part of the plan of Rybzavod. One of my tasks was to check that the requirements of the plan were met. The reports from the individual fishing hamlets were submitted to me, and I then had to add up the individual catches and keep an account of the total. Every week I had to send a cable to the ministry in Moscow, stating the total catch of the week and the extent to which the annual plan was fulfilled.

There was no radio communication between the fishing hamlets and Rybzavod, and the reports were sent in by motorboat in the summer and by dog sledge in the winter. Due to snowstorms, the reports often did not arrive in time, and this gave me huge problems when I had to send my weekly cables to Moscow. The reports and the statements that were to be sent on to the ministry in Moscow had to be signed and approved by Semikin, the manager, with whom I soon developed a certain rapport.

During the winter, which lasted for ten months, all fishing took place under the ice. This was a difficult procedure but the only one feasible. The nets were set up through holes in the ice and were checked every twenty-four hours. The fish that had been caught was left on the ice at the spot where it had been caught, and in the course of half an hour it was frozen and could remain where it was until collected. There were two kinds of fishermen at Rybzavod. One group consisted of the permanently employed fishermen, who received their salaries regardless of the volume of their catches. They were employed by the state, and their catches were subject to strict supervision—everything had to be handed over to the state. Under no circumstances were these fishermen to keep as much as a single fish of the catches they landed. One of the deportees from Lithuania who worked as a fisherman was careless enough one day to bring home some fish to his family. His act was discovered, and he was tried and sentenced to three years of labor camp for the theft of state-owned property.

The other group of fishermen was composed of people who caught fish on their own account. This meant that they only received payment for the fish they handed over to the state, and they were allowed to bring home all the fish they desired, as long as it was for their own consumption. These were the fishermen fishing for a livelihood. A separate group was composed of anglers, who were permitted to fish on the condition that they deliver the first eleven hundred pounds of fish to the state, and once this had been done, they were allowed to fish as much as they wanted for themselves.

One of the other deportees, my good friend Svirskiy, and I myself decided that we wanted to try our luck at fishing. Svirskiy was also employed in the bookkeeping department at Rybzavod. We were given all the necessary fishing tackle and merely needed instruction in the noble art of fishing. We found an old Yakut who became our teacher on the subject. He was illiterate but a competent fisherman who knew all the secrets of the trade. He took great pains explaining to us how to fish, and when we felt that we were able to do it, we went out on the ice and found a spot where we could throw our nets.

We had to wait for twenty-four hours, and we were very anxious to return to check our nets. To our great surprise and joy, we pulled a twenty-two-pound fish onto the ice—it was a nelma, one of the finest salmons found in the area. We returned home triumphantly with our catch and were received with enthusiasm.

When we told our teacher about our catch, he said with a smile that we would catch still another nelma the next day, for they always traveled in pairs. This proved to be true, for the next day we pulled onto the ice another nelma of almost the same size. It must have been beginner's luck, for we never succeeded in catching such fish again. However, we got other fish in our nets, and they made an important contribution to our diet. Svirskiy and I were proud as peacocks at our achievements. However, the eleven hundred pounds of fish, which the state required in return for allowing us to fish, were never handed over—we had "forgotten" that, and, apparently, nobody else thought about it.

At some point, a cable arrived from Moscow, ordering the fishermen at Rybzavod to start tending their nets twice every twenty-four hours.

Some shrewd person in the Ministry of Fisheries had figured out that if the nets were tended twice a day instead of once, the catches would become doubled. The manager and the other chiefs shook their heads in despair, but it was no use complaining about it, and the order was immediately passed on to the fishermen, who were told to comply with the new regulations from Moscow.

The fishermen, however, were stubborn and did not intend to simply give in to the whims of ignorant government officials in Moscow. The catches remained the same as prior to the new order from Moscow. For the fishermen knew that the water will have to calm down before the fish will approach the net, and tending the nets twice a day would be too much and would upset the fishing. The result would be smaller catches instead of the larger catches predicted by the ministry.

As a result of the new regulation, I got considerably more work. I now had to check whether all of the fishermen complied with the new directives from Moscow. From now on the fishermen were to state in their reports the extent to which they complied with the so-called plan for tending nets.

For example, a fisherman who had one hundred nets on the ice would, if tending his nets twice a day, have two hundred nets to tend. However, if he only tended ninety of his nets once a day, he would only have fulfilled the requirements of the plan by forty-five percent.

None of the fishermen tended their nets twice daily, but to avoid trouble and complaints from the management, most of them stated that they had and that they had thus met the requirements of the plan by one hundred percent. They could do this with a good conscience, for they were, of course, paid on the basis of the volume of fish they caught and not on the basis of the number of times they tended their nets.

However, a few of the fishermen refused to write such false reports and indicated that they had tended their nets only once a day and had thus defied the directives from Moscow. The individual reports were entered into a ledger, and every fifth day I sent Moscow my report on the catches and the extent to which the fishermen had complied with the new plan.

Semikin, the manager, was well aware of the fact that the plan for tending the nets was not complied with one hundred percent, and he instructed me to alter the reports somewhat so that the difference between the plan and the actual results became as small as possible. I followed the directives of the manager, and everything went well until an auditor from Moscow all of a sudden emerged at Rybzavod and, like a bolt from the blue, swooped down upon the bookkeeping department. He had traveled thousands of miles and had had a long and difficult trip, the last twenty-five miles by dog sledge in order to come and check whether Rybzavod complied with the new plan.

I was the first one to be approached by the auditor, and he asked me to show him the latest report, which was under preparation. I promised him to do my best to complete it by the end of the workday. While I was altering the report according to the instructions given me by Semikin, Semikin himself came into my office and told me not to hand over the report to the auditor until he had returned to the office himself. When it was getting close to five o'clock and Semikin had still not shown up, I became somewhat nervous and did not quite know what to do. Instead of Semikin, the auditor himself came into my office, asking me to hand over the report and all of the background material. I dared not decline his request and handed all of the papers over to him. The auditor first examined all of the background material and then began to check all of my accounts and calculations. It did not take him long to figure out that there was something wrong and that the background material did not agree with the figures of the report. The auditor looked at me with skepticism, asking me about my education. I told him that I had completed the seventh grade, to which he answered dryly that it was completely beyond him to understand how it would be possible after seven years of schooling to possess as little knowledge of basic arithmetic as my

72

reports showed. Without any further comments, he took all the papers with him and allowed me to go home.

My spirits were extremely low on the way home and throughout the night. I had difficulty falling asleep and could not help worrying about the consequences of my lack of knowledge of arithmetic. I was quite certain that, at best, they would charge me with slovenliness and negligence and that, as a result, I would be fired. But I also risked being charged with sabotage through manipulation and alteration of government documents of great importance to the economy, and that might result in ten years of labor camp. Never before or after have I been as impatient to get to work as the next morning—I had to find out what was awaiting me.

As soon as Semikin arrived, he asked me to come into his office. On his desk was my report with all the errors I had made. On the last page, I saw Semikin's signature. "Sign," he told me, and his voice and appearance betrayed a certain amount of nervousness and tension. By signing the report he had undertaken the full responsibility for its contents and did not leave me as the scapegoat, which would have been extremely easy for him to do. I never learned what Semikin had told the auditor or what he had done with him. It was impossible to tell whether the two men had discussed the new plan for tending nets and all of its unreasonable aspects and faults, and whether Semikin had succeeded in convincing the auditor of the uselessness of the method, that it did more harm than good. Nor is it known how many bottles of vodka were emptied that December night—that was not entered anywhere and did not appear in any reports.

The next day the auditor went back to Moscow; I was dismissed and had to leave my job by the end of December. It may sound strange, but I was happy about the dismissal, for I had feared that the whole affair might have a much more unhappy ending. Semikin told me that the auditor had demanded that I be fired. He offered me a job in one of the workshops by way of compensation, since I had not betrayed him but had kept silent about our manipulation of the reports.

I thanked him for his offer, telling him that I would rather not accept it, as I wanted above all to get away from Bykov Mys. I should be very grateful to him if he would help me and my family leave Bykov Mys. Semikin promised to do his best to fulfill my wish.

The NKVD was in charge of our supervision, and without a permit from the NKVD we could go nowhere. It was no easy matter obtaining such a permit, and one had to figure out some kind of clever solution. It was Semikin himself who found a way out. He provided me with a statement to the effect that, on account of my poor state of health, Rybzavod was no longer in a position to employ me. For that reason, I was transferred to the main office of Rybzavod and had to be moved to Yakutsk.

The only drawback to this excellent solution was that navigation on the Lena did not begin until July, and that meant that we would have to wait for nearly six months before being able to leave. This was not very encouraging, but there was no other or better solution, so we had to get through the coming months as best we could. We now had to live even more modestly than before and managed by selling some of our remaining things, by fishing, and by the help of our friends and acquaintances among the deportees.

Rachel · Israel

It was high time for us to leave. We were all in poor health and weakened after our stay in Bykov Mys. Israel, who had contracted scurvy, was worst off. In time, he suffered more and more from the disease—his legs swelled, and he had difficulty walking. The best medicine would be vitamin C, but it could be obtained neither in the form of pills nor in the form of fresh vegetables and fruit. We felt more and more strongly that it was now a race against time and that it was important for us to get away before any of us succumbed to the horrible conditions under which we lived. Long and painful were the months we waited for the sun, the light, and the heat to arrive and open up the navigation on the Lena, which would bring us a little closer to civilization and, at any rate, to better climatic conditions.

7

Rachel · Israel

The navigation on the Lena started unusually early that year, and already in early July the first steamboat arrived at Bykov Mys. It was now to take us south to Yakutsk. Actually, we had only been permitted to go to the town of Kyusyur, which was located in the same district as Bykov Mys, but we hoped that the paper which Semikin had given us would enable us to go all the way to Yakutsk.

On arriving at Kyusyur, all passengers were told to report to the local police office to show their identity cards and travel permits. We decided to take the chance and remain on board the ship. Israel had talked to the captain and told him that we would be extremely grateful to him if he would allow us to stay on board and continue to Yakutsk. The captain needed no further explanations to understand in which way our gratitude would be expressed, and he agreed to let us stay.

However, it was not all that easy to fool the authorities and escape their firm hold on us. It was not long before an NKVD officer, accompanied by a couple of men in civilian clothes, arrived to check everybody who was still on board. We were immediately ordered to report to the police office. After examining our papers, the local commander gave us a searching look and told us to wait outside his office. After about an hour, he came out to us, saying that we would not be allowed to continue but would have to remain in Kyusyur for the time being. We did not have the necessary permits and would have to remain within the limits of the district. We went sadly back to the ship, got our luggage together, and went ashore.

On our way down to the ship, we quite accidentally met another deported family, who offered us shelter when they heard what had happened to us. They lived in a one-room apartment—they were five, and we were five, but we all managed to fit.

We thought at first that we would be allowed to continue our trip in a couple of days. But the days and weeks went by without anything happening. When we understood that it might still be a long time before anything would happen, we moved in with a fisherman's family, who lived in a large yurt. The fisherman had gone on a long fishing expedition, so there was a fair amount of space for everybody.

When a month had gone by without anything happening, we started getting nervous about what would now be in store for us. However, a Russian proverb says that nothing is so bad that it is not good for something.

Rachel

Although Kyusyur was located about three hundred miles north of the Arctic Circle, the conditions here were nevertheless better than in Bykov Mys. The climate was milder and the vegetation considerably richer and more varied. The local people told me about an herb that was very helpful against scurvy. Every day I went out and picked a whole bowlful of these herbs for Israel. They were extremely sour and rich in vitamin C, and after Israel had eaten them for a few days, the daily improvement in his health was quite noticeable. After some time he had completely recovered from the unpleasant disease, and the rest of us were also much better off in Kyusyur.

Rachel · Israel

The change of climate had a favorable effect on our state of health, but our economic situation, on the other hand, was in extremely poor shape. It was of no use for Israel to try to find a job, for we expected and hoped to obtain our travel permit any time. We sold the last pieces of extra clothing that we had, hoping that our stay in Kyusyur would soon come to an end. However, after two months without change we began slowly to get adjusted to the idea that we would have to remain there during the winter.

We had sent several cables to Rybtrest, the chief organization of the fishing industry for the entire area with its main office in Yakutsk, but we received no reply. One day we were summoned before the NKVD officer, who told us with the same stony face as before that if we wanted to go to Yakutsk, the authorities would not prevent us from doing so. If we wanted to go?! But now all the transportation problems started. There was no regular connection from Kyusyur south to Yakutsk, and it was only accidentally that ships sailing by would call at the small harbor. If we wanted to board one of the ships calling at Kyusyur, we would have to keep constant watch down on the bank of the river and be ready to leave at short notice. We got hold of a tent, in which we placed our luggage and where we ourselves would be protected from the rain, and started taking turns to keep watch down on the riverbank.

The man at the harbor, known by everybody as the harbor chief, had told us that when we saw the smoke from the smokestack of a steamer appearing from behind the top of a mountain north of Kyusyur, we could expect the ship to arrive at Kyusyur about three hours later.

It was about five o'clock in the morning when, after several days of waiting, Baba came up to the house and woke us up to say that a ship was on its way with a whole convoy of dumb barges behind it. It was going to call at Kyusyur to unload barrels of gasoline.

We quickly packed the few things we had left in the house and hurried down to the bank.

It was September 3, 1943, a bleak, dark, and cold fall day. It was drizzling, and the clouds were low in the sky. After the ship had dropped its anchor, five dockworkers started unloading the barrels of gasoline. Two other families wanted to leave by the same convoy. A fisherman in a rowboat was to take all of us to one of the barges, which lay about a third of a mile from the bank. His boat would only hold two passengers and a few pieces of luggage at a time. When he had gone back and forth several times, it finally became our turn. People on the ship and in the barges had started becoming impatient, and the shouts of "Bystrey! Bystrey!" were now heard constantly. The fisherman in the rowboat had also become nervous and said in an annoyed voice that there were only a few minutes left before the ship would be leaving.

Israel

Rachel and the children sat down in the boat and were rowed over to one of the barges. As soon as they were on board, the fisherman began to row back for Baba and me. When he had got halfway back, there was a sudden deep hoot from the steamer, and before any of us had had time to react, it set into motion, pulling the entire convoy of barges along with it. I cried at the top of my voice to the ship to stop, but it was of course in vain. I just barely managed to shout to Rachel that Baba and I would take the plane to Yakutsk and meet her and the children in the harbor when they arrived.

Thousands of different ideas raced through my head as I watched Rachel and the children slowly sliding away from me on the barge, while I myself stood entirely helpless, left behind on the riverbank in a distant and godforsaken corner of northeastern Siberia. How were they to manage? For they had neither money nor ration cards with them—only a couple of bundles. Where were they to stay in Yakutsk? When were we to see one another again? Did Baba and I have enough money to pay for the airfare, that is, if we would at all be permitted to go by plane? Would there be any more ships arriving at Kyusyur before the ice would prevent all navigation? Would we be separated from Rachel and the children till next summer by being forced to spend the winter in Kyusyur?

During the first few minutes after the departure of the ship, it was difficult to grasp the full implications of our situation. We remained standing on the shore, following with our eyes the barge with Rachel and the children until it became a silhouette which finally disappeared entirely below the horizon.

For the first time since our deportation, the family had become split up, and I was worried about the consequences. Rachel would have difficulty managing without me, because her knowledge of Russian was still rather limited, and she would not be able to make her point if difficulties arose.

Baba was entirely crushed by despair. Under no circumstances would she fly, and if no more ships arrived, she would have to spend the winter in Kyusyur until navigation started anew the following year. I could not leave her behind here, nor could I leave Rachel and the children alone in Yakutsk. I felt completely powerless—here I was standing entirely alone in this huge country, while my wife and children were sailing toward an uncertain future, and there was nothing I could do about it. There was nobody to whom I could turn for help, and there was nothing that I could do myself.

The experience has deeply penetrated my consciousness. In the following years I often dreamed that I arrived too late to catch a ship or a train—it sailed or took off right in front of me, and I ran desperately to catch it but never succeeded.

Having thought the matter over after we had calmed down a little Baba and I decided to take the risk and to hope for the arrival of another ship that would take us along. We again settled on the bank of the river and started keeping watch. After three days' watch we were successful—a ship with two barges had to call at the harbor to load a cargo of coal. When the ship had moored at the quay, Baba contacted the wife of the captain and told her that we had been left behind and had become separated from our family. She promised to put a word in for us, and the captain permitted us and another deportee, Meir Slutskiy, who had also been left behind in Kyusyur, to take the boat to Yakutsk. We were relieved and happy to finally leave Kyusyur.

On board the ship we were shown to a tiny cabin, which could only be used for sleeping since there was no room for sitting or standing. However, we were quite content, as we were on our way south to be reunited with Rachel and the children, and we had no difficulty putting up with the lack of comfort. The ship was very old and run down and must have held the world record in production of black smoke and consumption of coal. It became one of the strangest voyages I have ever experienced.

On account of its enormous consumption of coal, the steamer was repeatedly forced to leave behind the two barges because it did not have enough coal to tow them to the next coal supply center. It therefore left the barges behind, sailed to the next harbor where coal was available, and then went back for the two barges. The result of this shuttle was that a distance of, say thirty miles became ninety miles. Navigation became hampered by the increasing number of ice floes, which started forming in the river and grew in size. When we realized how slowly we were proceeding, we began to worry that we should not be able to reach Yakutsk before the river froze over.

The last harbor at which we had to call before reaching Yakutsk was a small town by the name of Sangar-Khaya about 220 miles north of Yakutsk. However, like so many times before, the supply of coal of the ship was insufficient, and about thirty miles before Sangar-Khaya we again had to leave the two barges behind. When we arrived at Sangar-Khaya, we decided to go ashore in order to send a cable to Rachel to inform her of our arrival and to purchase food supplies for the latter part of our voyage, which would probably take another week. It would take about twenty-four hours for the ship to get back to Sangar-Khaya, and while Baba remained on board, I went ashore to take care of all the practical matters. Meir Slutskiy went ashore as well.

Slutskiy was a person of a very special cast, and when God distributed the various qualities among his children, he was not particularly generous toward Slutskiy. He was at the time a man of approximately fifty years, with a narrow face, grayish hair, brushed back, and small, sly eyes, which were never at rest. There was something nervous and frightened in his attitude but at the same time something inscrutable, so that you were always on your guard with him. On several occasions he proved that watchfulness and a guarded attitude toward him were not entirely unjustified.

When we landed at Sangar-Khaya, I immediately went to the post office to send a cable to some of our friends in Yakutsk, asking them to inform Rachel that we were on our way and that we would arrive in approximately four days.

When that had been taken care of, I went with Slutskiy to the town's only restaurant or, rather, dining hall, where the tables had been arranged in rows and where the food was handed out through a hatch. However, after the modest meals we had been served on the ship, the food was fantastic.

There were many people in the dining hall, and we clearly attracted the attention and interest of the local people, who were not used to seeing strangers around. We soon started talking with those who were sitting around us, telling them where we came from and where we were going. Across from me sat a beautiful and attractive Russian woman in her mid-thirties. She had gentle features, dark, warm eyes, and dark, strong hair, which she had put up in an elaborate hairdo. She asked me whether I knew her niece, Frosha, who had an important job at Rybzavod in Bykov Mys. I knew her very well indeed and was able to tell Tanya, which was the name of the woman, a good deal about Frosha and her work.

I had had trouble finding lodgings for the night, and after I had spoken to Tanya for some time, I asked her whether she could help me find a place where I could spend the night. She told me that she herself had rented a room with an elderly couple, and she immediately offered to ask her host and hostess whether they might be able to put me up for a single night. Tanya worked as manager of the only shop in town and told me to come and see her later in the day when she would know whether they were able to accommodate me. She also offered to try to find lodgings for Slutskiy.

I went to her shop just before closing time, and Tanya told me that everything was in order. Her host and hostess did not mind my spending the night with them, and she had managed to put Slutskiy up with some acquaintances.

I helped Slutskiy find the house where he would be spending the night, and we agreed to meet on the bank of the river the next morning to wait for the ship.

When I arrived at the house of Tanya and her hosts, a lavish sight awaited me—in the center of the small room was a table laden with all kinds of dishes and several bottles. There were piroshki, salads, and various meat dishes, the existence of all of which I had almost forgotten, for I had not seen them for the last two or three years.

The host proposed a toast for peace and friendship, welcomed me to his house, and wished us all a good appetite. He need not have worried on that account—at least not as far as I was concerned. Tanya and her hostess proved to be excellent cooks, and the food was so delicious that I could not remember when I had last enjoyed a meal so much. One toast speech followed another, and we became more and more animated as the contents of the bottles decreased. It was as if all the barriers that separated us from one another were dismantled, and we simply enjoyed one another's company and talked freely about everything under the sun.

However, in the middle of it all, the door suddenly opened, and Slutskiy entered, downcast. Nobody in the company was particularly happy to see the unexpected guest, for we were just having such a good time and did not feel the least like breaking up. I asked Slutskiy what was wrong with him, knowing that nothing good would be forthcoming. He looked at me with the most pitiful expression and told me in a tremulous voice that he was afraid of spending the night with the people who had offered to put him up. He believed that they would murder him as soon as he had fallen asleep and steal his watch and wedding band. He was quite aware that his explanation was not well received, but he begged me to have mercy on him and ask my host and hostess to allow him to spend the night in their house. He would be happy merely to sit on the kitchen floor in the corner.

I did not know whether to laugh or cry, but we could not send Slutskiy back into the street. I told Tanya and her host and hostess about the

Rachel and Israel Rachlin

problem, and they, of course, immediately agreed to allow Slutskiy to stay with them. Our spirits were high—in a toast we had agreed to address one another informally and addressed one another as "dear friend." Space was easily made for Slutskiy because he was an acquaintance of mine. A bed was prepared for him in a corner on the floor, and he went to sleep.

However, shortly afterward there was another knock at the door. Now it was one of Tanya's girlfriends who came to ask us whether we would like to see a film with her in the local cinema. We accepted her invitation, and I did not mind being rid of Slutskiy for a couple of hours.

When we got back, Tanya brought out a bottle of nice Georgian wine, which she had kept for special occasions, and we sat down at the table again and listened to the latest news from Moscow over the loudspeaker, which had been placed in a corner of the living room.

A little past midnight we suddenly heard the whistle of a ship down at the river. Slutskiy started up, saying that it must be our ship. It could not possibly have been, for it could not have managed to be back already, but it was impossible to reason with Slutskiy, and we were unable to convince him that it had to be another ship. He panicked, gathered his things together, and quickly took leave of Tanya and our hosts. I did not at all feel like leaving the hospitable home and starting out into the night. But should it after all turn out to be our ship, what would my mother then think of me? I reluctantly got ready to leave, thanked Tanya and her hosts for their hospitality, and apologized for having to break up so suddenly. They told me that they would leave the door open so that I could come back if it turned out that it was not our ship.

It was rather difficult getting down to the river—it was pitch-dark, and we had to follow a small path down a steep slope. It turned out, of course, that it was not our ship. I was rather annoyed with Slutskiy, but it was too late, and I was too tired to return, so we spent the night in a small guardhouse down at the river.

The next morning at around ten o'clock our ship arrived. I told my mother what I had done during my stay in Sangar-Khaya and about the hospitality of Tanya and her hosts. The ship was not scheduled to leave immediately, and my mother and I took the opportunity to walk up to Tanya and thank her once more. My mother gave her two beautiful handkerchiefs, which she had embroidered on the ship.

One invariably associates each stop, however brief, in a new place with the people one meets and the experiences one has with them.

When I think back at the hours I spent in Sangar-Khaya, I think of Tanya . . . and of Slutskiy.

After another four days of sailing, we finally arrived in Yakutsk. The date was October 12, and our ship was the last one to get into the harbor of Yakutsk during that navigation period.

However, contrary to all of my expectations, Rachel and the children were not at the harbor to meet us. My disappointment soon changed into concern at what might have happened to them. We had been separated for five weeks, and that is a long time when one is constantly worried, not knowing how one's beloved ones are doing. I had no idea how Rachel and the children had managed the long trip, what they had had to eat on the boat, and where they would now be staying. The most obvious reason why nobody had come to meet us—that my cable had not arrived—did not occur to me. As it turned out, my cable only arrived two days after I did. I now had to find out whether Rachel was in Yakutsk and where she was staying with the children. I had the address of our friends and decided to look them up immediately. Baba remained at the harbor to watch our luggage, and I started out for the town—a walk of four and a half miles.

Rachel

I shall never forget the moment when I was standing at the rail of the barge with the children and the convoy suddenly started moving, while Israel and Baba were still standing on the bank. I was seized with panic when I realized what had happened. However, I soon regained my composure lest my panic should make the children afraid. While I was standing waving at Israel and Baba, I desperately wondered how I would manage till I got to Yakutsk. Israel shouted something about taking a plane, but I did not quite understand him.

I had quite unexpectedly landed in a dreadful situation, and there was not much I could do to get out of it. I was suddenly standing entirely alone with two children on board a barge surrounded by strangers. During the two years we had been living in Siberia, I had never been alone or been in a situation where I did not have Israel or Baba to help me. I still was not quite able to manage in Russian—it is true that I understood a good deal of the language and that I was able to say a few things, but I had to ask Israel or Baba to help me whenever the conversation became a bit involved. The worst thing, however, was that I had no ration cards—they had remained with Israel, for he always carried them on him. Nobody had been able to foresee our situation. Fortunately, there was some flour in our luggage, and with that we were able to manage, at least for part of the voyage.

The passenger barge we had boarded was the rearmost in the convoy, which was approximately a third of a mile long. The convoy was pulled by a motor vessel by the name of *Pyatiletka*, which, I was told, means "the five-year plan." I was also told that the ship was the largest one on the Lena and that the majority of the cargo on board consisted of merchandise from the United States. The goods had been shipped to Tiksi at the mouth of the Lena and were now to be sent on to Yakutsk and still farther south.

The passenger barge had a large, covered room with a great number of primitive benches on which we sat during the day and slept during the night. It reminded me of some of the many waiting rooms we had seen during our train trip through Siberia. The cooking took place on a huge stove, which had been placed in the rear of the barge in a makeshift kitchen. There was always a crowd around the stove, and people were always tense and unfriendly.

With the flour I had taken along, I baked some flatbreads, which the children ate with a healthy appetite. These flatbreads were called *lepeshki* and were made with flour, water, and a bit of salt kneaded into a firm dough that was placed directly on the hot stove top, after having been divided into small portions and pressed completely flat. I had often seen Russians and Yakuts bake bread in this way and therefore had some idea of how to go about it. During the three weeks en route to Yakutsk, I became quite an expert at baking lepeshki.

The sanitary conditions on board the barge were, to put it mildly, primitive, and washing the children or our clothes was always an ordeal. However, apart from all of the practical difficulties, I did, indeed, feel somewhat relieved knowing that we were now on our way south to a friendlier climate and hopefully better life. During the daytime, we often sat on the deck, enjoying the sunshine and the scenery around us. The children did very well on board the barge and enjoyed all of the fresh air. There were two other families from Lithuania on board—like us, they had ended up in Kyusyur and were now on their way to Yakutsk. I was able to speak German with them, and I took advantage of this when problems arose with the Russian language.

Naturally, my thoughts were usually with Israel and Baba, and I wondered how long it would be before we should be united again. I also thought back to our stay in Kyusyur and at the way human beings adapt. After the ordeals we had experienced in Bykov Mys, our arrival at Kyusyur was a liberation. We were still in a godforsaken place far away from civilization and thousands of miles from our homes in Lithuania and Denmark, but our conditions had definitely improved, and we were happy to have escaped from Bykov Mys.

For an entire year we had not seen a single flower, but in Kyusyur we saw a lot of spring flowers, which resembled anemones, with frail, hairy stems and large, bright yellow petals. They shone brightly at us from a long distance, as if welcoming us to the warmer regions, and the children rushed to them, picking large bunches for me and Baba.

During the two months we had spent in Kyusyur, we had managed to recover our health, especially Israel, who had got completely rid of the scurvy he had contracted during our stay in Bykov Mys.

After three weeks of sailing we approached Yakutsk, and when, on September 23, we arrived at the harbor, I was convinced that Israel and Baba would be standing on the quay to meet us. Although I had difficulty hearing it, I was certain that, when he was standing on the shore as we started sailing, Israel had shouted that they would take a plane to Yakutsk.

But nobody was there to receive us—neither Israel nor Baba, nor any of our friends. I knew the address of the Bernstein family, our good friends from Lithuania, and I had no other choice than to look them up. I got a lift to town, and after having looked for some time, I found the house of the Bernsteins. The entire family gave us a warm welcome, but, unfortunately, they could not give us any information about Israel and Baba. This worried me—I could not understand what had happened, and I had no idea how to go about looking for Israel and Baba or to get in contact with them. The Bernsteins immediately started looking for a place where I could stay with the children. By afternoon, they managed to find a woman, Olga Nikolayevna, who lived on Gor'kiy Street not far from the Bernsteins and who had a room she was able to rent to us. We immediately moved in with her.

The rumor quickly spread among the other deportees in Yakutsk that I had arrived in town with the children, and the very same day several of our friends came to see us to find out what we needed and how they could help us. One of our very close friends from Lithuania, Joseph Lavit, also came by, and when he heard that we had neither bread nor ration cards, he took all three of us with him to an office, dragging us along from one window to the next. Joseph shouted and his gestures became increasingly frantic, but it was all to no avail. I had some difficulty following the emotional discussion, but after some parleying, Joseph apparently succeeded, and shortly afterward we departed with a pile of ration cards allotted to me and the children. We went directly to a bread shop and got our ration of bread. It tasted heavenly. The children loved the bread and ate it more or less as if it were chocolate.

It now became Schneur's task to help me with the shopping, and every day he went to the bread shop to purchase our ration of bread. There was not much traffic—it was mostly horse-drawn vehicles, and only once in a while did a car come by, so I was not nervous about letting Schneur walk alone in the streets. I had enough to do myself, obtaining food and shopping. That was no easy task in September of 1943. With our ration cards, we were able to obtain bread, sugar, butter, and grits, but the rations were small, and we had to obtain other food supplies to manage. The other purchases had to be made in the private market, where prices were sky-high and cheating quite common. It took me some time to learn how to shop in the private market without being taken in.

As the days went by, I became increasingly concerned that I had still not heard from Israel and Baba. I could not understand why he did not send a cable from Kyusyur or some other place to some of our friends in Yakutsk. I knew that it was possible to send a cable either from Kyusyur or from some other town on the way to Yakutsk. But I had to wait for another three long weeks without any sign from him. On October 12, I sent Schneur out on his usual shopping trip to the bread shop. As he had done several times before, he took his friend Kolya along—Kolya was one of Olga Nikolayevna's three sons.

Israel

Sometimes reality surpasses one's imagination. On our way from the harbor into town, I stopped a truck, and for fifty rubles I was given a lift almost to the center of town. After having been dropped off, I asked some passersby for directions to the address of the Bernsteins. On my way to their house, I suddenly noticed two boys on the other side of the street. One of the boys stopped suddenly, looked attentively at me, and shouted "Papa," rushing head over heels toward me. They were Schneur and Kolya on their way to the bread shop. Schneur flung his arms round my neck, and after we had both recovered from the big surprise, the two boys immediately took me to Olga Nikolayevna's house, where Rachel became quite speechless when she saw me standing bodily in front of her. Tears of joy, laughter, reproaches, and a lot of questions intermingled amid all of our joy at seeing each other again. After the first hurried explanations and assurances that everything was all right, I had to arrange for a horse and a carriage to take me back to the harbor for Baba and our luggage. It was late in the evening by the time I got back to the house with Baba. We were all tired, confused, and very happy to have become reunited.

Pokrovsk, 1953. Rachel and Harrietta right behind our house on the slope leading down to the Lena. From that spot we often looked up the river, wondering when we would be sailing in that direction.

Pokrovsk, 1953. Rachel and Harrietta in front of the house, feeding the chickens. On the front steps is our water container, and on the wall behind it is our bathtub. Next to the wall to the right is the chicken coop, which was taken into the kitchen during the winter.

Pokrovsk, 1952. The first class graduating from the school of Pokrovsk. The teachers are sitting in the front row; Israel is standing to the extreme right. Seven of the graduates are Russians; the rest are Yakuts.

Yakutsk, 1954. Israel, Schneur, Samuel, and our lodger, Sasha Veksler, in front of the house. They had just fetched water in the barrel by sleigh. It is still early winter—later on we had water delivered in the form of large ice blocks, which were piled up right in front of the house. The small waterworks was located approximately two-thirds of a mile from the house.

Schneur and his fellow students helping with the harvest at the collective farm of Pyatiletka outside Yakutsk in 1954.

Baba's grave in the Jewish cemetery in Yakutsk. At the fence is a board in Hebrew and Russian. In the middle of the grave is a block of larch wood, which was used instead of a tombstone. Larch contains a natural preservative, which practically makes it last forever.

Copenhagen, 1957. The first photograph taken on our arrival in Copenhagen on July 22. It was taken right after our disembarkment at Langelinie in the harbor of Copenhagen.

8

Rachel · Israel

In Yakutia they have a saying, which we had already encountered many times: "We have twelve months of winter, and the rest is summer." That, of course, is an exaggeration, but in the course of the years, we had ample opportunity to experience the severe climate. Only about one hundred days a year were without frost, and even if we were about one thousand miles south of Bykov Mys, it was much colder in the winter than it ever was in Bykov Mys. The weather described was a typical continental climate at its worst, with temperatures dropping to fifty-eight to sixty-seven degrees Fahrenheit below zero in the winter and exceeding eighty-six degrees Fahrenheit on the warmest days of the hot and dry summer.

The town of Yakutsk is the capital of the Yakut Autonomous Soviet Socialist Republic, an enormous area measuring approximately 1.2 million square miles in the northeastern part of Siberia. The republic was only formed in 1922, five years after the October revolution. The local population did not want to recognize the Soviet power and waged a long and bitter war against the new regime. In 1922, however, all resistance was finally defeated, and Yakutia became one of the autonomous republics of the Soviet Union.

The town of Yakutsk was founded as early as 1642 when Russian colonizers pushed forward through Siberia. The town started as a minor fortress, built on the western bank of the Lena in an inaccessible swamp. The founders, the Russian colonizers, had chosen the spot quite deliberately to make it more difficult for their enemies to approach the fortress. The indigenous nomadic tribes fought the Russian colonizers, attacking them when and wherever possible.

The small fortress grew increasingly larger through the centuries, and at the time of our arrival, Yakutsk was a rather large town. At the time, in 1943, population statistics were considered state secrets, and it was impossible to estimate the exact number of inhabitants. However, the figure was probably somewhere between fifty and seventy thousand. Yakutsk was the administrative, economic, and cultural center of the republic. There were many schools in the town, a couple of scientific institutes, a couple of museums, and one theater. By the standards of the time, it was a rather civilized town.

The vast majority of the houses in Yakutsk were wooden structures, most of them single-story houses but a few with two stories. Wooden houses were easier to heat in the winter but were also better suited to the climate. The few brick houses in Yakutsk were all askew and contained huge cracks in their masonry on account of the permafrost, which caused shifts in the earth when the temperature rose and fell between seasons. Only in the sixties was a special building technique developed for regions subject to permafrost, making it possible on the basis of pile foundations to construct houses of masonry several stories high. In 1943, however, nearly all of the houses were wooden structures, either ordinary log cabins or cabins furbished up with clay and painted in all kinds of strange colors. Located in the middle of a swampy area, they were surrounded by hardly any vegetation at all. No bushes or trees would grow, making the town even more drab and unfriendly.

The population of Yakutia was rather composite. There were the native Yakuts and several other minor Eskimo tribes, who were originally nomads and had earned their livelihood through fishing or hunting. The Russians living in the area could be divided into two groups: the permanent residents and those who had been posted there. The latter came from all parts of the Soviet Union and had been posted in the area according to a rule, which still applies today, requiring all graduates, on completion of their college or university education, to work for three years within their profession in a place designated by the state. According to the official philosophy, it is the duty of every student or candidate to undertake this task as a kind of payment to the state for the free instruction and education he or she has received. This principle is strictly adhered to, and it is very difficult for the young men and women fresh from college or university to escape it.

Those who were posted in Yakutia were the least fortunate ones, and many regarded those years as a kind of deportation, even though they knew that they would be allowed to return home after three years. By way of compensation for the difficult conditions prevailing in Yakutia, they received a special allowance in addition to their basic pay, enjoyed longer vacations, and were given several other special privileges.

Then there were the deportees. These included Germans, Karelians, a large group of Poles, and people from the Baltic States, the majority of whom were Jewish and non-Jewish Lithuanians. In addition, there was a small group of Chinese and Koreans who somehow or other had ended up in Yakutia. They were important to all of us, since they grew and sold most of the vegetables available in the local markets.

Yakutia has always been the favorite area for deportations. As early as the nineteenth century, political opponents and other undesirable elements were deported to that area. That tradition developed steadily over the years and was carried on with special enthusiasm by Stalin. Under his leadership, the deportations to Yakutia assumed hitherto unknown proportions—millions of people were sent there. Though many were deported like ourselves, even larger numbers were sent to labor camps, often never to return.

After having lived in the area ourselves, we understood why Russian rulers through the ages have chosen Yakutia for their deportees. It was a punishment in itself to live under such difficult and unhealthy climatic conditions.

When temperatures dropped to less than fifty-eight degrees Fahrenheit below zero, it was, for several reasons, quite dangerous to go outside. The dreadful cold was often accompanied by dense fog, which reduced visibility to six or seven feet. The combination of severe cold and fog made it especially difficult to be outside and even to breathe. For the elderly and those of delicate health, it was thus especially dangerous to venture out in that kind of weather, and one only did so in heavy and uncomfortable clothes. On the head one wore a fur cap with earflaps, and to cover the nose and mouth, leaving only the eyes free, it was often necessary to wear a scarf. Those who were lucky had long fur coats or padded jackets or coats. Padded pants also constituted a vital part of one's clothing, as did knee-high felt boots. Felt boots were the only form of footwear used in the winter. In this entire outfit, one looked like a cross between a bank robber and a space pilot.

Another reason why it was difficult to go out was the high crime rate in Yakutsk. The town was the reception area for all prisoners who had been released from labor camps and were on their way home. During the winter there were always particularly large numbers of released prisoners in Yakutsk, because they were unable to get any farther until the navigation on the Lena River started anew. From October to May,

Yakutsk was more or less flooded with former prisoners arriving from labor camps to the north and east of Yakutsk, among them Kolyma and Verkhoyansk. A large number of those released were criminals whose only means of providing for the continuation of their trip was the same activity that had led to their imprisonment. Robberies and assaults were common during the daytime and especially during the evening throughout the winter months. The bandits did not merely rob people of their money when they succeeded in holding them up in the dark streets. They often forced people to undress, regardless of the cold weather. They left their victims without caps and coats in the icy cold streets, where they were in danger of freezing to death unless they succeeded in finding shelter very quickly. Not many people were outside after dark. If one had to go outside, one always made an endeavor to find someone to go along.

One had to be alert during the daytime too, when pickpockets infested the shops and the market.

Each winter the air in town was thick with hair-raising rumors of nightly assaults, of people being undressed in the street, and of murders. The local newspaper naturally never reported these crimes, for, officially, such serious crimes do not occur in a socialist state. That circumstance, of course, did not make one feel safer when forced to go outside in the winter night.

In Olga Nikolayevna's house we lived in a small room where we more or less had to sleep on top of each other. The entire house covered an area of about 430 square feet, and in addition to the five of use, the house accommodated Olga Nikolayevna herself, her three children, and a third family with two children.

However primitive, these conditions were, nevertheless, better than those in Bykov Mys. We gradually adjusted to the new situation, receiving help and advice from the friends and acquaintances who had been among the lucky ones to remain in Yakutsk when we were transported from Altayskiy Kray to Bykov Mys the year before. They had adapted quite well and been given positions in various organizations and institutes of education, which were in great need of college and university graduates. All of the deportees from Lithuania formed a kind of small colony, and we tried to stick together as much as possible to help each other adjust. The unity and willingness to help in these hard years heartened us, and the friendships that developed were deep and warm, the likes of which few of us were to experience later on in life.

Many people contracted tuberculosis, which was probably the most widespread disease at the time. Yakuts especially suffered from the disease, most likely because they lived under extremely primitive and unsanitary conditions. However, the deportees were quite susceptible too. In this connection, a rather gruesome case in point involved our good friends the Broyde family.

The Broydes had two sons, Allik and Boris, and one day a medical checkup revealed that Boris had contracted tuberculosis. The ability of the doctors to treat the disease was extremely limited, since no effective medicine had been discovered and the disease often proved fatal.

Mrs. Broyde was terribly upset and did not know what to do to help her son. We had all heard that the Yakuts used the lard of dogs in their treatment of tuberculosis, and it was said that it was by far the most effective remedy against the disease. After some reflection, Mrs. Broyde got hold of a puppy, which she started fattening in her home as if it were some kind of fatted calf. The two unsuspecting sons played with the dog and did their best to train it. Mrs. Broyde, however, had quite different plans for the puppy, which was never permitted to run into the street and which was looked after with great care. On account of the special diet it received, the dog's appearance became quite strange, and when it had become sufficiently large and fat, it disappeared without a trace.

Allik and Boris started looking for it, for their mother had told them that the dog had run away, but their efforts were in vain. In reality, when the boys were at school, Mrs. Broyde had handed the dog over to a Yakut to have it slaughtered in order to get the lard for her special recipe.

The lard of the puppy was melted in a saucepan, mixed with spices and onions, and afterward mixed into hot milk, which Boris was to drink. There is no way of knowing how the mixture tasted, but it was administered to Boris several times daily for a prolonged period of time. After completion of the treatment, he recovered entirely and has never since suffered from tuberculosis. We do not know whether he was ever told of the secret behind the miraculous treatment, but we know that several other deportees later on used the same recipe from the Yakut folk medicine.

Baba and Rachel were in charge of the housekeeping, which was an especially difficult job because of the extreme shortage of goods and the long queues everywhere. They often had to stand in line for several hours for their bread rations. Many articles, such as milk, meat, potatoes, and eggs, were not available in the state shops at all. They had to purchase these articles in the private market, where the prices were exorbitant. Baba and Rachel took turns shopping, and the children were always anxious to find out what they brought home from their shopping trips. They often came back with things that they had not at all intended to purchase, being often unable to buy what they did need. We quickly learned that when we saw an item we would need eventually, we ought to buy it, for the next day it would probably be gone.

Our room with Olga Nikolayevna on Gor'kiy Street was our seventh home since our deportation. We were to remain there for six months, what proved to be a time of many problems and much illness.

Israel

There is no unemployment in the Soviet Union—this claim is made by the Soviet propaganda machine with as much emphasis and pride today as it was then, and for the Soviets it provides irrefutable proof of the advantages of the socialist society over the capitalist society, where wage earners live under the constant threat of being fired and ending up unemployed.

After our arrival in Yakutsk, I was unemployed for some time. The first few days I spent recovering from the long and strenuous trip. I subsequently began looking for a job, and after a few days of job hunting, thanks to a tip from some friends, I got the job of bookkeeper in an organization that supplied machinery and spare parts to agriculture. When appointed, not only was I promised that I would receive a dwelling but also that the workplace would provide me with firewood and water. I soon realized, however, that I would never succeed in putting the accounts in order. Because they had been neglected for a long time, it was an impossible task for one man to systematize them. I had been appointed on trial and therefore was able to leave the job without difficulty after two weeks. At the time, I had already found out that there were many organizations in Yakutsk that needed economists and that I would therefore stand a good chance of getting a job as planner. Job discrimination was not known by name in the Soviet Union in 1943. As a special deportee I had all of the civil rights under Soviet law, for the idea was to turn us into law-abiding Soviet citizens. Officially, we were only restricted in our freedom of movement in that we were not allowed to travel to or move to any other place without special permits. However, I soon discovered that what may be true in theory does not necessarily exist in practice.

At the first commercial organization where I applied for a job, the manager told me that they were looking for a man of my very qualifications and that I would get the job immediately. I merely had to settle some formalities in the personnel department first.

The personnel manager was very kind and obliging, and after we had talked with one another for some time, he asked to see my passport. I told him that I had no passport and that I was a special deportee. His expression changed immediately, and he looked at me more or less as if I had cheated him. He shook his head, saying that I could not get the vacant position.

I made several attempts in other organizations—with the same result. One day, after having been rejected once again, I was in a depressed state of mind. As I walked along the street, wondering what to do, for we would not be able to manage if I did not soon get a fixed income, I suddenly noticed a sign for the Ministry of Education. I had nothing to lose and immediately decided to go into the ministry and try my luck.

Having been taught by bitter experience, I approached the personnel manager directly, telling him that I was a deportee and did not have any of my certificates but hoped to be able to get a job after all. He asked me about my qualifications, and I told him that I had a German baccalaureate and had completed a five-year study of economics at the University of Leipzig. When I noticed that he hesitated, I suggested that he subject me to a test, if the ministry had a consultant in the instruction of the German language. After considering the matter for a few seconds, he agreed, saying that they had a consultant, a comrade by the name of Rund, who would find out whether I fulfilled the qualifications for teaching German.

Comrade Gerda Rund turned out to be a German lady from Berlin. She possessed a doctorate in German and had served as lecturer at the University of Moscow. She had been a member of the Communist Party and had come to Moscow years before as one of the many idealists wanting to participate in the development of the socialist society. And she suffered the same fate as many of her comrades who had been similarly disposed—she held her job as lecturer at the University of Moscow for only six months, when she was arrested for being indiscreet and making critical remarks about the many shortcomings and errors she saw in the system around her. The end result was that she was forced to move to Yakutia—a better fate, after all, than that of many other foreign communists, many of whom disappeared without a trace in prisons and labor camps.

Right from our first encounter we spoke only German together and quickly took a liking to each other. Fräulein Rund, as I called her when we were alone, was a cultured and intelligent person who suffered a great deal from the deportation, the severe climate, and loneliness. She always looked very depressed and often gave expression to her despair. We met several times by virtue of our official duties, and she was always happy to talk to me. We often talked about Berlin, our student days, and the trips we had made around Europe. At our very first meeting, Fräulein Rund said that she would see to it that I be employed as teacher of German. After some time I received a written declaration to the effect that I was competent and qualified to teach German, and the road to my teaching career was now open.

Fräulein Rund died some years later lonely and unhappy—one of the many tragic lives that, through the unpredictability of life, had ended in Siberia.

A Russian saying has it that people only know one another very well after having eaten a whole *pud* of salt together. The Russian unit of measure is equivalent to approximately thirty-six pounds. I do not know how many pounds of salt I have eaten in the course of my years in the Soviet Union, though it is enough for me to believe that I know the Russians fairly well.

Despite our status as social outcasts and the many difficulties and shortcomings of the war years, throughout the years and wherever we went in Siberia, we met people who were friendly and helpful toward us. It is true that we also had less pleasant experiences and even humiliating and nerve-racking confrontations with some of the system's official representatives, who maliciously wanted to make life even more difficult for us. However, most of the people we met during our sixteen years in Siberia were people whom we today remember for their goodness and human warmth. They were people from all walks of life—ordinary laborers and artisans, managers and scientists, teachers and engineers, and many, many others.

That which we especially remember about these people is their sensitivity, hospitality, and readiness to help people in distress. Once one had become close to them and been accepted by them, they were willing to share their last piece of bread or clothing if one was in need. The Russians are quite sentimental, and it is characteristic of their temperament that, unlike the Scandinavians, they are not constrained when it comes to opening their hearts to another person and giving expression to their feelings.

That description does not, of course, fit everybody. The principal of

School No. 16 definitely belonged to the group of Russians who possessed less admirable qualities.

Shortly after having passed my "exam," I was appointed teacher of German at School No. 16—Soviet schools are, in general, given numbers instead of names. At this point, Soviet schools were divided into all-girl and all-boy schools, with School No. 16 being a school for boys. Most of the teachers were women—the teaching profession was traditionally dominated by women in the Soviet Union, and now that most men had been drafted, the difference was even more noticeable. The principal, whose name was Sevastyanov, was happy to get a male teacher, saying that men are better at making themselves respected and maintaining strict discipline. The principal and his wife, who taught Russian at the school, had just been evacuated from the beleaguered Leningrad.

I soon established a good rapport with my colleagues at the school, and most of them proved to be friendly and obliging people who were always ready to lend me advice and assistance. I also developed excellent relations with my students and had no special problems with any of them. Unfortunately, it soon turned out that Sevastyanov, the principal, was not a very kind person or, rather, comrade. He always flashed a friendly smile and spoke in a soft, calm voice, but behind the facade a calculating and evil disposition lurked. Even if we had no confrontations at all, I soon noticed that the feelings flowing toward me from Sevastyanov were anything but sympathetic. He seized every opportunity to strike at me, well aware that, due to my position as a special deportee, there was nothing I could do.

Like most other Soviet organizations, the schools in the Soviet Union have a so-called *zavkhoz*, a man or a woman who sees to it that all practical things function in the way they are supposed to. The zavkhoz supervises the buildings and checks that the heating system, water supply system, and other installations are functioning properly. At School No. 16 it was also the task of the zavkhoz to collect and distribute ration cards. However, Ivanov, our zavkhoz, was a war cripple and an alcoholic; rather negligent when it came to discharging his duties, he found it especially difficult to collect and distribute the ration cards. Several people complained to the principal about the zavkhoz, but he dared not fire him because he was a war veteran. Sevastyanov soon found a way out.

One day he called me into his office and, with his usual, ingratiating smile, told me that the school was in a difficult situation. He asked me to take over the work in connection with the ration cards as an honorary job, adding that he and the other teachers would be very grateful and that he would soon try to find another zavkhoz. However, that was not his intention at all, and during the next few months it became my burdensome job to handle the ration cards. I had to collect the cards myself from an office that was located far away, and each time I had to walk the long distance of several miles by foot. This task was difficult enough as it was and so became even more burdensome during the winter when the temperature dropped to forty degrees Fahrenheit below zero. Distributing the ration cards and keeping the accounts was quite a job. I was not paid a kopeck for the several hours of work I put in several days a week, for it was an honorary job, as stated by the cunning principal. I dared not turn down this honorary task for fear of losing my job and being regarded as an antisocial element who did not want to participate in the life and work of the collective.

Nor would it have been any use approaching the teachers' association. In short, there was not a single person who would lift a finger to help me, and there was nothing for me to do but to dig in my toes and endure.

Like all other Soviet citizens, at the time of my appointment I was given a conduct book, which accompanied me everywhere throughout our years in Siberia. Such a book contained information on the education, career, and work activities of the holder. It gave all of the particulars on promotions, transfers from one job to another, and censures of the holder. When a person left his job, it was indicated in his conduct book. He was also graded on his participation in public life. The latter statements were extremely important when he applied for a new job.

Serfdom was abolished in Russia in the nineteenth century, but the conduct book survived as some kind of relic from those days, despite the fact that it was not entirely in accordance with Soviet statements on the privileges of the workers in the workers' state.

Instruction in foreign languages in the Soviet Union commences in the fifth grade. My youngest students were twelve years old, a rather difficult age anywhere in the world, but perhaps particularly difficult for a German teacher in the Soviet Union in the war year of 1943. Germany, the Germans, and everything that had to do with them naturally caused violent reactions among the vast majority of Russians, and the children were, therefore, not particularly motivated to learn German. Many had relatives fighting at the front, and several had lost close relatives in the bombardment of towns in the European part of the Soviet Union. Some of the students simply refused to have anything to do with the German language. "We do not want to concern ourselves with the language of the fascists!" they said. It took a lot of effort and much patience on my part to convince them of the importance of knowing the language of the enemy both in times of war and peace.

I told them that German fascism would be overcome and that there would then be a demand for people proficient in German to talk to people in the occupied parts of Germany. I did not yet realize how right I was, but my arguments influenced only a few of the students. The hard core stubbornly refused to learn German.

Finally, however, I succeeded in breaking down even their resistance when we entered into a gentlemen's agreement. Educationally, it was probably not quite the right thing to do, but it worked very well. We agreed that if the students worked hard, did their homework, and were attentive in class, they would be allowed to ask me questions about life in Germany. Most of the students knew nothing of life in a big city, having only seen Yakutsk, and were impatient to hear about life in the outside world.

They had never seen a house of more than two stories, nor a train, nor a streetcar. They could not conceive of a house with a built-in water supply system nor of an indoor toilet. One of the many questions asked of me was: "How do people living on the fifth floor of a house get eggs, for they cannot keep chickens on the fifth floor?"

The students knew that I was a deportee, but in all the years I worked as a schoolteacher in the Soviet Union I never sensed any form of distrust or reserve on their part. Apart from some innocent pranks, I never had any difficulties with them. On the contrary, they often showed me affection, cheering me up very much in the midst of all my difficulties outside of work.

I had no particular difficulty in adjusting to the Soviet system of education, although it deviates greatly from the principles of education followed in the West. The most important requirement of a Soviet teacher is that he teach his students in such a way as to contribute to their education in the spirit of communism, influencing them to respect and honor the leaders of the country and to be obedient and patriotic. The same textbooks are used in schools all over the country, and the objectives are the same everywhere. Throughout the school years, great emphasis is placed on conduct, and all students from the first to the tenth grade are graded on conduct. All grades are on a scale of one to five.

Anna und Marta baden. This was the first sentence of the German textbook used in Soviet schools. The sentence may appear strange, but actually it is not. There are no short and long vowels in the Russian language, and to demonstrate that the case is different in German, the sentence *Anna und Marta baden* was made up. In that sentence *Anna* has got a short *a, und* a long *u,* and so forth. B*aden* was the first German word the students were taught, and with their usual ingenuity, it did not take long for them to give me the nickname of "Baden," which stuck with me during most of the years I taught German. After break when I was on my way to the classroom, I often heard my students shouting, "Baden is coming!"

When Schneur reached the fifth grade several years later and became one of my students, the name of Baden was also given to him, and he was called "Badenuol"—probably the only word coined in the German and Yakut languages at once. The word *uol* means "boy."

9

Rachel

In mid-December, in the very darkest time of the year, Harrietta suddenly became ill. We summoned a doctor, and after having examined her, he said that she had to go to the hospital at once. He saw to it that an ambulance was sent for. It turned out that she had contracted diphtheria. Neither she nor Schneur had been vaccinated against that dreadful disease. Harrietta was three years old at the time and spoke only German, because we spoke German among ourselves. I therefore had to accompany her to the hospital and remain with her during her serious illness for six weeks. The following weeks were a difficult time for the entire family and not least for Baba, who bore the brunt of it, since she was now the only one to attend to the housework, and since she also had to bring food to Harrietta and me at the hospital every single day. It was fortunate for us that the chief physician of the department of children's infectious diseases was another deportee from Lithuania, a woman by the name of Dr. Joffe. My knowledge of Russian was still not too good, and it was a great help to me that I was able to speak German with Dr. Joffe. I must admit that the treatment we received at the hospital was good, everything considered. Although Harrietta was given rather large doses of serum injections, it took her a long time to recover. Only after six long and difficult weeks was she declared well and free of infection and discharged. We were all relieved and happy, but unfortunately we got only a short respite.

Only a few weeks after our return, Schneur became ill. He too was taken to the hospital at once. The doctors at the hospital could not understand how he had become infected, for Harrietta had been checked thoroughly before being discharged.

Schneur became even more ill than Harrietta and was given even larger doses of serum than she. His condition was so serious that the doctors wanted him to have a blood transfusion. I went to the hospital to donate blood for him, and after the transfusion Schneur became somewhat better.

It was a mystery to the doctors how Schneur had become infected, and Dr. Joffe started asking me questions about our living conditions. I told her that we lived with two other families with children, and that two of the girls attended a nursery school. She immediately began to suspect that the girls might be carriers of the disease and that they had first given it to Harrietta and later on to Schneur.

The two girls were taken to the hospital to be examined, and it turned out that Dr. Joffe was right. The elder girl was the carrier of the disease without being ill herself. She was, of course, treated at the hospital immediately.

We unfortunately came to realize the truth of the old saying that misfortunes seldom come in single doses. While Schneur was recovering from his illness, Baba had an accident.

Valenki, special Russian felt boots, were the only form of footwear one could wear in the winter. The boots were the only thing that could protect the feet against the cold, and one would not slip in them as long as one took care that they did not become damp. The first thing one did upon getting home was to take off one's valenki and place them near the stove to dry. If the boots were not entirely dry when one got outside again, a layer of ice would quickly form on the soles, and the boots would then become highly dangerous to walk in.

Baba probably had not been careful enough in drying her boots. One day while she was out doing her daily shopping, she slipped on the pavement and fell in such an unfortunate way as to break her left upper arm. She immediately went to the emergency room of the neighborhood outpatients' clinic, where she waited a long time for her turn to come. The doctor examined her and gave her an admittance slip, but she had to get to the hospital at the other end of town herself. On her way, she stopped by our house, and I then accompanied her to the hospital. On our way there, she complained of much pain in her arm.

When we look back upon those days today, we cannot at all comprehend how Baba was able to cope with all these trials and how she summoned the strength to walk several miles at forty degrees below zero while suffering such severe pain. But it was, of course, the only thing we could do—we could not call a taxi, and we risked having to wait for several hours if we sent for an ambulance.

Baba only stayed in the hospital for a few days and returned home with her arm in a plaster cast, which she had to wear for six weeks. After this final sad event, we hoped that our series of misfortunes had finally reached its end. There was only one remaining problem: We could no longer tolerate our dreadful housing conditions. After a long search, we finally managed to leave the place.

We found a small house that had originally been used as a cow shed but had been converted into a dwelling and provided with a stove and a chimney. The house was located in a courtyard right next to the owner Krasnov's log house, which appeared very elegant and spacious to us, more or less like a palace. The old cow shed covered an area of about two hundred square feet, which, of course, was not much space for five people, but we were happy to be entirely on our own. It was a great improvement over our former living quarters.

Schneur had still not been discharged from the hospital, and the doctor allowed me to stay with him all the time, for his condition remained serious and he required a lot of care. In between my hospital stays, I went home to help Baba with the household, for there was a limit to what she could do with her broken arm. Israel was very busy at work and returned home each day quite exhausted after the long walk from the school.

Passover was approaching, and we were looking forward to having the entire family assembled to celebrate the big holiday. But it was not to be—Schneur had not yet been discharged and remained in the hospital much longer than we expected.

Together with several of our friends, we baked matzos, the traditional Passover breads, and Passover was celebrated with a feast consisting of gefilte fish, meat, and soup—it was a dinner we did not often have. In the evening I went back to the hospital, for I would still spend the night there to be with Schneur.

One morning a few days after Passover, Israel unexpectedly came to the hospital, asking me to come home with him, for Baba had become seriously ill. We hurried back, and as soon as I saw Baba, I realized that she was in a very poor shape. Her legs had become entirely blue, and she complained of severe stomachaches. I ran out to get an ambulance. When it arrived, Baba got dressed on her own and got into the ambulance without anybody's help. Israel accompanied her to the hospital where the doctors, after examining her, told him that Baba had volvulus.

The doctor on duty said that it was too late to operate on her and that they had to await further developments in her condition. Israel wanted to stay with Baba, but she told him that she did not want him to stay away from the school and his students because of her. After all, there was nothing he could help her with right now, she said. Complying with Baba's wish, Israel left and went back to his school. It was to be her last wish.

Baba died a few hours later. When I arrived to visit her, I was met by a nurse who told me that Baba had died. She had been fully conscious all the time but had apparently not realized how serious her condition was. According to Jewish custom, Baba was buried the next day in the Jewish cemetery in Yakutsk. A small group of our Jewish friends and acquaintances accompanied her on her last trip. Her coffin was placed on a horse-drawn sleigh. The small group of mourners walked behind the sleigh on its way through the town all the way out to the stadium, where the Jewish cemetery was located behind a wooden fence. After a brief ceremony, during which the Jewish prayers were said, the simple wooden coffin of rough boards was lowered into the frozen ground.

The Jewish cemetery in Yakutsk was rather old. Already during the czarist regime, many Jews were deported to that area because they were politically active and had fought the system. Many of them had dreamed of creating a socialist state, which became a reality after 1917. Little did they dream of the oppression and political persecution that would arise in the Soviet state under the new rulers. Baba's grave in the Jewish cemetery became one of the many new graves that remained as the only memorials to entirely innocent people who paid with their lives for Stalin's persecution of imaginary enemies.

About a week after Baba's funeral, Schneur was finally discharged from the hospital. The first thing he asked upon his return was why Baba was not yet home. He knew that Baba had been taken to the hospital, but we dared not tell him the truth yet. He had been immensely fond of his grandmother, and we simply dared not subject him to the emotional strain while he was still extremely weak from his long and severe illness. At first we managed to divert his attention, and he busied himself with exploring our new home and its surroundings. After a few days he nevertheless sensed that something was wrong and kept asking why we were not visiting Baba at the hospital. Finally, we both had to sit down and tell him in as gentle a manner as possible what had happened while he was in the hospital.

Baba's death was a great loss and meant a great change for all of us. We had loved her and been very attached to her. During the upheavals in our life, she had proved a wise and noble human being who, in her modest and self-denying manner, had done everything she could to help us in our distress. And even if she had been used to an entirely different life, she accepted her fate with great dignity and proved capable of adjusting to the most impossible circumstances. Our family had always been very close, but the conditions in Siberia made us even more strongly attached to one another. My relations with Baba were entirely different from the usual relations between a mother-in-law and a daughter-in-law. We were two women suffering a common fate, and we both regarded it as our most important task to see to it that our family, and especially our children, did not suffer any hardships. We both did what we could to give the children as much security and warmth as possible. Wherever we were, we endeavored to make our lives as comfortable as possible and to protect the children against the dangers of the outside world. Even in the darkest and most difficult hours, each helped the other keep up her spirits, and we never lost hope or our joy in life. It was hard to become reconciled to the idea that Baba was no more, and I could not at all imagine how we would manage during the coming years without her support and guidance. Baba had reached the age of sixty-two years.

Time seemed to drag on, but the weather started getting warmer and the days became longer. Around mid-May, spring slowly appeared, and we were all looking forward to the warm sun and warm weather. The reports from the front became increasingly encouraging. The Soviet Army was advancing on all fronts, and we started hoping that, as soon as the war was over, our deportation would be lifted and we would be allowed to leave Yakutsk and go somewhere else in the Soviet Union where the climate was better and the conditions more civilized.

Our financial situation caused us constant difficulties. Even if a teacher was relatively well paid, we were unable to manage on Israel's salary. We had to live in a very modest way and count every single ruble we spent. Our money was spent only on food and firewood—firewood was very expensive, but it was, of course, impossible to cut down our consumption of firewood in the cold weather of Yakutia.

We were able to manage for ten to twelve days on Israel's salary, and then we once again had to find things that we could spare from our suitcases and wardrobe. We had no problems selling clothes, since nearly everything would sell, including jewelry.

Among the deportees in Yakutsk were approximately one thousand Polish Jews. In 1944, parts of Poland had become liberated, and as increasingly larger parts of the country became liberated, the deportees from Poland were allowed to return home. During their years in Yakutsk, many of the Poles had proved extremely adaptable and had been able to "save" considerable sums of money. I do not know how they managed to do it, but I have the feeling that it was not always done in an entirely legal manner. Many of them wanted to spend their money on purchasing valuables before returning to Poland, where their rubles would have absolutely no value.

We realized that the time had now come to part with a valuable ring that we had managed to keep, despite the many raids to which we had been subjected. It was a diamond ring with a large 2.75-carat stone of very fine quality. The ring had its own history.

It was an heirloom, and it was presented to me at Schneur's birth. One day after the Soviet occupation of Lithuania, I decided to hide the ring, although I did not at the time have the faintest idea of the trials we would soon be undergoing. The air was already thick with rumors of raids on the homes of well-to-do people and seizures of all of their valuables. We ourselves had already been visited by several so-called committees, who came to "borrow" furniture, which they felt we did not need. It was therefore only to be expected that a committee arrive at any point in time and express an interest in our jewelry and other valuables, which, in their opinion, we did not need.

I did not know how to best hide the ring, but one day as I was sitting knitting a sweater, it suddenly occurred to me that the best place in which to hide it would be inside the ball of wool lying in my lap. It proved to be a good idea.

All of our things were thoroughly searched several times, and several NKVD officers had held my knitting in their hands without suspecting anything. Of course, it is not the easiest thing in the world to unwind an entire ball of wool. But in that manner I managed to hold on to my ring throughout all their searches. Finally, however, I had to take the ring out of its safe hiding place, for it now had to be sold in order for us to survive. It turned out that several people were interested in buying it, but we did not know what to ask for it. There was no possibility of having the ring evaluated anywhere. After much reflection and many comparisons and calculations, we finally decided on the price of forty-five thousand rubles.

It was a lot of money for us, for Israel would have to work as a teacher for three and a half years to earn that amount. For the same amount of money we would be able to purchase a milk cow. The question was: Did a teacher make too little money, or was a milk cow too expensive? I am unable to make the necessary calculations to answer that question, but the ring was sold to one of the Polish deportees for forty-two thousand rubles. No milk cow was purchased with the money, but it helped us make ends meet for nearly twelve months.

As had been the case elsewhere, our circle of friends in Yakutsk was mainly composed of other deportees from Lithuania. We could not do a great deal of entertaining under the circumstances, but we nevertheless got together at regular intervals in one another's homes for a cup of tea. We would then discuss our common problems, of which we had a great deal, dwelling on the past and wondering what the future might have in store for us. The hours we spent together with our friends were among the few bright spots in our life.

I often thought of Denmark and of my relatives, with whom I had had no contact for such a long time. What would they think of me and my family, given that they had not heard from us? It was quite strange thinking back to Denmark—my life in Copenhagen now seemed so distant as to appear almost unreal. I often felt overcome with grief at the thought of Denmark and my family there, for in Yakutsk, in the midst of that huge, unknown land stretching for thousands of miles in all directions, the idea of ever seeing my native land and my family appeared as inconceivable as the possibility of flying to another planet.

As spring approached, life became somewhat easier. We no longer needed as much firewood, and we got rid of the heavy winter clothes and the uncomfortable valenki boots. More vegetables began to appear in the local market, with the Chinese and Koreans offering to sell, in their broken Russian, chives and radishes—a welcome supplement to our vitamin-deficient diet. After all of the difficulties and severe illnesses of the past winter, we began to relax and enjoy the long days full of warmth and sunshine. Later on in the summer the children were able to play outside late at night, for it never got entirely dark at that time of the year. However, the peace which seemed to surround us did not last long.

Israel

Fear and uncertainty were our constant companions throughout our years in Siberia. The threat of new difficulties, transfers, or other such arbitrary decisions always hung over us. Nor could we be certain that we would not one day be arrested, charged with some crime or other, and subsequently locked up in a prison or sent off to a labor camp. There were quite a number of such cases among our friends and acquaintances. As time passed and months gradually became years, our uncertainty concerning the authorities' plans for us became increasingly intolerable.

Thus I finally decided one day to look up the NKVD's top official, who was in charge of all of the deportees in Yakutia. However, this proved to be no easy matter. Colonel Karelin was not someone who could be approached by a deportee without difficulty. The outcome of my first attempt was a flat refusal, in which Colonel Karelin explained that he did not discuss individual cases and that all applications had to be made in writing. I did not give up, and after several weeks of oral and written exchanges, I finally succeeded in obtaining an interview with the top NKVD official himself.

Karelin turned out to be a tall and handsome man in his forties. He had blond hair, which he brushed back, and blue eyes that inspired confidence and peace of mind, and like all high-ranking NKVD officials, he acted in such a polite and punctilious manner that one was almost induced to believe that his attitude toward one was friendly and accommodating. It appeared rather incongruous that this man had far-reaching powers over the fates of thousands of deportees and that one word or the stroke of his pen could have far reaching effects on their lives in one way or the other.

However, although it was difficult at first to place Karelin in the right context, the big photo of Stalin hanging on the wall behind Karelin's desk made a visitor soon realize where he was and with whom he was dealing. The powerful ruler, shown in a full-length portrait wearing his generalissimo uniform, looked down on one with small, sly eyes and an inscrutable smile concealed behind his black moustache. His expression and his look certainly did not seem promising.

Karelin asked me to sit down on a chair on the other side of his desk. He put his hands together beneath his chin, palm against palm as if in an Indian greeting, and said that he was ready to listen to me.

I thanked him for having given me the possibility of meeting with him and told him briefly that I had asked to see him to have our situation somewhat clarified. I, moreover, told him that our deportation had now lasted for three years and that nobody had as yet told us the reason for our deportation, how long we were to remain, and what we were to expect as far as our future was concerned. I concluded by saying that a punishment without a time limit was a very severe one.

Karelin listened attentively, and when I finished, he looked at me with a disarming smile, saying in a gentle, friendly voice that I was by no means to regard my deportation as a punishment. To prove his claim, he went on to say, "You are working as a teacher in a Soviet school, and that in itself is a proof of the confidence the authorities have placed in you. Being a teacher in the Soviet Union and participating in the education of the new generations is a great honor."

After that explanation Karelin phoned his aide-de-camp, asking him to bring my file. I was rather surprised to see the thick file the aide-de-camp brought back. Karelin started leafing through the documents and then began to furnish me with information on myself and my family. He produced one document after the other, reading from them in an almost triumphant voice. Karelin told me things about myself and my family that I had completely forgotten over the years. There was information on trips abroad, which I had undertaken from Lithuania, on various family matters involving some of my uncles and relatives, on purchases and sales of property, and other financial matters in connection with the operation of our business. I could not understand why he reeled off all of that information. Did he want to show me how efficient and comprehensive the system of the NKVD was in collecting information on the persons with whom it dealt? Or did he believe that the information he reeled off revealed what a scoundrel I had been and how well deserved our deportation therefore was? I could not figure it out, but when he had finished, I asked him once more if it would be possible for him to tell me how long our deportation would last. Karelin did not give any answer. But upon closing my dossier and thus letting me know that the session was over, he said that as long as the war continued, it would not be possible to take a position on the question of the deportees. I ought to understand that.

When, somewhat later, I again found myself in the street on my way home, Goethe's words cropped up in my memory:

Da steh ich nun, ich armer Thor   Here I stand, I, poor fool
Und bin so klug als wie zuvor.   And am as clever as before.

I do not know if it was my visit to Karelin which triggered the following act on the part of the authorities. At any rate, one day shortly afterward, as the school year was drawing to a close, there was a knock on our door. We did not expect any visitors, and we had long ago become used to the idea that an unexpected visit was no good thing. Each time it

112

happened we feared further troubles and difficulties. This time it turned out that our fears were entirely justified. We opened the door and found an NKVD officer standing outside, asking us permission to enter. He did so immediately, and without beating about the bush or giving us any explanations, he said that we would have to make ourselves ready to leave for the town of Pokrovsk, which was located fifty-five miles south of Yakutsk on the banks of the Lena. The officer added that we would probably be leaving in two days.

I naturally wondered a great deal whether our transfer was the result of my talk with Karelin and whether the NKVD wanted to teach me still another lesson for having tried to extort from them an answer to my questions. Afterward, however, I found out that I might as well have saved my speculations. Several other families among the deportees from Lithuania had been given the same order as we. Unofficially, we were told that the reason for the transfer was that the NKVD had found out that deportees were not allowed to stay in the capital of the republic.

Although I gradually came to realize that it was useless to search for a rationale for the actions and decisions of the Soviet authorities, I could not reconcile myself to being uprooted once more and moved elsewhere. For nearly an entire school year I had been teaching German to about 120 students and had achieved good results. I had excellent relations with both my students and my colleagues, and it was obvious that the school would have difficulty finding a teacher with the same qualifications. Now I was forced to leave to work in some sort of brickworks where they needed a clerk for various tasks that did not require any special qualifications or skills. Despite Karelin's assurances that we were not being punished and despite the honors which he said the Soviet power bestowed upon us, we knew that we remained slaves— we had no legal rights, and the state could do as it liked with us without anybody lifting a finger to help us.

Some of the other families who had been told to move to Pokrovsk succeeded in being allowed to remain in Yakutsk after all. Several of the men went to the managers at their workplaces to tell them what was about to happen, whereupon their managers immediately contacted the NKVD to tell them that they would not be able to do without the deportees, for there was no one to replace them.

I tried the same thing, telling Sevastyanov, the principal, that a request from him might induce the NKVD to reverse its decision. But Sevastyanov did not want to hear of it at all. Apparently, he was afraid that such a request might be detrimental to him, since he might appear to speak in defense of a deportee.

He raised his arms in a gesture of despair, saying, "I cannot at all interfere with the decisions of the NKVD." In his usual fawning manner, he expressed his regret that I had to leave the school and that he was unable to help me.

There was nothing to do. I took leave of my students and my colleagues, who all understood that my sudden departure was involuntary, even though I had not told anybody the reason. My career at School No. 16 had come to an end.

10

Rachel · Israel

Two days after the visit of the NKVD officer, a truck drove up in front of our house early in the morning. In a matter of minutes, our few belongings were placed in the back of the truck, and sitting down on top of them, we left for Pokrovsk.

Looking back at the nine months we spent in Yakutsk, we found that they had not given us much joy. It had been a difficult time with many hardships and illnesses, and we had lost our beloved Baba, without whom we were now setting out on a trip for the first time. The day before our departure we had all been out at the cemetery to take leave of Baba—it might be the last time that we would ever see her grave. Indeed, Yakutsk had not been good to us, and in the final analysis, we were not all too sad to leave that town.

At the same time, of course, we did not know what lay in the future, but we had been in this situation several times before. The children found it exciting that we were leaving and were looking forward to the drive.

The trip to Pokrovsk took about two hours. The road was bumpy and dusty and passed now through wooded areas, now through swampy terrain or fields with sparse vegetation. Several times during our trip, we saw flocks of kites circling high in the air or sitting around a carcass on the ground. Upon arriving at Pokrovsk, we found the town to be a group of houses on either side of the road—one row facing the Lena and the other the *taiga*, the Siberian primeval forest.

We were immediately taken to the brickworks in the southern part of Pokrovsk. We were given a room in a log house and were told to report to the office of the brickworks the next morning to be assigned work. However, as always, it turned out that nothing had been organized after all and that there were other job opportunities that the authorities had not revealed. People at the brickworks told us immediately that it was not a good place to work, advising us to apply for work somewhere else immediately. But the possibilities of finding a job in Pokrovsk were, of course, limited, and the fact that we were deportees did not improve Israel's chances.

Israel

The day after our arrival, I looked up the principal of the local school. His name was Aleksandr Pavlov, and he proved very understanding and friendly when I explained my visit and offered to teach German at the school. He regretted having to tell me that, for one thing, the time schedule for the next school year had already been set up and, for another, the curriculum of the school did not yet include German. Pavlov felt, however, that the school would be offering instruction in the German language in a few years, and he asked me to contact him again then.

The brickworks in Pokrovsk provided most of the jobs in town. There were no other industrial plants. There was some fishing, agriculture, and hunting, and a few people worked in the administrative and commercial sectors. The town had a fairly small hospital, a pharmacy, and some shops. Pokrovsk had probably been founded in connection with the brickworks and had slowly grown into a town of six to seven thousand inhabitants.

In inquiring about the possibilities of work, I was told that in the opposite direction of the brickworks, in the northern part of Pokrovsk, was a plant research station by the name of Selektsionnaya Stantsiya. Several people recommended that I try my luck there, saying that I probably would be better off getting a job there than anywhere else in Pokrovsk. I had nothing to lose and therefore set out for Selektsionnaya Stantsiya to meet the manager, Jacob Ivanovich Klimov.

As soon as he heard what I wanted and who I was, he told me that I was the very man he needed for the job of deputy accountant. Klimov told me that with the job came housing and the possibility of purchasing milk and vegetables at prices that were a mere fraction of the prices in the market. Selektsionnaya, as the research station was called locally, had a canteen, where the staff could eat or purchase food at a low cost.

Bookkeeping was indeed not my favorite pursuit, but I did not have second thoughts about accepting Klimov's offer.

Klimov was a man of around forty. He was tall and stately and seemed to bubble over with vitality. Even if our meeting did not last very long, he talked to me in a good-natured and friendly manner. I secretly hoped that my impression was correct and that I would be able to establish good relations with my new boss.

Rachel · Israel

We fully realized that when he spoke of housing, Klimov had not implied any kind of villa or single-family home. But then, we were no longer used to much space and were willing to accept what we could get. We were allotted a room in a log house, which already housed two families. The house had an entrance hall that gave access to the rooms of the two other families. A partition wall was put up in the entrance hall, which provided us with a room of about 130 square feet, with the rest remaining as the entrance hall. However, there was no stove in our room, and Klimov said that it would probably be another month before we could move in.

After about three weeks, the remodeling had been completed, and we moved in. It was wonderful to get away from the dismal and dusty environment of the brickworks and to arrive at Selektsionnaya, which was located in a beautiful green area on a slope leading down to the Lena. There are many plant research stations of that kind around the Soviet Union. Selektsionnaya in Pokrovsk, which had an area of approximately three hundred acres at its disposal, had been given the task of developing grain and vegetable strains suited for the northern regions and their very special and difficult climatic conditions. With the one hundred frost-free days a year, the growth period in Yakutia was very brief, and this placed very special demands on the plants and the methods of cultivation. The annual amount of precipitation in the area was about ten inches. At Selektsionnaya, a number of various grain and vegetable strains were cultivated in well-defined areas under highly uniform conditions. In the fall the crops of each area were harvested separately and carefully examined, weighed, and analyzed. The following spring only the grain and seeds of the areas that had shown the best results were sown. In this way, the best-suited strains were arrived at, and that is briefly what is understood by selection in the cultivation of plants and grain.

Selektsionnaya was actually a small village, and compared to Yakutsk, it made us feel as if we lived out in the countryside. The combination of fresh air, green areas, and the proximity of the river made us feel much better than in Yakutsk. The climate was considerably better because there were no swampy areas around Pokrovsk, as there had been in Yakutsk.

Selektsionnaya had a school, a nursery school, an infant day-care center, and its own small shop with foodstuffs. The shop was located right next to our house, and the canteen, which we occasionally used, was not far away either. Each day, all employees at Selektsionnaya were allowed to purchase a quart of milk, which came from Selektsionnaya's own herd of cattle. The milk cost two rubles per quart, which was very cheap, for in the market it could cost as much as twenty-four rubles per quart.

Selektsionnaya's water carrier, Savin, saw to it that all residents were provided with water from the river. He drove around town with a large wooden barrel on top of his horse-drawn carriage, carrying the water in buckets to each individual family.

At Selektsionnaya, there was also a club that worked as a kind of community center. On Sundays it showed films. Most of these were Soviet films, but once in a while we saw old, worn, and scratched copies of foreign films, including German, English, and American ones.

We always went to see the foreign films, even if it was a somewhat special experience to watch these films in a primitive movie theater in the wilds of Siberia. The films, many of which we had already seen, were like a breath of air from the past, from a world that had once been ours but now appeared distant and unreal.

Selektsionnaya, of course, also had its own banya, which was very well maintained. Like all the other inhabitants, we took advantage of it. It was only heated, however, during the weekend. On Saturdays it was open for men and on Sundays for women. Visiting the banya is a ritual for Russians, and it is not merely a question of washing oneself or being whipped with scented birch rods. It is just as much a social occasion, a time to spend together with one's friends in a relaxed atmosphere of good fellowship. People take drinks and food along with them to the banya and have a pleasant time talking to various people—exchanging the latest news, discussing the world situation, and telling the latest jokes. The banya is a cultural element of great importance to the emotional well-being of the Russian people.

Selektsionnaya did a lot to provide for its residents, and the atmosphere among them was always positive. One area, however, they left to the residents themselves to take care of, and that was the area of firewood. The residents had to go into the taiga themselves to fell trees for firewood. For a reasonable amount of money it was possible to hire a horse-drawn carriage on Sundays and take off into the woods to cut trees. Sometime in the fall we decided to go to the woods to secure a supply of firewood for ourselves for the winter. We managed to rent a horse-drawn carriage and procure the necessary tools, and then we took off together for the taiga. We had to go rather far into the woods, for it was prohibited to fell trees within an area of two to two and a half miles from the Lena.

We had never felled trees in woods before, but between us we managed to fell quite a few. We took only larch trees, for they were in the majority, and they yielded the most heat. We stripped the felled trees of their branches and cut them into lengths that would be easy for us to transport when we came to collect them after the first snow had fallen. We had to await the arrival of the snow to transport the trunks on a sleigh. It was impossible to transport such a load on a carriage through the taiga, for there were no roads. Naturally, the trees we had felled were not among the largest. They would have been impossible for us to fell, and we would not have been able to bring them back with us afterward. We chose the trees we could manage, and the children were good at helping us gather the branches together.

Our trip into the woods to cut firewood was a wonderful outing. It was still rather warm, the sun was shining, and we had taken food and drink as for a picnic. The children played, picked the last lingonberries and wild strawberries of the season, and had lots of fun.

At the end of the day, we gathered all of the trunks together into a big heap, and surveying our achievement, we felt no small amount of pride. Before leaving, we had been somewhat skeptical of being able to handle the task, but we now felt that we had done it almost as well as the native Siberians who had lived all of their lives in the taiga. Before leaving to go back to Selektsionnaya, we marked all of the trunks with a sign, so that we would be able to recognize them when we came back for them in the winter. Such was the custom of everyone preparing his firewood in the woods.

It was getting dark when, tired and happy, we arrived back at Selekt-sionnaya.

When the snow arrived, we were unable to leave the first Sunday because others had already reserved the available sleighs. We decided to go into the woods the following Sunday.

That Monday, however, we saw a big heap of firewood not far from our house. All of the trunks were marked with our sign. The next Sunday we went into the woods to find out if we had been mistaken. But true enough—all of our firewood was gone. When we got back, we discovered who had taken our firewood—it was a young fellow by the name of Nikolay Oglobin, whose father was at the front. Nikolay Oglobin, however, denied having taken our firewood, stubbornly maintaining that he had himself been in the woods in the autumn, felling the trunks he had now transported back. We decided to drop the matter in order to avoid trouble.

Now that the snow had fallen, it was much more difficult to cut down trees. We ended up by joining forces with other deportees from Lithuania and going into the woods to perform the task together. It was very hard work, but we managed to fell the trees and provide everybody with firewood for the long winter.

Among our many memories of our stay at Selektsionnaya is an event we recall very vividly both because it was rather amusing and because it was very characteristic of the conditions prevailing in the Soviet Union.

In late July or early August, shortly after our arrival at Selektsionnaya, the rumor that a high-ranking foreign politician would pay a visit to Selektsionnaya spread like wildfire through the research station. It proved to be the American vice president, Henry A. Wallace himself, who was on an official visit to the Soviet Union. On his trip around the country, he would visit Yakutsk, from which he would make a small detour to Pokrovsk to inspect Selektsionnaya Stantsiya. It was said that Henry A. Wallace was very interested in agriculture and that one of the objectives of his visit to Siberia was to inspect the research work on the development of special grain and plant species suitable for the rough northern climate. Selektsionnaya was the obvious research station to receive the important visitor.

Information on the visit, with instructions on how to receive the guest, that is, what the visitor was to be shown and probably what he was not to be shown, came from the highest authorities in Moscow. The local authorities in Yakutsk were to be the hosts of the American vice president during his visit, and they were also to assume all of the costs in connection with his visit to Selektsionnaya.

Once all of the details of the visit had been decided upon, Selektsionnaya began to hum with activity. The management launched a cleaning campaign throughout the area of the research station. They swept, weeded, and cleaned more than ever. The building where the reception for Wallace was to take place was refurbished from top to bottom. Ceilings were whitewashed, new wallpaper was put up, and all of the woodwork was given a fresh coat of paint. Suddenly, all of the materials that were normally impossible to obtain were available in large quantities. Now there was no scarcity anywhere. The first party secretary from Yakutsk arrived personally to inspect the preparations. He was not quite content with the reception rooms, and they were consequently whitewashed and painted once more. The local commercial organization, Selpo, at Pokrovsk was to provide all of the food and liquor for the feast, and the amount of eight thousand rubles was decided upon to cover the costs. Cutlery and tablecloths were provided by the restaurant in Pokrovsk. In the course of the hectic preparations, somebody suddenly realized that problems would arise if Wallace wished to wash his hands before the meal. There were no washbasins, only primitive containers filled with water, and when a small tap at the bottom of the container was pushed with the flat of the hand, water would pour out. That would not suffice for the vice president. After much worry and a long search, they succeeded in locating a washstand—a rare object in this part of the country—and the owner of it was delighted to make it available for the occasion to help save the honor of Pokrovsk.

All the students at the school at Selektsionnaya were to have the day off when Wallace arrived—not so that they might participate in welcoming him but to get rid of them in the movie theater where they would be shown a free film. An extra film had been made available in case Wallace's visit should be prolonged. Nothing was left to chance—there was to be nothing whatsoever with which the American vice president could find fault during his brief visit.

Finally, the day everybody had been anxiously awaiting arrived, and in midmorning a motorcade arrived from Yakutsk. Never before had Pokrovsk seen such a motorcade and probably never after. Wallace and his retinue were received with all the pomp and circumstance the town was able to muster—Soviet and American flags, a small orchestra that had been put together in a hurry, streamers with words of welcome, flower arrangements, and spotlessly clean buildings and greenhouses. Wallace was subsequently shown around Selektsionnaya by the manager and some of the agronomists, who told him about the work and research carried out on the premises. The route followed during the tour of the station had been carefully planned, and nothing that had not been included in the original plan was shown to Wallace. Apparently, everything went very well, and everybody was satisfied.

After the tour of the plant and a discussion with Wallace, everybody was ready to sit down and enjoy the banquet. A couple of women, appointed from the bookkeeping department to serve the meal, guided the American guests to the table. According to Russian custom, all of the food had been put on the table beforehand. The table groaned under the weight of sliced meat and all kinds of delicacies fetched from far and near. There were herring, caviar, various kinds of smoked fish, various meat dishes, several kinds of piroshki, and, of course, a wide selection of drinks—wine, vodka, cognac, and champagne. It was an impressive sight, especially in view of the fact that the war was still going on and the country was subject to a strict rationing system.

After Wallace had sat down, he searched around for something on the well-provided table. Everybody at Selektsionnaya held his breath, wondering terror-struck what might be missing. Wallace approached his interpreter, who, to everybody's relief, explained that the vice president would like to have a glass of milk. The danger had passed. Nobody had imagined that an American vice president would drink milk. Fortunately, Selektsionnaya did not lack milk, but the kitchen did not quite know how to serve the milk, as it had been procured with lightning speed. Finally, they decided that a wine decanter would be suitable.

The meal lasted a little over an hour. Wallace had a tight schedule, and he had to see a few other grain fields before his return to Yakutsk. Wallace gave expression to his admiration for the work carried out by the agronomists at Selektsionnaya, and he did not hesitate to say that he had not expected to see such luxuriant and well-kept fields and such highly developed farming systems so far north.

Before taking leave of his hosts at Selektsionnaya, Wallace asked to see the guest book. Again his request took his hosts by surprise, since they had not taken this small detail into account and did not wish to lose face at the last moment after everything had gone so well. A man set off for the bookkeeping department and returned out of breath with an account book which would have to do as a guest book. Wallace initiated the new guest book of Selektsionnaya, expressing his thanks for the warm reception he had been given. He wished all of the staff at Selektsionnaya success with their impressive work, with which he was gratified to have become acquainted.

And then came the time for giving thanks, shaking hands, and waving until the motorcade disappeared around the bend. Everybody at Selektsionnaya breathed a sigh of relief—everything had gone perfectly, and they had solved the difficult task to the satisfaction of all in an honorable manner. But this was only act one.

Israel

Almost immediately after Wallace's departure, some people arrived from Selpo, which had supplied everything for the feast, and in a very short time they managed to collect all that was left of the food and liquor. When they had cleared everything away, they took off, and later in the day we learned that the entire staff of Selpo had gone to a small island in the middle of the Lena where they had had an incredible feast on the leftovers from the lunch at Selektsionnaya. The picnic ended late in the night.

The following day, a Selpo employee arrived at Selektsionnaya with a bill of eight thousand rubles for the food and liquor supplied at the official luncheon. Klimov, the manager, flatly refused to pay the bill, claiming that it was not Selektsionnaya which was to pay for the luncheon, since Selektsionnaya's sole task had been to organize the visit and the meal, while all of the costs were to be defrayed by the government in Yakutsk.

Some time went by without any further occurrence, but suddenly Selektsionnaya received a summons from Selpo, which now wanted to recover its eight thousand rubles through legal means. Klimov let the accountant, Ivan Mikhaylovich Churkin, handle the matter. He was a Sakhalyar, that is, a Russian born and raised in Yakutia. He was in his late fifties and was fond of liquor.

Churkin had apparently had difficulties with the authorities at some point earlier in his life, for he was terrified of the authorities, especially of the police and the courts. When he heard what Klimov wanted him to do, he went to him, begging him to relieve him of the task. That is how I came to represent Selektsionnaya in court.

Churkin provided me with all of the particulars and vouchers available in connection with the supplies from Selpo, but I was not too enthusiastic about the task. It was an obvious handicap for me in the court that I was a deportee and thus not on an equal footing with my counterpart. Any success on my part would therefore be limited. On the other hand, I could not refuse the job, for I felt that I had to do something in return for all of the friendliness and helpfulness we had encountered at Selektsionnaya.

I was not too knowledgeable in legal matters and had only been in court once before. That was in Lithuania in 1935 when I applied for a new birth certificate, which I needed to be married in Copenhagen, because I had lost the original. I was rather anxious about the proceedings, and I was fully determined to do everything in my power to defend the interests of Selektsionnaya.

Following a brief introductory procedure, the representative of Selpo was called upon to speak. He gave a long and detailed account of the entire course of events and produced a large number of bills. My speech for the defense was brief. I stated that Selektsionnaya was not to pay for the banquet, since it was not we who had ordered the food and liquor. It was thus that Selpo could not produce any receipt. I asked the court to reject all of Selpo's claims and to suggest that the trade organization approach the party that ought to pay for the luncheon, that is, the government in Yakutsk.

The end of the matter was that the court upheld my contention, the claim from Selpo was rejected, and Selektsionnaya won a definite victory. The management of Selektsionnaya was very satisfied with my achievement, and in reward I was allowed to buy two quarts of cream in the canteen. The last traces of Vice President Wallace's visit to Selektsionnaya appeared in a number of delicious dishes prepared by Rachel from the cream.

Later on, I became the permanent representative of Selektsionnaya in all the legal matters in which the research station became involved. It often happened that privately owned cows broke through the fences surrounding the fields of the research station and ate from the crops, thus making them useless for further research. The responsible owner had to pay compensation and a fairly stiff fine, and when he refused to do so, as happened fairly often, the matter was decided in court. I had to represent the research station in quite a few cases over the course of time.

At the time, one quart of milk in the open market cost twenty to twenty-five rubles. The owners of the cows were therefore soon able to recover their losses. Twenty rubles was a fairly large amount of money at the time. By way of comparison, my monthly salary amounted to approximately twelve hundred rubles.

In time it became quite a habit for Selektsionnaya to assign me tasks that were somewhat beyond my usual routine. Each year a big report had to be written on the scientific work carried out at Selektsionnaya, and the report was to be handed over in five copies. It was Klimov himself who had to go to Moscow to bring the report to the Ministry of Agriculture, and the deadline was January 15. In late December, when the secretary had only written about one fourth of the report, she found to her dismay that she had no more carbon paper left, and it would be impossible to meet the deadline if she had to write the rest of the report without copies, that is, in five originals. The research station was in trouble, for Klimov could under no circumstances arrive in Moscow late. Klimov called me into his office and told me about the matter, explaining that I had to go to Yakutsk to procure the needed amount of carbon paper, whatever the cost. I was given a letter for the Ministry of Commerce in Yakutsk and provided with a huge fur coat for the trip, for it was now the coldest time of the year, with temperatures as low as fifty-eight degrees Fahrenheit below zero. A big truck was made available for me for carrying out my special mission, and with a young driver by the name of Yegorov at the wheel, I left for Yakutsk.

When we arrived in the town of Yakutsk, we stopped briefly at the house of a close friend of mine, Ellik Rakhmilevich, since his house was located right on the road leading to the center of town. When Ellik heard about my mission, he looked very skeptical, not believing that I would succeed in bringing any carbon paper back with me. Incidentally, I experienced a minor incident, which I later on found quite amusing. When we were about to leave, I told Ellik that I should like to use his privy and asked him where it was located. Ellik laughed, saying that this was, unfortunately, not possible, for somebody had stolen the entire structure, apparently to use the boards for firewood. However, he would be happy to accompany me to the neighbor's privy, which was watched by a huge and ferocious dog. Such minor, absurd incidents did after all add a bit of color to our situation, and we were able to laugh both at ourselves and the crazy situations we got into.

After visiting Ellik, I started my hunt for carbon paper. I first approached a section chief in the Ministry of Commerce, but he reported being unable to help me. A trip to most of the shops and storehouses in town also failed to produce any results.

Later in the afternoon, I went to the Ministry of Agriculture, to which I had to give some seed samples from Selektsionnaya. I was taken to an agronomist, whom I recognized from his several visits to Selektsionnaya. He noticed my exhaustion and dejection and asked me what was wrong. I told him the entire story, whereupon he said, "I shall write a few words to my brother. He may be able to help you."

A little later, I was on my way to his brother at the other end of town. It turned out that he was a discharged officer who had recently returned from Germany. I do not know why he was in possession of carbon paper—perhaps it was part of the spoils of war he had brought home with him, being well aware that carbon paper was always in short supply. At any rate, he asked me how many sheets I needed. I got a hundred sheets, he got two hundred rubles, and we were both satisfied with the deal.

The trip back to Pokrovsk was rather dramatic. We had been told to take a woman along with us back to Pokrovsk. It turned out to be the manager of the infant day-care center, who carried an infant in her arms. I was compelled to let her have my seat next to the driver and climbed into the back of the truck, where I wrapped myself up in my big fur coat and huddled into a corner right behind the driver's cab.

Halfway back to Pokrovsk there was a small house the highway authorities had turned into some kind of lay-by. When we got in the vicinity of it, the engine began to misfire. We managed, however, to get to the lay-by, where Yegorov, the driver, discovered that water had got into the gasoline, in which tiny needles of ice were floating.

Yegorov immediately started emptying the tank, after which he filtered the gasoline through a piece of felt to get rid of the small particles of ice. The light available was not too good, and though it was not the first time that Yegorov had had this task to perform, he accidentally spilled some gasoline on his hands without paying any attention to it. The combination of gasoline and intense cold is extremely bad, but Yegorov did not realize what had happened until we drove on. Only then did he notice that his fingers were frostbitten. It got worse and worse, and he barely made it back to Pokrovsk. Here he was immediately seen by a doctor but was nevertheless in such a bad shape that he had to take sick leave. Both of his hands were bandaged for several weeks. However, he suffered no permanent damage and started working again as a driver after his sick leave.

Mission "Carbon Paper" had been a success, and I had once more become the hero of the day at Selektsionnaya.

Rachel · Israel

Schneur's schooling had got a rather confused start. In the Soviet Union, children begin school at the age of seven. In Bykov Mys Schneur had received private instruction, corresponding to the first grade, with three other children. In Yakutsk he had started in the second grade, but because of his illness and long stay in the hospital, he missed a lot of the school year and had to begin again at Selektsionnaya. It was an elementary school with four grades.

We got Harrietta into the local nursery school, which was not very large but was an excellent school. The teachers were very competent and interested in the children, and we felt quite comfortable leaving her there. The children were given three meals a day at the school.

Rachel

Now that the children had become older and I no longer had to be with them all the time, I started thinking about getting a job. That my Russian was still not very good presented some problems in this respect. At home we still spoke German, even with the children. I believe that we kept speaking German because it gave us the feeling that we belonged to a different world, which still existed somewhere or other. But there was also a different reason—human beings are, after all, constituted in such a way that they do not give up hope even in the most hopeless and desperate situations. Somehow or other, we still nurtured the hope that our deportation would be over someday and that we would be allowed to leave the Soviet Union and perhaps go back to Denmark or to some other country where the children would be able to use their knowledge of German. I did not think of speaking Danish with the children, for I was the only one who could speak it, and it would, no doubt, have confused the children to learn three different languages at once. Israel did not speak Danish and knew only a few words.

One day I decided to go and see Klimov and try to explain to him what it was that I wanted to do. Klimov was all smiles when I came into his office, and he listened attentively while I presented my plan to him in broken Russian. He could not help laughing at the way I mishandled the Russian language, but the most important thing was the he understood what I was interested in doing.

A little later I left his office with a letter addressed to the nursery school, requesting it to employ me as a substitute teacher. I was very happy, for it was the very job I wanted. The head of the nursery school was extremely friendly to me from the very start, and after I had started working there, she was always ready to help me and show me how to perform my tasks. Due to my work with the children and my contact with the other teachers, my knowledge of the Russian language soon improved considerably.

It was only now, after more than three years in Siberia, that I really came into contact with the Russians, and it was a rather overwhelming experience for me. Only now did I understand what they were saying, and only now was I able to get real insight into their world, their thoughts, and their feelings. I experienced an intense human companionship I had not known before. We met and spent our time with many warm-hearted people who were unbelievably helpful and hospitable. They more or less competed in inviting us to their homes, for it was very unusual and exciting for them to be with such strange birds as we. People from the West did not often visit these regions.

The way Russian women were able to arrange their homes under such primitive conditions and their ingenuity in cooking and preparing exciting dishes with their limited means made a deep impression on me. They were especially good at making piroshki, which they filled with meat, fish, preserved berries—or cabbage when they had difficulty getting anything better. One of our neighbors, a wise elderly woman, Anna Semyonovna Makrygina, was an artist at cooking, and she gave me a lot of good advice and recipes, some of which I still use. And Israel and the children loved it when I invented and served new and exciting dishes.

Among all of the places we had lived, Selektsionnaya was the one where we settled down most quickly, and we never felt as well at any point during our deportation as we did there.

The war was drawing to a close, and it was probably in anticipation of the victory and subsequent peace that the day of the revolution, November 7, 1944, was celebrated in such an elaborate manner. Never before had we experienced anything like it. Everybody at Selektsionnaya participated in the celebration, and everybody had an enormous amount to drink. There was a lot of food—a vast selection of various piroshki, meat and fish dishes, salads, and, naturally, salted cucumbers and sauerkraut. The most popular drink was one by the name of brazhka, a home-brewed beer with a high alcohol content but with a terrible taste and an unappetizing, dull brownish color. It made one quickly drunk but also very ill afterward. Thus most people drank brazhka not because they liked it but in order to become drunk.

The children felt happy at Selektsionnaya. Schneur had found some friends to play with and was already an avid reader of children's books. He was now eight years old, and Harrietta was four. It was difficult getting toys for Harrietta, for there was nothing available in the shops in Pokrovsk. We had an old rag doll we had taken along with us from Lithuania, a sailor with which Harrietta often played, and I made her small rag dolls. These few toys were enough for her to create her own fairyland, and she would spend hours absorbed in it.

On Sundays we would go into the woods or down to the river, where there was always something that might catch the attention of the children. I always went to great pains to tell them about nature and taught them to appreciate flowers and animals. Both children now spoke fluent Russian, in Harrietta's case almost too well.

One day in the fall, I was standing outside our house, listening at a distance to Harrietta playing with some other children. She spoke Russian as well as the other children and very rapidly. As I stood there lost in reverie and filled with maternal pride, one of the neighboring women came up to me and asked me if I knew what my little daughter was saying. I shook my head, not understanding what she meant, whereupon she explained that Harrietta was using some of the worst curses and words of abuse existing in the Russian language. I was quite shocked to hear it, but my neighbor consoled me, telling me not to be too upset about it but to explain to Harrietta that they were ugly words, which a little girl should not use. The woman knew where Harrietta had picked up her vocabulary—in the house next door there lived a family that was notorious all over Selektsionnaya for cursing and swearing, and quick children did not take long to pick up some of the worst words of abuse.

In the early part of the winter, the children were able to play outside and would skate, ski, or go sledding in the nearby hills. However, once winter really set in, they were unable to venture out very much and had to spend most of the time indoors. It was a long and difficult time for all of us.

Our small room, which served as kitchen, living room, and bedroom at the same time, had but one small window, which became frozen and covered with a heavy layer of ice and white frost, so that very little light penetrated into our room. We did what we could to provide the children with a sense of security and to make them feel as happy as possible. During the long winter evenings, we amused ourselves reading, playing various games, and watching our "Siberian TV"—the fire burned continuously in our walled-in stove, and we would sit in front of it, keeping the stove door open so that we could watch the embers and the burning pieces of wood. The embers and flames formed all kinds of pictures of animals and buildings, forests and towns, and many other kinds of things, depending on our imagination. When we had figured out what we were able to see inside the stove, I began to tell the children all kinds of fairy tales, both well-known ones and some that I invented on the spot, while they stared into the stove, completely absorbed, the bright glow of the fire dancing on their small innocent faces. These were moments the children loved and came to remember for the rest of their lives.

11

---•·•---

Rachel · Israel

Like all other Soviet citizens, we had a loudspeaker hanging in a corner of our room. It was an extremely small loudspeaker, encircled by stiff black paper shaped like a cone. The loudspeaker was connected to the local radio station and gave access to only one program. Each day we listened to the news from Moscow. It was the only way in which we could keep informed of world events. Even if the news did not provide us with a complete picture of the world situation, we were able to form a rather clear idea of what was going on, of the ravages caused by the war in Europe. We often wondered how our relatives in Lithuania and Denmark were doing, and the scanty information to which we had access caused us deep concern about their fate. We realized that in the midst of all of our misfortunes, we were, indeed, fortunate to be so far removed from the war and its horrors. Despite the sufferings and the privations we had to undergo as deportees, we were happy that we had escaped the war.

Even though we had settled down comfortably at Selektsionnaya, the insecurity and uncertainty kept bothering us. On the first Tuesday of every month, we had to appear before the local NKVD commander for registration. And each time we felt insecure and worried that we might again be told to move. Several times during the monthly registration, we were asked to fill in long, detailed questionnaires concerning our relatives abroad, the foreign languages we spoke, and many other pieces of information that appeared senseless and irrelevant to us. The commander emphasized that we not go beyond a range of three miles from Pokrovsk without special permits.

Among our new experiences in Pokrovsk were the so-called *zakrytyye magaziny*, which, literally translated, means "closed shops." That it is not

131

immediately clear what the term stands for is not the fault of the translation but due to its interpretation. It was not the shops that were closed but the circles of people who were allowed to use them. These circles were composed of privileged party people and people in leading positions, in short, the elite or the new class. In closed shops this population group was able to buy goods that were rationed in normal shops or often were not available anywhere else.

One day, as spring slowly began to show signs of approaching, we were told that we would be allowed to move into a larger "dwelling." In April of 1945, we moved into the house next door, where we had been allocated a larger room. The room was twice as large as our previous room and was considerably brighter, since it contained a large window. At the front of the room, a thin partition wall surrounded a small walled-in stove to form our kitchen. The building was a large log house with a long corridor and rooms on both sides. Here some of the other employees at Selektsionnaya lived under as crowded and primitive conditions as we.

The spring of 1945 liberated us from the severe winter, but that spring also brought us another liberation—the end of the war. Now only good news came from the front, and the radio brought one message of victory after the other. The Soviet Army was approaching Berlin, and the days of the Nazi terrorist regime were numbered. Everybody's spirits at Selektsionnaya rose higher every day.

The first of May was celebrated in due manner with a big party. There were lots of food and drink and many speeches on the victorious Soviet Army, the brave Soviet people, and, last but certainly not least, our "leader and teacher Joseph Vissarionovich Stalin." Many toasts were proposed for our "father" Stalin, and in such toasts one's glass always had to be emptied entirely. Nobody dared not do so.

The following week saw still another celebration. On May 9 at ten o'clock in the morning, we heard the message of peace on the radio. It was Levitan, the famous radio speaker, who read the message about the victory and the capitulation of the German troops on all fronts. The war was over!

As soon as the happy news had reached everybody, the schools were told to give the children the rest of the day off, and everybody else was excused from work. Two trucks were sent off to collect the people working in the fields. All of Selektsionnaya was rapidly transformed into a motley crowd of happy people, singing, cheering, and running around embracing and congratulating one another on the end of the war. Bottles that had been kept for a long time for this very occasion were now opened, and people kept drinking and toasting. Laughter and tears of joy kept giving way to each other, and there simply was no end to the joy and enthusiasm. In the evening the victory was celebrated with a big gathering in the office building, and the celebration went on till early morning.

There was hardly a family in the Soviet Union that did not have a relative in the war and that was thus not directly affected by the war. Now everybody was anxiously awaiting the return of his loved ones, and everybody was hoping for better times after the five years of endless hardships. We now started entertaining hopes of getting in contact with our relatives and having our deportation lifted. But, as always, the joy of expectation turned out to be the best one.

Many of those expecting the return of their husbands, sons, fathers, or other relatives were to be disappointed. Instead, they received letters saying that their beloved ones had been killed in the struggle against the fascist forces. Many others returned home disabled and had to start a difficult retraining program to learn to live with their handicaps.

As far as we were concerned, the peace did not cause any major change in our lives. We remained deportees, and the conclusion of the war did not bring about any changes in the conditions under which we had to live. We had to get used to the idea of remaining there indefinitely.

In late May the time had come to plant potatoes. We had been allocated a plot of land of about fifty-five hundred square feet, and for the second time during our stay in Siberia, we were to plant potatoes. We hoped for a good harvest, for it would mean a necessary improvement in our financial situation if, in the course of the winter, we were able to use our own supply of potatoes. However, the conditions for growing potatoes were not as good as in Altayskiy Kray, and even if we tended our crops carefully, earthing up our potatoes according to all of the directives, their yield was modest. People told us that there had been too little rain that summer.

On the other hand, the cabbage crop at Selektsionnaya was excellent, and, like all of the others, we were allowed to purchase 220 pounds of cabbage. What did we do with all that cabbage? Most of it was used for making sauerkraut, which was to last us the whole winter. In the wintertime no vegetables were available, and the only way in which we would be able to satisfy our vitamin C requirements would be to see to it that we had as much sauerkraut and as many lingonberries as possible. We picked the lingonberries ourselves every fall and kept them in a large barrel in a shed, where they froze automatically as soon as it got cold enough. In this way, we had berries the entire winter.

Rachel

It was Anna Semyonovna, our neighbor, who taught me how to prepare sauerkraut. I had actually never tried it before, but she gave me a very easy recipe, and the result was excellent. Since then, I have often wondered why Danish recipes for making sauerkraut are so complicated. The recipe I got at Selektsionnaya merely called for shredding the cabbage finely and mixing it with thin slices of carrots. Caraway seeds and dill seeds were also added, and then only salt was needed. After a week of fermentation under pressure in a large wooden barrel, the sauerkraut was ready and was placed outside in the cold. Throughout the winter we were able to go to the shed and fetch a bowl of frozen sauerkraut, which thawed after a while at room temperature and tasted excellent.

Israel

The bookkeeping department where I worked had seven employees. Our boss, Ivan Mikhaylovich Churkin, was a cheerful but somewhat unpredictable person. He was small and of fragile build and walked with a heavy limp. For this reason he had been rejected by the draft board. He was an excellent accordian player and equally good at drinking vodka or whatever he could get hold of. These two talents went very well together—since he was the only person at Selektsionnaya who could play the accordian, he was invited to all the parties, which suited him very well. When he came to work on Mondays, he usually had quite a hangover and was rather desperate for a drink. I was his substitute, and when he stayed at home, as was often the case, I had to see to it that everything went according to schedule in the bookkeeping department.

Selektsionnaya was administered directly by the Ministry of Agriculture in Moscow, and all expenditures of the plant had been arranged beforehand in the ministry's budget. This saved a lot of work, and the most important task of the bookkeeping department was to see to it that the amounts specified for the individual items under the budget were not exceeded. The work of the bookkeeping department was quiet and uncomplicated, and we were all on good terms with one another.

I had gradually become quite good at using the abacus. Like all of the others, I had learned to roll my own cigarettes from newspaper and to smoke the strong Makhorka, a special, coarse tobacco. I no longer differed as much from the others and was more or less considered one of them. The same thing applied to Rachel and the children, and if this had been the objective of Stalin and his helpers responsible for our deportation, one would have to admit that they had succeeded.

Some of the agronomists at Selektsionnaya wanted to improve their rather modest knowledge of foreign languages and asked me to teach them English. I agreed to it and taught them two hours a week. I rather enjoyed being a teacher again.

My students were interested and industrious, and even if they were all cultured people, they revealed a profound ignorance of conditions in the West, about which they were very much interested in learning. None of them had been abroad, and they had a very distorted idea of life in the West. Frequently, they refused to believe what I told them about the rights and opportunities of the citizens in Western countries. The lessons often became quite long because we kept talking and discussing.

One day in the middle of the fall of 1945, I was called into the office of Klimov, who told me that I would unfortunately have to leave my job in the bookkeeping department, since the man for whom I had been substituting had recently returned from the Army and would be returning to his job immediately. I was rather distressed to hear it, but Klimov told me at once not to worry, because he would find me another suitable job.

A few days later I was again called into the office of Klimov, who told me with a smile that I could start working in the tomato section as Viktor Vasil'yevich Tarasov's right-hand man. He described the assignment more literally than I had imagined. A few days before the end of the war, Tarasov had lost his right hand in combat in one of the suburbs of Berlin. Tarasov was an agronomist in the tomato section, and when he returned, he was given his former position. The plants had to be followed closely, and many notes and reports had to be made. Until Tarasov had learned to write with his left hand, I was to perform all of the written work and to help him with his work in every conceivable manner.

I was given the title of "senior technician in tomato cultivation" and immediately set to work learning my new profession. The number-three man in the tomato section was Sun Sian Tin, or "the Misha Chinese," as everybody at Selektsionnaya called him. He was one of the many Chinese who had come to Russia before the revolution and had settled down as nurserymen. Misha had worked at Selektsionnaya since the early thirties when the research station was first founded. Misha held the title of technician and was in charge of all of the practical work of tending the greenhouses and the hotbeds.

Sun Sian Tin was the first Chinese with whom I had any real contact, and in time we became very good friends. I grew quite fond of Misha, with his wise, peaceful eyes and quick, energetic movements. He was of medium height and fragile build. He was a superb nurseryman and probably one of the most diligent and conscientious people I ever met. Misha became my teacher in tomato cultivation, and it did not take me long to start enjoying my new profession. I shall never forget my teacher and the hours we spent in each other's company.

The climate in Yakutia was not very suitable for the cultivation of tomatoes, and the task of Selektsionnaya was to develop types that would yield the best results under the difficult growing conditions. Our work was based on an American type of tomato by the name of "Bison," and we proceeded according to the method of selection. When the plants had attained a certain size, they were moved to hotbeds. The nights, however, were so cold that it was necessary to cover the hotbeds each night with straw mats to protect the fragile plants. In the morning we removed the mats and opened up the hotbeds. Around June 15, the tomatoes were ready to be planted in the open.

As early as August it started freezing, and to protect the plants we had to make big fires and thus keep the cold away from them. It was Misha and I who were in charge of the nightly fires. After having started the fires, we sat down in a small primitive tent, which had been pitched for the purpose, and smoked Makhorka cigarettes rolled from newspaper. We told each other about our former lives and of the places we had seen and asked each other questions. We greatly enjoyed the hours we spent together on those nightly jobs. Misha liked to tell me about China and Chinese customs. I remember, for example, how shocked he was at the lack of culture manifest in the European and

Russian modes of preparing and serving food. Misha told me that, according to a Chinese custom, only four persons were to be seated around a table, the reason being that a greater number would make it impossible to carry on a decent conversation. The Chinese, moreover, did not have more than one dish on their plates at a time. It was barbaric and uncultured to mix several dishes on one's plate. At least eight dishes had to be served for guests. The maximum number of dishes was forty-eight.

My good friend Misha was not satisfied with just the strong Makhorka tobacco—he also smoked opium. He did not try to conceal it from me and often told me how much he enjoyed it. Off and on, Misha would smoke during the working hours.

One day we were going by horse-drawn carriage to a plot of land with tomato plants several miles from Selektsionnaya. We had been out there several times before, and Misha was usually the driver, holding the reins in his hands. I was sitting right next to him. Suddenly, I discovered that Misha was completely gone and had got a strange, glassy, and vacant expression in his eyes. His eyes were open, but he paid no attention to anything whatsoever and seemed to be in a different world. Nothing happened, however, for the horse knew the way, and there was no oncoming traffic. When we reached our destination, I went around inspecting the plants and taking notes. When I had finished and got back to the carriage again, I saw that Misha had awakened from his intoxication and was again cheerful and in good shape. I noticed several times that when he awoke from an intoxication, he literally bubbled over with vitality, and everything was done at an enormously fast rate. Indeed, it more or less looked as if he were doing magic tricks.

Misha grew his own Makhorka, and his tobacco purse was full throughout the year. Our boss, Tarasov, smoked quite a lot but seldom carried any tobacco with him. Each time he saw Misha, he therefore asked, "Misha, would you happen to have some tobacco for a cigarette?" And each time Misha handed him his tobacco purse with a friendly smile. Tarasov took the purse and each time rolled a huge cigarette—he had taught himself to roll cigarettes with his left hand long before he had learned to write with it. Misha always put his purse back in his pocket without comments, but one day he could not help himself, and after Tarasov had left, he said to me, "I do not mind that he rolls his cigarettes with my tobacco, but I cannot understand why he always has to make them so thick."

Rachel

I had come to like my work in the nursery school a great deal, but one day I was called into the office of the principal, who told me that they were in a difficult situation because the children's nurse in the infant day-care center next door had to leave. They wanted me to take over her job, since they felt that I was the one best suited for the job. The very next day I started working in the infant day-care center.

It was not a difficult transition for me. Every morning, I would receive the children and would at once proceed to wash and dress those who needed it. I treated them the same way I treated my own children when they were small. Actually, in time I came to like this work even better than my work in the nursery school. It was very rewarding to watch those of the children who were neglected grow into lovely, well-cared-for babies. Several of the children suffered from favus, impetigo, and other diseases. We treated them and gave them cod-liver oil, and the parents were always very grateful to us when they saw their children recover in our care.

In the spring of 1946, we received an offer to move to a big room in the house where the scientific leader of Selektsionnaya, Nurgaliy Habibulovich Sagitov, a Bashkir, lived with his wife and son, Volodya. We naturally accepted the offer immediately and moved into the new room. It was a sturdy log house with three rooms, an entrance hall, and a kitchen. The room we were given was rather big and had two windows. It was, without a doubt, the best room in which we had lived since our deportation, and we were all happy with the improvement.

My happiness at the improved housing situation grew when, sometime later, I discovered that I had become pregnant. When we lived in Lithuania, I had wanted many children and had wished to give them a secure and protected life, as was indeed possible under the circumstances at the time. Now that we were living as persecuted deportees without any legal rights or certainty about the future, bringing a child into the world was an entirely different matter. What could I offer a child under these circumstances, how could I be certain that it would have a normal and secure childhood, and did we indeed have the right to add a child to our family when we and our two other children had such difficulty making ends meet? These and many other considerations overwhelmed me when I found out that I had become pregnant. It was not easy to decide what was right or wrong in our situation. But consid-

138

ering the cycle of life and man's ability to survive, and desiring to stand up to hardship and show that my vital force was not to be broken even under the worst conditions, I made my decision. That child was to be allowed to live, and I could only trust that one day it would come to experience a better and friendlier world than the one that now surrounded us. It turned out that Sagitov's wife, Aleksandra Sergeyevna, was also pregnant and was to give birth at about the same time as I. She was clearly a woman used to a high standard of living, and it was hardly easy for her to get used to the living conditions here at Selektsionnaya. She belonged to the Soviet upper class, and it was the first time that I had the occasion to become acquainted with a woman of that class of society.

Just as different as our backgrounds were the conditions under which we lived. Sagitov, who belonged to one of the numerous national minorities, the Bashkirs, was a party member and an esteemed scientist enjoying concomitant advantages and privileges. He was stationed at Selektsionnaya for a limited period of time to complete a scientific project and was to subsequently return to his institute not far from Moscow. He received a high salary and was, in addition, paid the special allowance given to people working under difficult conditions. The Sagitov family shopped in the "closed shop" and were not familiar with the problems we encountered in procuring the most basic food items.

Rationing had ended now that the war was over, and it had become much more difficult to buy bread and sugar, not to mention butter. With our ration cards, we were at least ensured a minimum of food. Now we had no guarantee whatsoever. We were referred to the private market, where prices had soared to even higher levels—levels at which we could not afford to pay.

Aleksandra Sergeyevna was a beautiful woman and appeared elegant and refined, and I kept thinking how difficult it must be for her to adjust to life here. It was some consolation that we were not the only ones subjected to these rough conditions. Aleksandra Segeyevna was only in charge of the cooking, for everything else was done by her husband and her maid, who worked full-time for them. For example, the maid took care of and milked the cow they owned. I soon developed an excellent relationship with Aleksandra Sergeyevna, and we had a lot to talk about now that we were both pregnant. She told me about their life before coming to Selektsionnaya, about their home in a town southwest of Moscow, and about the plans they had when they would return from

Selektsionnaya. She was very interested in life in the West and was always full of admiration for the few Western belongings we still had left.

We were on good terms with each other and never had any problems sharing the common kitchen. On the contrary, we often helped each other cope with the practical things in the household. My Russian was now quite good, and I no longer had any difficulties with the language. I had started reading a lot and found the time to read some of the great Russian classics, becoming acquainted with Pushkin, Tolstoy, Turgenev, Dostoyevsky, and several other great authors whom I had not read in Danish. There was a quite excellent library at Selektsionnaya, and I came to make diligent use of it.

Now that I started talking freely, several people told me how difficult it had been to understand me at first. Indeed, it had not been possible to make head or tail of anything I said. They had simply nodded their heads, pretending to understand all of it even if they did not understand a word.

One day—I believe it was in the early part of July of 1946—I read a notice in one of the papers that several of the Western countries that had been occupied by the Germans during World War II had now reopened their embassies and legations in Moscow. Denmark, too, had reopened its embassy. I recall reading it with a beating heart. I immediately got the idea of contacting the Danish Embassy but did not know how to go about it. Israel and I had a long discussion on the risks associated with contacting Danish diplomats in Moscow. One possibility not to be precluded was that the Soviet authorities would react very strongly to it and subject us to even greater hardships, on the pretext that we had attempted to contact a foreign power with anti-Soviet intentions, or for whatever other reason that might occur to them. We had gradually come to realize that the Soviet authorities did not lack ingenuity in that respect.

At that time, Israel received an answer to his inquiry about his family in Lithuania. The authorities had not been able to trace any of his relatives—all of them, without exception, had been killed by the Germans. We contemplated the matter for a long time, discussing the dangers to which we exposed ourselves and the best possible way to arrange it. The matter was, however, soon solved in an unexpected manner. One day, we learned that Jacob Ivanovich Klimov was going to Moscow on a business trip, and Israel decided to explain the matter to him. He told Klimov that I would like to contact the Danish Embassy in Moscow to make inquiries about my relatives in Denmark, but we dared not send our letter through the mail, and we wished him to take the letter and see to it that it reached the Danish Embassy. Klimov promptly said that he would do it, adding that it was no problem at all.

That there were no problems at all involved was hardly correct, though, for if it were discovered that he had acted as courier for some of the deportees wishing to contact a Western embassy, he might get into serious trouble, despite his high position and long-standing membership in the party. In those days, people were punished with imprisonment and labor camp for even slighter offenses. I believe that Klimov himself was fully aware of the risks involved but that he nevertheless did not hesitate to take our letter along for humane reasons, probably feeling that he could not reconcile rejection of such a request with his sense of honor and self-respect. His action was one of the most courageous tasks performed to help us during all the years of our deportation, and it later on turned out to have a decisive effect on our fate. We shall forever be grateful to this human being who so readily undertook a task that appeared to be extremely simple and innocent but that actually involved a serious danger to both his life and career and might also have had far-reaching consequences for us.

On the evening we had decided that I should write the letter, I sat down to write it with a beating heart and a multitude of thoughts going through my head. It was to be my first letter in Danish in six years.

Pokrovsk, July 22, 1946

The Danish Embassy
and Consulate

Dear Sirs:

I take the liberty of approaching you with the following request.

I would like you to help me find my parents, brothers, and sisters who lived in Copenhagen in June of 1941.

My parents, Mr. and Mrs. M. Epstein, lived at 12 Krystalgade, 5th floor. My brother, Eyzik Lachmann, lived at 51 Raadmandsgade, 4th floor.

Since my departure from Kybartai, Lithuania, in June of 1941, there has been no sign of life from my beloved ones, and I am naturally very concerned.

I should be very grateful to the Danish Embassy for complying with my request.

At the same time, I would ask you to kindly give me the address of Mr. Høgsbro Holm, formerly at Akselborg, Copenhagen V.

Rachel and Israel Rachlin

If possible, please inform my parents that my husband, our two children, and I are well and healthy.

Yours sincerely,
Rachel Rachlin
born Lachmann
Address: Selektsionnaya Station
Pokrovsk, Yakutia

The contents of that letter were to reestablish contact with our relatives and the world from which we had been cut off for six long years. I wrote it after much reflection, fully aware of the fact that I was not to write anything that might be detrimental to Klimov or ourselves should the letter be intercepted. I was, for example, unable to state directly that we had been deported and that this was the reason for our remote place of abode in Yakutia. However, by stating that we had left Lithuania in June of 1941, I assumed that the recipient of the letter would grasp the connection and realize how we had ended up in Yakutia.

Through the names and addresses of my relatives, the embassy would be able to identify me, and if it should turn out that it could not trace my relatives, it could find out who I was via Høgsbro Holm, the secretary-general of the Agricultural Council of Denmark. In conjunction with the import of Lithuanian horses to Denmark, Høgsbro Holm had gone to Lithuania in 1937 and had visited us in Kybartai. With him, and a Danish delegation, we had been invited to visit Germany's largest stud farm, Trakehnen, in East Prussia—a very great honor for non-Aryans such as Israel and I. Later, we were to meet with Høgsbro Holm on several occasions in Copenhagen.

Naturally, I wondered a great deal how they would react to my letter at the Danish Embassy. For it would more or less be like a sign of life from outer space—they did not know who had sent the letter, under what conditions the person concerned lived, or how it would be possible to maintain contact. I imagined the astonishment my letter would cause and the thoughts and speculation to which it would give rise among the Danish diplomats. At the same time, however, I had no doubt whatsoever that they would do what they could to contact us and try to help us, provided our letter reached them.

I have no idea how the letter reached the Danish Embassy in Moscow. Only many years later did I learn that it had taken one and a half months. In mid-October the postman delivered us a letter, and from the

142

very envelope we could see that it did not come from a Soviet organization. The sender was the Royal Danish Embassy in Moscow.

I was completely beside myself with excitement, and with trembling hands, I managed to open the letter. It had been written by Charge d'Affaires Døssing, who confirmed the receipt of my letter, stating that they had contacted my relatives in Copenhagen. He conveyed their greetings, telling us that they were all alive and well.

I was seized with indescribable joy and happiness to learn that all of my beloved ones were alive and well. At the same time, I was entirely overwhelmed at the thought that contact had now been made with the Danish authorities and that we would from now on be able to write to them and, in time, perhaps start applying for exit permits to Denmark. I gave quite a start when I realized what an incredible and daring idea it was. Our hope had now been given a more concrete existence than ever before. Little did we realize the many years and the many difficulties we would have to go through before our hope became a reality.

It was a long time before I got another letter from the Danish Embassy and even longer before I had established contact with my relatives in Copenhagen. The most important thing, however, was that the first contact and exchange of letters had taken place and that somebody from "our part of the world" knew where we were and what had happened to us.

My pregnancy proceeded without complications. I did nothing in the form of birth preparations, gymnastics, or relaxation exercises, and there were no regular examinations by a physician. I was entirely on my own but managed very well.

Baby clothes, naturally, presented a problem. There was nothing to be had in the shops, but, fortunately, I still had a few of Harrietta's baby clothes, and I also managed to sew and knit quite a few things during the nine months. In addition, I should not forget to mention that the state presented each newborn baby with nine yards of white flannel. People said that it was a personal gift from Stalin himself. By the New Year I had gathered quite a lot of baby clothing and felt that, by Soviet standards, my baby would be quite well equipped. I kept working in the infant day-care center as long as I could in order to save up as much maternity leave as possible for the time after the birth of the baby. A total of seventy-two days of maternity leave was allowed.

One day, not long before our babies were due, Aleksandra Sergeyevna and I asked our doctor to examine us. Our doctor, Nina Ivanovna, was a plump, middle-aged woman who had been kind and attentive to us and who, incidentally, had bought several things from us. As they do today, the Russians at the time went into complete raptures over anything from the West, and Nina Ivanovna had purchased some skirts and dresses from me.

After examining us, she told us that we would give birth within a week. Aleksandra Sergeyevna was told that she would have a girl, while I would have a boy.

Less than a week later, on Saturday night, January 11, Aleksandra Sergeyevna started suffering labor pains and was immediately taken to the hospital by a horse-drawn sleigh, as arranged by her husband. The winter was a terribly cold one that year, and at this time the thermometer almost always registered fifty-eight degrees Fahrenheit below zero and sometimes dropped as low as sixty-seven degrees Fahrenheit below zero. It was close to ten o'clock in the evening when Sagitov came back with his horse and sleigh. He entered our room to tell us that he would leave the horse close to the house, for we would probably need the sleigh soon ourselves.

It turned out to be correct. A few hours later, my first labor pains set in, and Israel said that we ought to go to the hospital immediately and take advantage of the availability of the horse. We put on big fur coats and departed. On our arrival at the maternity ward, we were immediately told that Aleksandra Sergeyevna had already had her baby and that it was a healthy baby girl. She was very happy when I came to see her in her room—she had wished for a girl.

Incidentally, Israel was not at all permitted to enter the maternity ward, since men were strictly prohibited from doing so. We took leave at the door, and Israel said that he would come back the next morning to find out how I was doing.

My pains disappeared again, and a whole day went by without anything happening. Not until the next evening did my pains resume, and I felt that the time had come. I had the baby around ten o'clock in the evening, and Nina Ivanovna was right: it was a boy, whom the midwife held up in front of me with a smile. I would have liked to hold him immediately, but this was not permitted. The babies were washed and immediately taken away to a room with other newborn babies, only returning when they had to be breast-fed.

I was not afraid that my baby would be mixed up with another baby, for it was not possible to mistake him for any of the other Russian or

Yakut children. But a Yakut mother lying next to me had an experience she never forgot.

The woman, who was a teacher at the school in Pokrovsk, had had a daughter the day before my child was born. Each morning the nurses arrived with our newborn babies in order for us to breast-feed them. To me, all of the Yakut babies looked exactly the same, but as my neighbor was nursing her daughter, I suddenly noticed that the child had less hair on her head than the last time I saw her. I told the mother, who summoned one of the nurses to look into the matter. And sure enough, the name band on the wrist of her baby had been exchanged with somebody else's, and my neighbor had been given another child. It created quite a stir in the ward, although they soon corrected the matter, so that the two babies were returned to their own mothers. They never managed to find out how the mix-up had occurred. The teacher, whose name I have forgotten, kept thanking me, assuring me that she would never forget me. She said that she doubted that she would have discovered the mix-up herself. Later on, when we ran into one another in the street or in a shop, she would always thank me, telling me how her little girl was doing.

Apart from that, I must admit that we were treated quite well in the maternity ward, despite some shortcomings and the rather primitive conditions. I shall never forget my midwife, Maria Ivanovna, who was extremely kind and attentive to me. She did not leave me during the delivery and knew how to reassure me, telling me what to do. Under her guidance the delivery proceeded entirely without complications. It is true that the technical facilities were deficient, but we could not complain of the careful treatment and friendly attitude toward us on the part of the staff.

I was discharged after a week, but with the temperature outside still sixty-seven degrees Fahrenheit below zero, I had no idea how to bring the baby home. I told Maria Ivanovna that I dared not transport the baby home, and she offered to help us. She packed the baby into a blanket, so that it was completely enclosed in a bundle, and when we got out into the sleigh where Israel was waiting for us, the bundle was packed into a big fur coat, which Maria Ivanovna took on her lap. To feel the breath of the baby, she put her hand through the many layers, holding it right over the baby's mouth. I was terribly worried that the child might suffocate or suffer harm from the cold, which might reach him through the various layers. Never had a ride seemed so long to me as the ride from the hospital to Selektsionnaya. Maria Ivanovna, however, did her best to calm me during the trip, assuring me that she had certainly experienced the same thing many times before, and no babies had ever been harmed by the cold.

I was extremely relieved when, at long last, we arrived home and got the baby out of the bundle. Schneur and Harrietta gave us a warm welcome, jumping up and down to see their baby brother. They had already found several names and competed with each other to suggest funny names. Harrietta had thus suggested that we call him "Chulok" (stocking). We asked Maria Ivanovna to stay and eat dinner with us. Israel had prepared dinner and had made a delicious beef soup. It did not happen often that Israel did the cooking, but he had nevertheless succeeded in preparing a delicious dinner, which we ate with a hearty appetite after our drive.

When Maria Ivanovna was about to leave, we wanted to give her a small present in thanks for her good treatment, but she said that it was entirely out of the question. She had merely performed her duty as midwife, and she was paid to do that, so we should not think at all of giving her any presents.

Now a busy and difficult time began for all of us in our little home. It was not easy being five in such a small room, and our patience and endurance were often tried. Washing diapers, playing, eating, and studying took place in the same room, which, moreover, served as bedroom for all of us. The coming months were very taxing. When I think back to that time, I wonder how it was possible for all of it to take place in such a smooth manner and where we got the energy and persistence to cope with all of the difficulties. It is difficult to understand how we managed, but at the time we did not think of it. We were in the middle of it all, and it was merely a question of coping.

After considering the matter for a while, we decided on the name of Samuel for the new member of our family. He was sweet and easy to care for, and since I was able to breast-feed him, feeding him was no trouble. The winter of 1947 saw a serious shortage of foodstuffs, and following the discontinuation of the ration cards, the supply situation became even worse.

When my maternity leave was over, I decided to give up my job and remain at home. There was the possibility of placing Samuel in the infant day-care center, but we did not want to do so, and I felt, moreover, that it would be best for all of us if I could do the housekeeping myself and take good care of the children.

As in the worst months in Yakutsk, we now had to struggle with hunger. I still had a couple of beautiful nightgowns. I had held on to them hoping that one day I would be able to use them myself, but their turn had come.

One Sunday morning when Israel was at home and was able to look after the children, I took off for Pokrovsk with the nightgowns, which I wanted to sell to our doctor, Nina Ivanovna, who, as I have mentioned, had a weakness for beautiful things from the West. I also knew that she could afford such things, and I got a good price for the nightgowns as well as a few other small items I sold her at the same time. With the money we purchased bread and butter. On rare occasions, we also got meat—especially horse meat and reindeer meat from the private market. My trip to Pokrovsk had lasted several hours, and I hurried back to Selektsionnaya to breast-feed Samuel. However, when I returned out of breath to our room, I met with an entirely unexpected and rare sight: in the middle of the room I saw Aleksandra Sergeyevna breast-feeding Samuel. He had become restless after I had left and had begun crying. He had not stopped, and in the end, Aleksandra Sergeyevna had come in to help Israel and the children calm him down. However, as all their attempts at comforting him were in vain, she decided to breast-feed him. Apparently, it agreed with him, for he had calmed down immediately, and everything looked idyllic when I entered the room.

Schneur was now eleven years old and Harrietta six, and they were old enough to help me with the household and to look after their little brother. We were all looking forward to the spring and the summer, so that we could get outside into the fresh air and the sunshine—being confined within the small room with a baby for such a long time had been hard on us. With the summer came our liberation.

12

Israel

My career as a tomato expert lasted only for eight months, when I became a schoolteacher once again. Klimov's wife, Anastasiya Alekseyevna, taught Russian at the school in Pokrovsk. In August of 1947, when the school holidays ended, she asked me if I would like to start teaching German. She remembered that I had asked to teach German at the school immediately after our arrival from Yakutsk. I did not hesitate for a moment and gladly accepted her offer.

Anastasiya Alekseyevna's interest in providing me with a job as teacher of German was not entirely unselfish. Klimov had a daughter, Nina, who was entering the fifth grade, at which point instruction in German normally started. The parents did not want their daughter to know less of German than students in the more civilized parts of the country and thus contacted me.

Before I could start the job, the party district committee had to approve me. This presented no problem, however, since I had a certificate of competence, signed by Fräulein Rund and the Ministry of Education in Yakutsk, and since Klimov, who was an influential man, put in a word for me.

After my appointment, another complication arose, however—the school had no place for me to live; again, Klimov came to the rescue. Selektsionnaya agreed that we could remain in our room in Sagitov's house until the school had found an apartment for us. For the second time, I was to embark on the profession of teacher.

The textbook we used was again *Anna und Marta baden*, and some of my students apparently had been in contact with my former students in Yakutsk, for it did not take long for my former nickname of "Baden" to be resumed and for Schneur to be called "Badenuol." Some of my students were Yakuts, and most of the teachers were also Yakuts.

The school had a dormitory as well, and the students came from all over the district, which was half the size of Denmark but very sparsely populated—the entire area had only about sixteen thousand inhabitants. Many of the students were of the first generation in their families to learn to read and write. The struggle to overcome illiteracy in the wilds of Siberia had as yet failed to produce any impressive results.

The mentality of the Yakuts is very different from that of the Russians, and it takes one a long time to become familiar with their thinking and to understand their character. For centuries the Yakuts had been nomads, living by breeding reindeer, in addition to hunting and fishing.

They had no written language, and all of their legends and traditions were preserved by a very rich oral culture, which was maintained from generation to generation. Shamanism was deeply rooted in their culture, and it took the Soviet power many years to overcome it. Some of their traditional holidays took place in the summer, and on these occasions one clearly felt how bound they still were by their old cultural traditions. On those nights Pokrovsk resounded with a uniform, rhythmic singing accompanied by the characteristic mouth organs with their vibrant, wailing sounds and the simple tambourines struck with the hand or a specially cut piece of wood. The playing went on and on into the night, monotonously and ecstatically, and not to the unqualified enthusiasm of the rest of us. Only at the formation of the Yakut Autonomous Soviet Socialist Republic in 1922 were the Yakuts given a written language, which was first based on the Latin alphabet and then, in 1940, on the Russian alphabet. For the sounds that were not found in the Russian language, a few Latin letters were retained. Newspapers, magazines, and books started appearing in the Yakut language. Classical works both from Russian and foreign literature were translated into the Yakut language, and in Yakutsk a theater that performed both plays and operas in the Yakut language was opened. During the first four years of elementary school, instruction was given in the Yakut language. Nevertheless, the transition from a nomadic society to an urban one was difficult and took time. Like other oppressed minority groups, the Yakut people suffered under the cultural pressure to which they were subjected by the Russians. Relations between the Russians and the Yakut people have from time immemorial been strained, and things did not change, not during the revolution nor for many years to come. The mutual hostility was often evident in open conflicts with violent fighting, which often took place after heavy drinking.

Their behavior patterns differed greatly from what we had hitherto experienced. Many times during the winter, somebody would knock at

149

the door, and outside would be a Yakut who wanted to sell us something. He would murmur something or other incomprehensible in the Yakut language, and we would ask him inside. He would get inside and remain standing right inside the door, completely stiff and silent. It was almost as if he stood there thawing. When we met these people in midwinter, their eyebrows, eyelashes, and hair were covered with rime, or drops that had frozen to ice, and when they suddenly entered a warm room, they needed a bit of time to get used to the sudden change. It was considered impolite to address them too soon, and one simply had to leave them to recover inside the door. If one spoke to them before sufficient time had elapsed, one usually got no answer at all. On the other hand, one should not wait too long either, for they would never be the first ones to start talking. This was a small ritual that was repeated every time, and gradually we learned the rules of the game. They usually came to sell milk or reindeer meat. The milk was sold as frozen blocks of ice, which had been shaped in a deep plate or a bowl. The cream always gathered at the top right in the center of the round block, and the children loved to scrape the frozen cream off with a spoon and eat it like ice cream.

Once the trading had started and we had bought something from them, the ice was broken, and they started telling us about their experiences on their trip to Pokrovsk from their village or settlement in the taiga, or they would tell us how to best prepare the meat and how good it was for us to eat reindeer meat. And once the deal had been concluded, they disappeared into the cold to continue their trip on their reindeer sleigh to the next customer. Incidentally, sometimes they came to sell hares or other game, such as grouse and capercaillie, which were plentiful in the area.

The upheaval the Yakut people had experienced since the revolution had left its mark on them. The oppression and the discrimination they had experienced for years had made them sensitive and vulnerable. This gave non-Yakut teachers a difficult task. A thoughtless remark might release the most unexpected reactions. If one rebuked or spoke harshly to one of the Yakut students, one might risk that he or she become completely and permanently silent, and then it was impossible to establish contact with the student again. At other times, one might release angry reactions and be told that one had merely acted or spoken as one had because the student was a Yakut. It took me some months to learn how to deal with Yakut students: one should never raise one's voice, one should be very wary of making jokes and never use irony, lest they should feel ridiculed, and one should be extremely careful to be fair, so that they would not feel discriminated against compared to their Russian classmates.

Many of the students were extremely intelligent, bright, and perceptive, and they reacted quickly to something that did not conform to their conceptions. In one of the German lessons there was the sentence "The roof is red." One of the students spoke up quickly, insisting, "That is not right! A roof cannot be red!" There were no houses with tiled roofs in Yakutia, and each student evaluated all new information presented to him on the basis of his personal realm of experience.

At first I had difficulty distinguishing between my Yakut students and remembering their names. Most of their last names were formed of Russian first names with the ending -ov or -yev. Petrov, Nikolayev, Sidorov, Ivanov, and similar names reoccurred in all of the grades. As the Yakuts resemble one another very much with their typical Mongolian features—the slanting dark eyes, flat noses, and black hair—it was rather difficult to distinguish among them, and it took me a long time to figure out who was who.

The students had similar difficulties adjusting to the formal form of address used when speaking to their teachers. In the Yakut language, there is no formal address, only the familiar form. They applied this to Russian as well, and it took them several years to learn how to address a teacher.

However, after a while I developed excellent relations with my students. It made a great impression on them that I spoke five languages. Thanks to my knowledge of languages, I gained much respect and admiration among them. As in Yakutsk, I often had to answer questions that were not related to the subject of German.

The black American singer Paul Robeson was at the time one of the most popular foreign singers in the Soviet Union. Soviet newspapers often wrote that he was persecuted, partly because he was black and partly because he was a progressive advocate of civil rights for the blacks. One day, one of my students asked me why Paul Robeson did not leave the United States to settle in the Soviet Union, where he would be much better off. In answering questions like this one, it was extremely important to bear in mind the policy that the teacher had to follow and that one should not deviate too much from the official course. After a moment's reflection, I said that it was, of course, true that Paul Robeson would be treated well in the Soviet Union, but he had to remain in the United States to help the other blacks who were being discriminated against by the whites. He would not be able to fight for the rights and equality of the blacks if he lived outside his country.

In answering such questions, a teacher would always have to be ready to give an answer in conformity with the current party line. Athletes have to practice and train constantly to keep in shape. Similarly, all people holding responsible positions in the Soviet Union must constantly see to it that they keep in good shape politically. All teachers were required to participate in political study groups. We gathered once a week for two hours to discuss party history and current domestic and foreign policy issues.

It was compulsory for all teachers to participate in the political study groups, and in addition to our regular work of preparing our lessons, we had to spend a couple of hours each week familiarizing ourselves with dialectic materialism, party history, and the thinking and statements of Marx, Lenin, and, especially, Stalin on the class struggle, the economic development under socialism, and the role of the proletariat as the vanguard of the party. For each new meeting of the study group we had to prepare reports on the subjects we had examined at the previous meeting. It was important to keep well abreast of what was going on and to participate actively in the meetings, for at the end of the school year, a party secretary of the district committee arrived to test the participants in the study group. If the secretary was not satisfied with the achievements of the teachers, he reprimanded them, requesting that they start all over again and go through the same material the next year. Consequently, we all made an effort to pass the test and avoid reprimands from the district committee of the party. It was, as a rule, the party secretary of the school's own party organization who was the leader of the study group. Among the participants in the political study groups, I was the only one who knew any foreign languages and was familiar with Latin. My colleagues, therefore, often approached me, asking me to explain unfamiliar foreign words to them.

One day, as I was on my way home from a meeting in the study group, I was accompanied by a colleague who asked me to explain the meaning of the word *cosmopolitan*. I explained its definition and gave him an explanation of the Greek origin of the word. The interpretation I gave him of the term was a very positive one, that is, a citizen of the world who feels at home everywhere, irrespective of country and nationality, a human being who is very adaptable, versatile, and experienced. I did not attach any major importance to our brief conversation, which I found similar to all of the other instances when I had been asked by colleagues about the meaning of foreign words.

Shortly afterward, however, I got a different idea of the situation, for at that time Stalin started his campaign against cosmopolitans, a witch-hunt with distinct anti-Semitic undertones directed against all dissidents and against everybody who had or had had connections with the West or who at some time or other had given expression to sympathy for the Western culture and mode of life. The radio and all magazines and newspapers thundered against the "rootless cosmopolitans," and Stalin's interpretation of the word differed quite considerably from the explanation I had given my colleague.

The cunning cosmopolitans threatened to undermine the Soviet state from within; they had infiltrated the entire system, and all Soviet citizens were now requested to be on their guard and to watch for the intrigues and traps of the cosmopolitans. Soviet citizens were presented a frightening picture of these terrible cosmopolitans, who did not stop at anything to hinder socialist development.

I now grasped what was going on. My colleague was a party member and had been informed of the campaign against cosmopolitans beforehand, and that was the reason he had come up to me to ask me about the meaning of the word.

I was rather nervous in the time that followed, for if my colleague desired to put me in a difficult situation, he could most easily have done so by reporting my interpretation of the word. I feared that I would some day be pointed to as an example of a rootless cosmopolitan or a person sympathizing with such monsters. It would not, of course, take much imagination to present me as the archetype of a cosmopolitan. However, my colleague kept his information to himself, and nothing happened.

Rachel · Israel

Almost an entire year passed before we were able to move from Selektsionnaya to the small apartment that the school had allotted us. The apartment consisted of a narrow room, which was in turn divided into two rooms with a total of 240 square feet. There was a joint kitchen in the hallway, which we had to share with the family living in the other half of the house.

Our new apartment was greatly inferior to the one we had had at Selektsionnaya, but we had no choice and thus not much to ponder. We had but to settle down in the new apartment. As it turned out, it became the apartment in which we stayed the longest in the years of our deportation.

It was one of the typical Yakut log houses, but a very simple version. The roof was not pitched but flat and made of a mixture of soil and clay. The house was located at the end of a row of three houses, which were more or less built together. It was located close to the edge of the slope that led right down to the Lena, and both summer and winter we had a beautiful view of the river, which was several miles wide at that spot. The window at the other side of the house faced the taiga. We had to admit that the location was perfect with regard to both view and distance from the school, which was situated more or less next door. This was very important both for Israel and the children when they had to go back and forth during the cold winter.

We made the room facing the river into a bedroom for ourselves and Samuel, who slept in a tall crib. Schneur and Harrietta slept in the other room—now on a bench, now on a bunk. In the daytime the room functioned as the combined living and dining room of the entire family. Our spartan home here became the scene of the most stable and quiet period of our entire deportation.

We gradually got into a routine, a rhythm of life similar to that of most of the local people, greatly influenced by the harsh climate and the change of seasons. Fear and anxiety had not left us, but after some time they were not as pronounced as they had been in the preceding six to seven years. We were able to develop a certain calmness about our situation, coupled with resignation to the fate that had been allotted us. This did not mean that we had completely given up hope, for never did we lose all hope, not even in the most hopeless and desperate moments. It was somehow easier for us to adjust to the new situation, because we were able to calm down and were no longer haunted as much by uncertainty about the future.

It goes without saying that the things we had been through had made heavy demands on both of us, especially in our relations with each other. Neither of us had imagined when we got married that we would have to spend the best years of our lives under such conditions. We had both had dreams of our life together, but all of our dreams of trips, of family happiness, of contributing and creating something together were rolled down and crushed by all of the misfortunes that had overtaken us. Behind us were already quite a few dramas, traumas, and tragedies, and ahead were still the uncertainty and unknown trials. We knew, however, that we had each other's support and thus derived the strength to endure and persevere. At no point so far had either of us given a thought to the tests to which our relationship and love had been put during all of the hardships we had been through together. Via crooked paths our two fates had been united in love, and each of us had done what we could to protect the other and our family.

Indeed, we are not trying to idealize the situation or our relationship. As in any other family, disagreements and situations arose, which required indulgence and tolerance from either side. It was not always so easy to find the strength to cope with the problems of the home when our nerves were worn thin from the constant outside pressure to which we were both subject. However, in all our experiences of those years, we knew that no matter what happened, we had each other's support, and neither of us did at any point doubt our mutual love.

All of that had been so natural to both of us that neither of us had given it a thought in the years that went by, and only now that we had settled down in Pokrovsk and had more time for reflection did we truly understand how much we meant to each other and become even more closely attached.

In looking around us and regarding the marital problems of the present time, we almost feel that it was easier for us at the time. We see today how men and women confront each other with endless demands in their marriages, barricading themselves, each behind his or her own marital defenses. Nowadays, married life has, in our view, far too often assumed the character of a struggle, a bombardment in which the parties drown each other in arguments about equality, sex roles, women's liberation, oppression, and scores of other things concerning the present-day marital relations debate, which has proved endless. In our opinion, the most characteristic feature of a relationship between a man and a woman today is that each spends a great deal of his or her time determining which of them is better off. Everything is measured and weighed and settled on the basis of ready-made standards, which have been made the yardstick by now one movement, now the other, and which must now be applied to everybody forcefully.

It is possible that we are mistaken and that the entire upheaval we have witnessed through the seventies has benefited some people, but as far as we can see, they have, in the hurry, forgotten the individuality of human beings and the way they want to live their lives. It is possible

155

that the newly gained insight into the relations between man and woman and the liberty that the younger generations have come to enjoy may in time lead to greater happiness and joy in marriage. But so far, it seems to us as if men and women have been too busy watching over one another and making demands and, in all of their desperate attempts to achieve a good life, have forgotten to live. The result has far too often been that neither the woman, the man, nor the children of the marriage are very happy.

In a way, we had fewer problems in our married life because of outside circumstances, which made demands on us and forced us to act without attaching too much importance to each other's shortcomings or faults. According to modern standards of value, our relationship was marked by distinct sex roles with division of work as well as responsibility. It was never a question of measuring or weighing the contributions of each to our marriage, for we were two people who belonged together, who shared everything, and who strove for the same things. We were both aware of having given each other our lives, and we wanted to continue giving the best we had. That feeling has not changed after the many upheavals we have undergone since then.

Much of our time was spent surviving: supplying our family with enough to eat and sufficient clothing both summer and winter required much time, energy, and money. To supplement our supplies, we got a flock of chickens, or, rather, some chickens and one cock, which grew up and gave us both eggs and a new batch of chickens every summer. To keep poultry was not too easy, given the prevailing conditions, but it played an important role in our diet. Most of the other people kept poultry as well. And for us, chickens presented no problem during the summer, when the chicken house, or, rather, the chicken coop, was placed outside the house, right under our window, and the chickens were allowed to walk around outside all day, finding their food in the area around the house and in the vegetable garden. In the evening Schneur and Harrietta saw to it that the chickens got into their coop for the night.

We managed in time to become very good chicken breeders. Availing ourselves of our experience with seed growing from Selektsionnaya, we kept detailed accounts of each chicken's egg laying. When a new brood of chickens had to be hatched, we only took eggs from the chickens that had the best production both in number of eggs and size of individual eggs. We all followed with great interest the tables and statistical calculations made for each individual chicken. In this way we succeeded in the course of three or four years in breeding a really good stock.

All of our chickens belonged to the white Italian breed by the name of leghorn; each individual chicken had its own name, and we were able to distinguish among them. We had around twenty-two chickens, so there was quite a lot of work involved in looking after them. Gradually, our production became so great that we were able to start selling some of the eggs, and this became a considerable supplement to our income. Our record chicken laid 175 eggs in one season, and if we sold the production of a whole month, we were able to get nearly as much as half of Israel's monthly salary from the school. It was soon rumored among the local people in Pokrovsk that the deported Rachlin family were experts at chicken breeding, and people came from far and near to buy brood eggs from us, so that they could start their own good breed. We were quite proud of this.

Chicken breeding, however, involved a lot of work. During the winter months they always lacked calcium, and we solved that problem by means of a local recipe. Ox bones were burned and subsequently crushed into a fine powder, and the chickens were fed this special kind of bonemeal. It was an excellent remedy for calcium deficiency. Another treatment was to feed our chickens old newspapers, which were torn into tiny pieces—the paper contained some substance or other which the chickens needed.

The first eggs were usually laid in December or January and were awaited with great excitement. We had to be very careful to get to the eggs before the chickens could, for if we did not, they would attack them and eat them. Thus when the time for egg laying approached, we had to find out which chicken was laying the eggs. A small hood made from the bottom part of a sock was then pulled down over its head to prevent it from hacking its eggs to pieces. Once the egg laying had really started, we had to feel each chicken with a finger to find out if it had an egg inside, and if so, it was taken out of the cage and put into a box lined with hay to enable it to lay its egg in peace and quiet.

Samuel was the one who got the first egg of the season each year, and we always made it a special event to bring some cheer and festivity into our home during this dark time of the year.

Israel

Late in the summer, chickens were slaughtered. I was always the one who had to undertake the task. I did not particularly like it, but it had to be done. A huge sawed-off tree stump stood some distance from the house; it was the site of execution (I thought of it in these terms, as I believed the rest of the family did). It was no pleasant sight. Chickens that had had their heads cut off kept jumping around for some time with blood spurting from their necks. This was the way in which chickens were slaughtered here, and I had learned it from one of our neighbors. None of us ever got used to it, but there was no other solution. In the course of our stay, quite a few chickens lost their lives in this manner. I often think of these experiences when, nowadays, I pick up a ready-to-cook chicken from the deep-freeze section of the supermarket.

In the winter it was more difficult to breed chickens. When it got too cold outside, the chicken coop was carried inside the house and placed in the kitchen with our neighbors' coop. The immediate result was an enormous bustle and noise in the kitchen, and after some time a strong stench spread through both the kitchen and the rest of the house. We had to put up with it if we wanted to enjoy the advantages of having our own chickens. We did what we could to keep the coop clean, but we were unable to remove the smell.

In the worst winter months, nearly all of our activity took place inside the house. We only went outside when it was strictly necessary, and during the long winter nights, we sat at home, each occupied with his or her tasks—preparation of the next day's classes or repair of some clothing on our part, and homework or playing on the children's.

Rachel

I often read stories and fairy tales to the children, and our old game from Selektsionnaya—that of sitting in front of the open fire, looking into its flames and embers, and imagining—was resumed.

Samuel came to like this game very much as he grew older, and we would sit for a long time in front of the fire while I retold some of the fairy tales he already knew, pointing out the various figures in the embers and the flames to him.

The days went by, one after another, and time crawled by without any major events or experiences for us. We were happy as long as we were able to survive. It was not always easy, especially toward the end of the month. We had to pinch and scrape to get our money to last, and we did not always manage. I especially recall two events from those years when the situation became critical.

It was midsummer in the year of 1951. Israel had suffered an attack of malaria and was forced to remain in bed for several days. It was at the end of the month, and we had no money at all. We were literally destitute and had neither bread, butter, sugar, nor anything else left in the house to eat. We had no idea what to do, for there was nowhere we could go to borrow money. In the midst of our despair, Israel, however, suddenly got a bright idea.

Like all other working Soviet citizens, we held state bonds. Each year an amount equivalent to a month's salary was deducted from everybody's salary, and long-term state bonds were handed out in return. The transaction was said to be voluntary because the money the state received in this way would be used to develop and strengthen the Soviet society, but the truth was that everybody was obliged to purchase the bonds, and nobody dared refrain from doing so.

Israel's idea was for me to take all of the bonds to the savings bank to examine the most recent list of bonds drawn for redemption. We might be fortunate enough to have one of our bonds come out a winner. To be honest, I did not have much confidence in the idea, but since we had no better solution, I went to the bank with Samuel. One of the employees at the savings bank helped me check the drawing lists. He was very friendly, and I felt that he understood and sympathized with us. We had gone through nearly the entire bunch of bonds, and I had already given up hope, finding solace in the idea that the chance of winning had, of course, been quite negligible to begin with, when the man who helped me suddenly spread out his arms, exclaiming with undisguised enthusiasm, "You have won! You have won five hundred rubles!" I could hardly believe my own ears, but after having compared the number on my bond with that on the drawing list and the amount stated opposite it, I knew it to be true.

It was almost too good to be true, and my joy was indescribable. Samuel, who was four years old at the time, realized that something very wonderful had happened, and he shared my joy as we hurried to the nearest shop for food supplies.

We bought what we could get of canned food and other foodstuffs that were available, in addition to bread, butter, potatoes, sugar, and tea. I also bought a little bit of chocolate for the children to make them happy after their wants during the preceding days.

However, we had nothing in which to carry all of the things I had purchased, for I had not imagined that one of our bonds would be a winner. I, therefore, had to borrow a carrying net from the shop, but since that was not sufficient either, the shop assistant gave me a metal bucket in which to carry the rest of the goods. And I then took off with Samuel, who held the handle of the bucket with his small hand to help me carry it. With a shiny metal bucket filled to the rim with various goods in one hand and a full net in the other, and with Samuel next to me, I hurried home, hardly able to keep back my joy. Even in Pokrovsk I believe I was a strange sight that day, but I felt as if my return was a triumphal procession. When we returned to the house, we were received as heroes, and we very quickly started cooking. It became quite a big day in our little home.

The second episode took place six months later around the New Year. After the revolution all religious holidays were removed from the official Soviet calendar. Christmas and the Christmas tree were abolished. Instead, the New Year's tree was introduced in order not to rob people of all joys in that dark time of the year. New Year was now made into a holiday, which had all of the customs and traditions of Christmas but which was not to be associated with anything religious. Fir trees were decorated, in exactly the same manner as Christmas trees, with colorful glass balls, tinsel, festoons, cornets, and hearts. Santa Claus, who in Russian is called Grandfather Frost, was also to arrive with presents for the children. The days before the New Year were as hectic as the last days before Christmas in Denmark, and everybody was busy preparing for the festivities, decorating fir trees, cutting decorations, buying and wrapping presents, and, naturally, preparing festive meals.

Each year a big New Year's party was held at the school for the children. The children were dressed in amusing outfits, and there was dancing and games while everybody eagerly awaited the arrival of Grandfather Frost. He arrived, carrying a big bag over his shoulder with a small present for each child. The first time Samuel partook in the celebration and Grandfather Frost came up to him with a small bag of candy, he became terribly frightened. He cried at the top of his voice as he clung to me, showing that he did not want to have anything to do with Grandfather Frost at such a close range. He did not calm down until the disappointed Grandfather Frost, with his big white beard, withdrew to talk to some other and more reasonable children.

Later everybody walked around the New Year's tree while various songs were sung. The children loved all of it and were jubilant.

Now that the festivities around the New Year were again approaching, the excitement communicated itself to our children. Preparations were going on everywhere, and with decorations being cut and glued in all homes, all of the children talked of nothing else. Only in our home, nothing of the kind was in progress, because we did not celebrate Christmas. It is true that the New Year festivities had no relation to anything religious anymore, but, nevertheless, we associated it with something that did not agree with our Jewish traditions. A decorated fir tree, whether it was called a Christmas tree or a New Year's tree, did not belong in the home of a Jewish family, and we therefore never had it in our house. We explained to the children why we could not have a New Year's tree, and they accepted the explanation, although it was perhaps a little difficult for them to understand while they were small. However, they always participated in the festivities at the school and thus experienced some of the celebration.

That year, however, the temptation became irresistible, especially for Harrietta and Samuel, who kept begging us for a New Year's tree to decorate and dance around, as was done in every other home. They went on asking for a tree, and in the end we gave up, promising them to go into the woods together to cut one down. Two days before the New Year, we went to the woods to find a tree, which we felled and brought home in triumph. The children were wild with joy and immediately embarked on the preparations for the night of the New Year's festival. Everybody was cutting, gluing, and decorating with all his might, and the children had a wonderful time. Israel and I had somewhat mixed feelings about the whole thing, but we did not begrudge the children their joy, for there was not much to be joyful about in our otherwise quite dreary existence. The preparations coincided with the depletion of our funds. Once more, despite our efforts, we had not been able to make our money last till the end of the month, and there was no money left for purchasing New Year's presents nor food for a festive meal.

I managed to concoct a pitiful meal consisting of fried potatoes, sauerkraut, rye bread, and some kind of fruit stew, which I made from frozen lingonberries. Quite naturally, the luster of the festivities vanished like dew before the sun. It was not possible to maintain a festive atmosphere under the circumstances. While we sat around the table eating our modest meal in silence, the decorated New Year's tree stood in a corner, appearing out of place and superfluous. I understood that it was a mistake to have agreed to the New Year's tree, which now, somehow or other, was identified with the all but cheerful situation in which we found ourselves. When the very day after New Year's Eve we threw out the tree and the next day Israel was paid his salary, we breathed a sigh of relief. We have never had a New Year's tree or Christmas tree in our home since then.

At the time, we had already had contact with my relatives in Denmark and the Danish Embassy in Moscow for several years. A long time elapsed after I received my first letter from the Danish Embassy and before I managed to establish contacts with Denmark. First some letters were exchanged between me and the embassy, and one day—I believe it was in 1947—I wrote my first letter to my family in Copenhagen. Several months went by before the postman brought me the letter I had been awaiting with great eagerness. The letter was from my mother and my twin brother, Eyzik, who wrote me to tell me how my entire family in Denmark was doing. Somewhat later, I also managed to establish contact with my sister Doba, who lived in Göteborg, Sweden. Our correspondence was very irregular, with the letters often taking several months to reach their destinations or not arriving at all. However, contact with my family had been made, and in the course of the years, it became increasingly easier to maintain a regular exchange of letters. Of course, I was never able to write what I wanted to write and constantly had to seek ways of harmlessly writing my letters so that they reflected the actual state of affairs. The letters from my family and our contact with the Danish Embassy became our lifeline to the world from which we had been cut off. It was this lifeline that gave us the hope that we would one day leave this foreign country and return to the world where we felt we belonged.

It is possible that there was not too much basis for that hope at the time. The cold war was in full progress, and there was no indication at all that the Soviet authorities intended to change the status of the deportees and allow them to return home. Nevertheless, after the first contact with the Danish Embassy, we started looking into the possibilities of getting out of the Soviet Union and being reunited with my family in Denmark. In 1946, when the initial exchange of letters between me and the embassy took place, our difficult struggle to get home began. Fortunately, we had no idea of the many disappointments, humiliations, and trials awaiting us in the coming years.

Our contact with my family had another very important effect on our lives. After some time, we received our first parcel from my sister Doba, who in Göteborg had undertaken the task of seeking to help us by sending us parcels. She sent primarily clothing. Some of the clothes we needed ourselves, and others we were able to sell and thus acquire a much-needed supplement to our forever unstable financial situation. In the following years, her parcels played a very important role in our lives.

They arrived most irregularly, but each time we received the message that a parcel was waiting for us at the post office, it was a festive occasion for our family. How excited we all were in opening the parcel! The packages were usually big bags made out of strong material, which was sewn together around the contents. As we all stood together around the dining room table, we cut open the seams with a knife or a pair of scissors and poured out its contents. There were dresses and suits for us, as well as clothes for the children. Everything was held up and admired while we discussed whether it was something we ought to keep or sell. Once in a while, small surprises were concealed in the pockets of jackets or coats: boxes of Tobler chocolate, lozenges for the children, or vitamin pills. A couple of times, some food articles also reached us, but that was rare.

Once, the package from Doba contained a doll for Harrietta and a small yellow bear for Samuel. Both children became quite speechless with joy at the nice gifts, for neither of them had too many toys. The doll was immediately given a name and was called "Birgitta," while the bear had to be called "Misha"—that is the name given to all small bears in Russian. Birgitta was finely clothed in a dress with a petticoat, stockings, shoes, a chic little jacket, and an elegant hat on her dark brown hair. Unfortunately, the doll came to a bad end—one day when we were again out of money, we received a visit from a couple who wanted to buy clothing from us. They purchased quite a lot of things, and as they were about to leave, the woman caught sight of Birgitta and asked if she was for sale. She was not, we said, but as the woman offered more or less a fortune for the doll, we could not reject her offer, and Birgitta was sold. This happened several years later, and Harrietta was then so big that the loss of the doll was not too painful for her. Samuel, on the other hand, was allowed to keep his Misha, which he still holds on to as one of his Siberian treasures.

Another of his precious treasures from those days is a small wooden horse, which he received on his second birthday. Each time one of our children had a birthday, we had a terrible time finding presents. As Samuel's birthday approached, we again started worrying about what to do. There were no toys to be had in the shops in Pokrovsk, and we had no idea what to give to him. Somehow or other, however, one of Israel's Yakut students learned about the difficulties we were experiencing and came to our rescue. Like many other Yakuts, Popov was a very talented wood-carver. One day after a German class, he came up to Israel somewhat timidly and took out of his pocket a package wrapped in a piece of notebook paper. It was a small, well-made statue of a Yakut horse standing on a pedestal, carved from a piece of wood.

When on that special day of January Samuel woke up to unpack his birthday presents and discovered the horse, he was very happy. In addition to the horse, he received two pieces of chocolate from his older brother and sister. The horse became one of his most cherished toys and followed him through all the years as one of the tangible memories of his Siberian childhood.

Incidentally, both Birgitta and Misha were greatly admired both by children and adults when Harrietta and Samuel played with the toys with other children. Toys like these were a rare sight in this part of the world, and the neighborhood children always competed to play with the much desired doll and bear.

The packages often rescued us in the most hopeless situations, and we were always deeply grateful to Doba and the rest of the family for their contents. Some of the packages were lost in transit, for many that Doba wrote she had sent never arrived, but there was nothing we could do to obtain compensation. Other packages had their own stories.

Israel

On a Sunday afternoon in the winter of 1951 or 1952, we visited some friends, Masha and Zelig Kapul, who had lived with us in Pokrovsk for several years. Masha was a Russian woman whom Zelig had married in Yakutsk. She was a pharmacist by profession, and in Pokrovsk she had a good position as manager of the district pharmacy. A nice residence came with the job, and Zelig and Masha were rather well-off under the circumstances. They had invited us over because Mulya Svirskiy, my good friend and fishing partner from Bykov Mys, had arrived at Pokrovsk on a visit. We had not seen one another since our departure from Bykov Mys, and there was a lot to talk about. Zelig, Mulya, and I had known one another from Lithuania, where we had belonged to the same Jewish community. We were of the same age, had a lot in common, and always had a good time together. We exchanged experiences, relating all that had happened in the intervening years, and speculated about the future. While we were absorbed in our conversation, there was a sudden knock at the door, and Masha came into the room, announcing that there was a young man outside from the post office who wanted to talk to me. I went out into the hallway and saw one of my former students who now worked as a postman. He apologized for disturbing me, but he had been to our house, where he had been told that he might find me at the Kapuls. He said that the postmaster wished to talk to me and that it was urgent. I did not understand what could be so urgent but nevertheless accompanied him to the post office.

At the post office, the postmaster told me that a parcel had arrived for us from abroad but had unfortunately become damaged in a traffic accident in Yakutsk. A glass containing strawberry jam had broken, and the problem now was how the postal services were to replace the jam. It was impossible to find any strawberry jam in the shops, and the question was whether we would be willing to accept an appropriate amount of chocolate in exchange. I immediately told him that it was no problem and signed a form to the effect that I had accepted the offer and waived any further claim for compensation from the postal services. The postmaster was extremely content that the matter had been solved so easily and quickly. I went back to the Kapuls and told them about the story, which surprised all of us. However, we had so many other things to talk about that night that we forgot the incident and were soon absorbed in all the stories of big and small moments in our lives. We remained together till far into the night.

A couple of days later, we received the parcel and wondered why there were no traces of the strawberry jam on any of the clothes in the parcel. If the glass had broken inside the parcel, it would have left stains on the other things. In time we forgot the matter entirely, and it was only several years later that the mystery was solved. When we again returned to Yakutsk, an acquaintance at the main post office told us what had happened. At the sight of our foreign parcel, a young girl working in the parcel division of the post office had become tempted beyond her power of resistance and had managed to take the parcel to her home. The theft was discovered, and in a search of her home, the contents of the entire parcel were found, with the exception of the strawberry jam, which she had eaten. The poor girl had to appear in court and was sentenced to ten years in labor camp for her offense. Since the strawberry jam was listed in the papers accompanying the parcel, the authorities had been forced to invent a plausible explanation. A traffic accident was the best thing they were able to come up with.

A few months after our visit to Zelig's house, we received the sad news that Mulya Svirskiy had died. Mulya had got a job as accountant at Rybtrest—the same organization in which we were employed when we worked at Rybzavod in Bykov Mys. A large part of his work consisted in traveling around most of Yakutia, visiting various divisions of the large enterprise to check their accounts. On one of his trips way up north, Mulya had been on his way by dog sledge to a small town with an engineer from Moscow. A native dog sledge guide—a *kayur* as they are called in the Yakut language—accompanied them on the trip. Suddenly, they were taken by surprise by a purga, the notorious Yakut blizzard, and, suddenly, the horizon was blotted out. The experienced kayur knew exactly what to do to protect himself and his passengers from the purga. He gathered the dogs in a ring around the sledge, and all three of them crouched on the sledge covered with reindeer skins. In that way they were able to remain outside in the severe cold almost indefinitely without danger.

After a while the purga subsided almost as suddenly as it had started, and Mulya said that they immediately had to try to reach a settlement a few miles farther away. But the kayur flatly refused to continue, saying that every purga was followed by still another purga, which was not quite as strong but still too dangerous for anybody to travel in. He wanted them to stay and wait till the second purga was over, but Mulya was in a hurry and ignored the warnings of the kayur. He left by foot with the engineer, and that became the cause of his death. They had not gone very far when the purga started anew, and while they were struggling ahead as best they could, the engineer lost one of his gloves. Mulya, who felt responsible for him because he had insisted that they leave, gave him his own glove so that he would not get any frostbite.

As a result, Mulya's one hand became severely frostbitten. They reached the settlement after several hours of walking, and Mulya was extremely weak from exposure. He needed immediate medical attention, but several hours passed before a doctor arrived. Mulya had his hand amputated under very primitive conditions. Blood poisoning set in, and Mulya died shortly afterward, before they managed to get him to Yakutsk.

13

---·•·---

Rachel · Israel

Our relations with our neighbors in those years were not always entirely smooth. Four different families lived in the apartment next to us in the course of the years we spent there, and they were certainly not all of them equally friendly. Worst was the Popov family, who lived next to us for the last eighteen months. They were Yakuts and the husband taught at the school, although he was not a particularly well-educated man. He had a quiet and timid wife, whereas his two adolescent sons were wild and unruly. They also had a small girl by the name of Tanya, who suffered from trachoma, a very infectious eye disease from which many Yakuts suffered.

Popov was unfriendly, not to say downright unpleasant, and this triggered many conflicts in our joint kitchen. We lived close together, and there was ample occasion for conflict to arise if one did not show understanding and tolerance. Popov did not intend to do either. During the summer we had water brought up from the Lena by a driver who poured the water into a barrel, which stood on the steps outside the door. In the winter we either had to collect the water ourselves far out on the river, where we cut a hole in the ice, or we had it delivered in the form of huge blocks of ice, which the driver took right up to the house on his sledge. When we needed water, we would chop off some of the ice and put it in a saucepan or a kettle on the stove.

One morning in the summer, we saw to our great astonishment that little Tanya was standing on a stool, which she had brought up to the barrel of water outside, and was washing herself in the water we used for drinking and cooking. Even if she had not suffered from trachoma, it would not have been a very good idea to use our drinking water in that manner. When we told Popov what his daughter had done, he did not

167

show the least interest, remarking casually that we might, of course, have placed the barrel somewhere else where Tanya could not reach it. We understood that it was hopeless to reach an agreement with the man and decided to have as little as possible to do with him and his family.

There was often furious quarreling in Popov's apartment. The two sons and the father often quarreled, and sometimes the quarrels developed into fights, which caused the walls of our house to shake. Furniture was thrown about, and china was broken once the three men got started. One day the fighting in their apartment was particularly violent, and when, after a long time, it became quiet, we were able to see from the kitchen that one of the sons had been tied to the iron bed by his father and his brother and lay battered and exhausted on the floor without being able to move. It was best to stay on the right side of people like that and avoid any conflict with them.

The conditions under which we lived did not make it easy for us to adhere to the Jewish customs and traditions with which we had grown up. We were not orthodox but held on to our Jewish traditions and always celebrated the holidays as well as we could. As a rule, we got together on the holidays with a circle of friends or acquaintances to celebrate. These celebrations always took place rather quietly, since none of us wanted to attract unnecessary attention from the authorities, for we fully realized that they did not take a favorable view of religious practices. Despite the conditions and restrictions, we adhered to our Jewish traditions as much as we were able to and tried to bring up the children in the Jewish spirit. When Samuel was born, it was, of course, entirely impossible to have him circumcized in the hospital. We dared not even raise the question. Things were first put in order after we got to Denmark.

The women usually helped one another prepare the dishes that belonged to the various holidays. It was not merely a question of matzos for Passover and gefilte fish for some of the other holidays, for there were also special baked goods and sweets, such as small spiced buns made of a mixture of grated carrots and sugar, which the children especially loved.

We were not kosher and thus had no problems in that respect. But among our deported acquaintances were families who throughout the years observed the strict rules for cooking and housekeeping. This was quite an accomplishment under the conditions prevailing in Siberia, where it was difficult just to get enough to eat. Some of those religious families managed during those years by eating fish, which, of course, is kosher.

Buying foodstuffs anywhere in the Soviet Union always presented a problem. It was especially difficult to get meat in the shops. In the kolkhoz market, meat was always available, provided one was able to pay the very high prices.

Many of the Jewish deportees were orthodox and ate only kosher meat (meat from cattle or fowl, slaughtered in accordance with the Jewish religious directives). Since none of the Jewish deportees were able to undertake the slaughtering according to the religious demands, the orthodox had no possibility of eating meat in all the years they lived in Siberia. Being a vegetarian is not too hard, but if one lives in regions where the temperature in the winter may drop to seventy-five degrees Fahrenheit below zero and where at least two and a half ounces of fat are needed daily to cover the calorie requirements, life as a vegetarian is proof of the strength of one's will to adhere to the demands of one's faith. We had no problems, since we were not orthodox. We ate meat, no matter how the slaughtering had been carried out.

We have often been asked whether we suffered from anti-Semitism during those years.

Anti-Semitism has deep roots in Russia, and for many generations, Russian Jews have been subject to discrimination, both in czarist Russia and in the new Soviet state that arose after the revolution. It is not without reason that *pogrom*, the Russian word for persecution of Jews, which literally translated means "destruction," has been adopted in most other languages. The pogrom hordes attacked the Jews in czarist Russia under the notorious slogan "Beat the Jews and save Russia!" That in itself is a reflection of the deep-rooted hatred of Jews within sections of the population and the system, which was in a position to exploit anti-Semitism in its political manipulations.

After the revolution, the new rulers condemned anti-Semitism as an antisocial phenomenon, which was not to exist in the Soviet state. However, reality refused to comply with the handsome manifestos, since the hatred of Jews was far too deeply rooted in the population to be abolished by decrees or resolutions. Anti-Semitism survived, even if its worst and most pronounced manifestations were no longer public.

As far as we were personally concerned, anti-Semitism presented no problem during our deportation. Of course, through the years we experienced various episodes in which anti-Semitism would rear its ugly head, but it was always a question of individual, isolated incidents and never of any systematic persecution.

Stalin's witch-hunt for the so-called cosmopolitans in the late forties and his campaign against the Jews in the early fifties did not pass us unnoticed. The attitude of these campaigns spread to the authorities with whom we had to deal during our deportation and was noticeable just beneath the surface, although one never caught anybody making blatantly anti-Semitic remarks. One would notice the anti-Semitism when it began to play a role in one's career or education. It smoldered beneath the surface but was nothing that influenced our everyday life. When we encountered anti-Semitic insults, they nearly always came from people from the Ukraine or White Russia, where hatred of Jews was sown in traditionally fertile soil. We do not recall being subject to anti-Semitic malice on the part of the local people.

In Pokrovsk, we had neighbors by the name of Pomigalov. They were a family of four—husband, wife, their small son, Seryozha, who was a little older than Samuel, and the mother of the wife, a woman of around sixty. The husband worked for the NKVD and had been posted in Pokrovsk for a certain number of years. They had come from the Ukraine, and the old woman turned out to be an inveterate and hardened anti-Semite.

Not long after their arrival, she started abusing Rachel with the worst curses and anti-Semitic insults imaginable because one of her chickens had strayed into our chicken coop. This gave her the opportunity to accuse us of stealing and wanting to become rich at her cost, and she assured us that she would make sure we did not escape unpunished and that her son was not employed by the NKVD for nothing. We soon realized what type of person she was and, as we had done in the case of Popov, tried to avoid her, as well as the trying scenes with her in the yard in front of our house.

Her grandchild Seryozha was a very naughty child. Spoiled and hyperactive, he was the curse of the entire neighborhood. One day as Samuel squatted, relieving himself behind a hedge a distance from the house, Seryozha stole upon him and, with a well-directed blow, threw a broken brick right at the head of the unsuspecting Samuel. On another occasion he threw a big stone with an equally well-directed blow through the window of a neighbor's house. Trouble and scandal always surrounded the boy.

170

His grandmother had prepared a large bed of flowers in our joint garden, in which we all had small plots at our disposal. In her bed of flowers she planted huge poppies, which in late summer grew very beautiful. They were her great pride, and she spent several hours every day tending her beloved plants. One day when all of her poppies were in full bloom, displaying a profusion of color, we noticed through the kitchen window that the rascal Seryozha had crawled into the bed and had systematically started picking one poppy after the other. He did not stop until the last poppy had been picked and he was holding in his arms all of the beautiful flowers his grandmother had tended and protected against all sorts of danger for such a long time. He got out of the trampled bed and stalked out of the garden, proud as a peacock, while we followed the drama at a distance, and—we have to admit—not without a certain amount of glee. We walked out onto the front steps of the house in order not to miss the last part of the drama enacted right in front of us. Seryozha passed us and headed deliberately toward the entrance of the house of the Pomigalovs, when his grandmother came out and, with a shriek, rushed toward him. All of the oaths and curses the poisonous woman knew poured down over the head of her sinful grandchild. Before he knew it, she had seized him, causing the poppies to scatter in all directions, and her abusive language toward the little criminal was followed by a spanking. Crying, screaming, curses, and the petals of the fragile flowers filled the air while the grandmother dragged the little hooligan into the house. We have to confess that we were not entirely dissatisfied with the course of the drama, feeling that both of them had got what they deserved.

Another person who on various occasions gave expression to his anti-Semitic attitude toward us was the state attorney of Pokrovsk, and he also came to a bad end.

We had had several controversies with him in the course of time, and he was quite clearly intent on harassing us because we were Jews. The state attorney, however, came to feel how fickle life can be and how much truth there is to the saying "High to fly, far to fall."

At one point the state attorney became involved in a case of corruption, and within a fairly short time he was fired and had to leave Pokrovsk. He was fortunate to get off so lightly and not be taken to court.

Sometime later, we were in Yakutsk and happened to see him in the street as he passed by, driving a horse-drawn vehicle with a big barrel of water. *Sic transit gloria mundi.*

Our children, too, were occasionally subject to anti-Semitic harassment, but, as in our case, it was not something which came to mark their childhood and adolescence.

One day we received a visit from one of our acquaintances in Yakutsk—a teacher by the name of Pud Ilyich, who was a Yakut.

He was always impeccably dressed and had a weakness for straw hats and white shoes, which were a rare sight in that part of the world during those years and probably still are today.

We had got to know him in Yakutsk and came to appreciate him greatly as a very kindly and cultured person. He was staying in Pokrovsk for several days and took the opportunity to pay us a visit. When he arrived at our house, he was, as usual, very well dressed, and his impressive white shoes shone from afar. He smiled broadly and immediately began to tell us about a rather funny experience he had just had and in which Samuel had played the main role. On his way to our house, he had seen two boys involved in a furious fight with one another, and by the time he had reached them, they had let go of one another and were showering each other with curses at a respectful distance.

It turned out that one of them was our son Samuel and the other one a small Yakut boy.

Pud Ilyich could not avoid hearing the exchange of words between the two fighting boys, and suddenly the Yakut boy shouted to Samuel, "You little dirty sheeny." And Samuel quickly retorted, "That is what you are."

Pud Ilyich could not help being amused at the quarrel between a Yakut and a Jewish boy in the wilds of Siberia, where one would least have expected such exchanges between two small boys.

Conflicts among the various races, however, were quite frequent. The Russians and Yakuts especially had difficulty controlling themselves, and their differences often developed into physical conflicts. The worst we ever saw in Pokrovsk was a fight between a telephone fitter, Arseniy Yakovl'yev, who had for some time lived in the apartment next to us, and a Yakut from one of the houses in the neighborhood. Arseniy lived there with his wife, and both were very amiable and cooperative people with whom we got along very well. However, when he had been drinking, Arseniy became just as wild and unruly as he was good-natured and friendly when sober.

One Sunday in the summer, Arseniy and his wife had been partying with some friends, and judging from their voices and their singing, we knew that they had had plenty of vodka to drink. The weather outside was beautiful, and at some point, they decided to move their party outside and to continue their convivial gathering in the open. We do not know what happened then, but suddenly we heard agitated shouting and the hysterical screaming of women. We ran toward the window and watched Arseniy, foaming with anger, tear off his shirt. Dressed in a red undershirt, he rushed at a Yakut who had already taken off his shirt and stood with both of his clenched fists raised in a protective parry. A furious fight started, in the course of which both the Yakut and Arseniy showered each other with the worst curses and threats conceivable. Their clothes were torn to shreds, and blood flowed from both of them. They were apparently both dead drunk, and their blows rained down upon each other at random until some of the bystanders managed to intervene and separate the two bruised and bloody men. Arseniy kept cursing the Yakut and his entire race, whom he compared to ground squirrels, which had to be smoked out or drowned in their plague-stricken holes. Their fight was one of many instances showing that the coexistence of the various peoples of the multinational Soviet state left much to be desired, even if the Soviet propaganda machine liked to represent the relations among the various races as an idyllic brotherhood in a large and peaceful family.

We were one of the first families among the deportees from Lithuania to arrive at Pokrovsk, and in time, as an increasing number of our acquaintances and friends followed, a small colony developed. The new arrivals always looked us up as "veterans" for advice and guidance. They all started out at the brickworks, but after a while most of them managed to find more pleasant and healthy jobs. One of those who came to Pokrovsk and started working at the brickworks was Harry P., a tall, skinny pianist, in his late twenties. He was not at all used to physical work and nearly succumbed to the hard work after a week. He appeared very frail and had long, thin fingers not at all suitable for the hard physical work at the brickworks. Through us he managed to become employed as a music teacher at the school. Harry was a very gifted musician and, after a while, managed to set up a choir at the school. He arranged concerts and was extremely successful. Another of our acquaintances who came to Pokrovsk was Aron L., an engineer who became employed at the local power station. He had no place to live, and for several months he stayed with us in our small apartment. Aron was a very cheerful person and always spread joy and happiness about him, so we were very happy to have him stay with us. On account of his work, he sometimes returned home late at night. To tell us that he was on his way home, he usually gave us a signal—he pulled the main switch at the power station twice, causing the lights throughout Pokrovsk to go out in two brief flashes. This was a most efficient way of communication, and we found it most amusing. Each time Aron came home after having given his signal, hot tea awaited him.

In the course of the years, we came to live more and more like the rest of the population of Pokrovsk. Our life was not too different from the lives of those who had not been deported, the main difference being that we were not allowed to move freely beyond the fixed radius of three miles. If we had to go farther away, to Yakutsk, for example, we had to apply for permission very early and provide the NKVD with detailed reasons for our trip. Some of the deportees ventured to Yakutsk without having first obtained a permit, and it cost them a week's imprisonment on a bread and water diet. Apart from this, we were subject to the same conditions as most of the people in the area. We were regarded as Soviet citizens by the authorities, for, like the others, we had the right to go to the ballot boxes each time there was an election and cast our votes for candidates who had already been chosen. The election was, for the most part, a token one. The problem of abstainers did not exist, however, as the voting percentage was always close to one hundred.

Moreover, the children grew up as their peers did. Schneur was accepted in the Young Pioneers and later on in the Komsomol (Young Communist League), and the same applied to Harrietta when she reached the same age. Samuel was sent to nursery school during the periods when we were both employed.

We had learned to adjust to the special environment in which we found ourselves—to the political, the climatic, and the economic conditions. We knew by now how to conduct ourselves so as to avoid conflicts with the authorities and to be constantly careful not to make any rash statements of political content in the presence of others. As the saying goes, we learned that, when in Rome, you must do as the Romans do. On the other hand, we also learned to enjoy every minute we spent with friends and acquaintances from Lithuania, with whom we were able to discuss freely and without danger anything that was on our minds.

Over the years we became as good as the local people at preparing ourselves for the winter and storing up supplies of berries, mushrooms, and sauerkraut for the long and dark winter. We had also learned to purchase supplies in the shops as soon as there was anything worth purchasing, for because of the constant shortage of goods, one could never be certain of finding things in the shops when one needed them.

In this respect, one might very well claim that the authorities had succeeded in their endeavors to change us from "upper-class citizens" in a capitalist country to regular Siberians or Yakuts in the classless Soviet society.

However, this "conversion" did not at any point affect our inner emotions and beliefs. Our minds remained as alien to the system as ever, and at no time did we develop any real appreciation, let alone sympathy, for the system and the results it had produced. We were well aware of the fact that much had been accomplished to create equality among and social benefits for all of the citizens, and we were also aware of the slow economic growth throughout the post–World War II years, but we never felt that such progress concerned us, for it was not our country, not our culture. We did not hate the system, but neither did we love it, given all that we had suffered—we merely did not belong to it, and our only desire was to be allowed to leave the country and become reunited with our family and the world that was ours.

Thus, if the objective of our deportation had been to make us loyal and devoted Soviet citizens, the entire effort had been a failure, both in our case and in the case of the other deportees. If the Soviet Union wished to convince others of the virtues of the Soviet system—of its fairness and of the many advantages and privileges Soviet citizens had compared to people in capitalist countries—it should not have allowed anybody to live in the country long enough to be able to reach below the surface and see the other side of the fine and shiny coin.

14

Israel

As had been the case in Yakutsk, my job as teacher in Pokrovsk involved various other jobs and tasks. One summer I was asked by the school authorities to participate in the school's camp, where I was to be in charge of finances and catering. Again, the request was made in such a manner that I had no choice but to accept the job. Actually, it was not the worst job that one might be asked to do, but I would have preferred to spend the time with Rachel and the children. However, I was paid a little extra for my efforts, and Harrietta was allowed to come along.

The summer camp was located about eight miles from Pokrovsk in a beautiful region near a forest and several lakes. Participation in a summer camp was an opportunity open to most children in the Soviet Union. Everywhere in the country, so-called Pioneer Camps were set up where the children could spend several weeks under the supervision of teachers and young instructors. The time was devoted to sports, hikes, and several other activites, to which were added beneficial activities in the form of lectures, study groups, and political indoctrination of the children.

There were about fifty children and three teachers to look after them. In addition, the camp had a manager, a cook, and myself. My main task was to handle the catering and supplies. I had to see to it that we did not exceed the budget that had been fixed for the camp and that we did not use more provisions than stipulated in the instructions we had been given. The amounts to be used for each meal had been specified in great detail.

In the mornings pancakes of some sort were served to the children. The evening before, I handed over the needed amounts of flour and butter to the cook. After a few days the manager asked me how much butter I gave the cook for the pancakes. I answered that she got the exact quantity prescribed. The manager was somewhat surprised, saying that she could not understand why the pancakes were burned every single day. She asked that in the future I give the cook the ingredients early in the morning instead of the evening before. As a result, I had to get up at six o'clock every morning. Also, two of the older students were asked to help the cook in the kitchen. The pancakes were never burned again.

The children were taken good care of, and the conditions were as good as might be expected in the wilds of Siberia. I was also in charge of the water supply, which was brought in a big barrel on top of a cart drawn by an ox. A young man from a neighboring village transported the water from the Lena, which was located about three miles from the camp. The ox belonged to the camp and turned out to be of vital importance to all of us. One day it suddenly took off, disappearing into the taiga, just as it was to be used to transport a load of water. Everything came to a standstill. The children were not able to wash themselves, and no cooking could be done in the kitchen. The entire camp as well as the people of the neighboring village were alerted, and a hunt was held in the taiga. Only late in the afternoon did we succeed in finding the ox, which was grazing quietly in the forest. The children drove the ox back to the camp triumphantly, and normal life in the camp was resumed.

At the end of the summer camp, all of the children were weighed, for the result, or, rather, the benefits, of the stay had to be measured in pounds and ounces. They had all been weighed the first day, and the authorities now wanted to find out how much they had gained. It goes without saying that the camp had a weight-growth plan, which had to be met. As it turned out, the results were satisfactory, and the children had gained as planned.

After World War II, the number of boarders at the school had increased sharply, and an expansion of the building was started to accommodate additional boarders. In 1950, the new addition was completed, and the new premises were to be inaugurated with a special celebration. All party heads and other important people from Pokrovsk and the vicinity were invited to the party, and for some reason or other, I was asked by the party secretary of the school to make the chief speech of the evening on behalf of the faculty. There was no way out, so I thanked him for the honor and started preparing the speech according to the rules of the game. One had to be extremely careful neither to say anything that might be misunderstood nor to forget to thank the party, the state, and, first and foremost, Stalin for their care and interest. There were also other rules to be followed in composing such speeches, and as long as these were observed, one would not get into trouble. I began and concluded my speech with thanks and tribute to the country's incomparable leader and ruler, Joseph Vissarionovich Stalin. In such a wrapping, my speech could hardly go wrong, and as it turned out, it was well received and applauded. Everybody got up to drink a toast to Stalin and to our school. As was the custom at parties at the time, people sang a song when they toasted. Their glasses filled with vodka swinging back and forth, they sang:

> Let us drink to the fatherland,
> Let us drink to Stalin,
> Let us drink
> And refill our glasses!

This song was repeated over and over till late into the night. It was also sung in the spring of 1951, when we had a celebration in honor of the first graduates of the high school. During World War II, the school had taught only eight age groups, but after the war the school was expanded to include two more age groups, and in 1951, our first students graduated. This was, of course, a big event in the history of the school, and it had to be celebrated properly.

A committee, of which I became a member, was set up to organize the party. It was to collect funds for the party and for gifts to the students, who were to be presented with special remembrances for being the first class graduating from the school in Pokrovsk. Huge amounts of food, wine, and vodka were purchased, and teachers, students, and volunteers cooked for several days in preparation. It was to be a celebration that would be remembered for many years to come.

And I must say that it was quite a celebration. Toasts, cheers, singing, and ovations continued indefinitely. Everybody drank and ate huge amounts. The students were sent home at midnight, while the teachers and the invited guests continued the festivities till four o'clock in the morning.

At some point during the celebration, the principal came up to me, drawing me discreetly aside. He asked me to hide two bottles of vodka, which we could take out as a surprise when all of the supplies had run out later in the night. I took the two bottles into the teachers' lounge, where I hid them in a large stove. I was convinced that a better and safer place could not be found for the precious bottles. When, later in the night, the wine and vodka were gone, the principal signaled me with an air of immense satisfaction to bring in the surprise. I went into the teachers' lounge and up to the stove, only to discover that the bottles had disappeared without a trace. It was somewhat of a shock to me and pained me greatly. I do not believe that the principal suspected me, for I am sure that he had quite deliberately given me the responsibility because he knew that I did not drink. Still, it was not too pleasant having to explain to him what had happened.

We saved the situation with the assistance of Dr. Nina Ivanovna, who was the guest of honor at the celebration. She saw to it that a bottle of pure spirits was fetched from the pharmacy. It was mixed with one quart of water and consumed with relish in place of the vodka that had disappeared. We never managed to find out who had committed the theft, but it was assumed that, in the course of the night, the corpus delicti went the way it would have gone sooner or later.

At the end of each school year, postgraduate courses were arranged, and one year I was sent to Yakutsk to participate in a summer course for foreign language teachers. Our course instructors were not particularly competent or knowledgeable, but they were party members, and that was more important than professional qualifications. Our course plan included a series of lectures, of which a librarian was in charge, on the literature of the West.

All Western authors were divided in two groups. Those who took a positive view of the Soviet Union were progressive, while most of the others were reactionaries. Anna Seghers, Martin Andersen Nexø, Howard Fast, and Upton Sinclair were all referred to as examples of progressive writers. At some point, one of the participants in the course asked to which category Sinclair Lewis belonged. The poor librarian was clearly uncomfortable with the question, but after having bitten his lip for a few seconds, he managed to find a diplomatic answer: "So far, we regard him as being progressive." The librarian did not know Sinclair Lewis and therefore did not know to which category he belonged, but his answer was sufficiently vague to cover all circumstances.

All of the participants sighed with relief when the course was over after two long and strenuous weeks. July is the warmest month, and everybody was completely exhausted after six hours in school. We were presented with diplomas, and I spent the rest of the day before my

return to Pokrovsk visiting friends and shopping. However, I had to undergo still another test before I was to be allowed to return home.

At the modest hotel where we had been put up, I shared a room with
three party officials who had also come to Yakutsk to take a course. I
had not seen much of them during the past two weeks, and the last
evening I was so exhausted that I went right to bed before they even
got back. However, late in the evening I was awakened by loud voices
and clinking glasses. The party officials were celebrating the end of
their course in due fashion with lots of vodka. They sat around a small
table with three bottles of vodka, two of which had already been emptied. When they realized that I was awake, they immediately invited me
to join them in drinking a glass of vodka. I regretted immediately having
let them know that I was awake, for I was well aware that one of the
worst things one could do to a Russian was refuse to drink a glass of
vodka with him. It was regarded as an insult and showed lack of respect.
I did not feel much like drinking vodka at that time of the night and
tried to avoid it by saying that I was too sleepy and that they should
continue and not pay any attention to me. But there was nothing I could
do. However, they were kind enough to suggest a compromise—I
would be allowed to remain in bed but had to have a glass of vodka in
any case. The glass was a tea glass which they filled almost to the brim
with vodka and gave to me. We touched glasses, and they concluded by
shouting "Do Dna!", which means "Bottoms up!" I drank the vodka at a
single draught, as my hardened drinking companions had done, and
more or less fell over in my bed as soon as I had emptied my glass. I got
up the next morning with a dreadful hangover. So far, it has been my
record in vodka drinking.

In 1950, I became a homeroom teacher for the first time, and that
involved quite a few new tasks. It is true that a homeroom teacher received extra pay, but at the same time he also had additional duties
and problems. At least twice a year the homeroom teacher had to pay
visits to the homes of his students to discuss with their parents their
levels of achievement, conduct, and maturity. The homeroom teacher
had to write a report on his visits, describe the family relations, and
present the information at the faculty meetings. In addition, the homeroom teacher met with the entire class each week to discuss the course
of events during the preceding week, including individual students'
achievements or offenses, which had to be brought to the attention of
the principal.

One of my students was the daughter of the local NKVD chief. His name was Fedotov, and he was in charge of all of the deportees in Pokrovsk. I had to visit him and his wife just as I had visited the parents of the other students. It was a somewhat peculiar situation, and I always went with mixed feelings. On the other hand, it was my task to educate his daughter, Nina, who was a sweet and intelligent girl. However, I myself was in Pokrovsk to be educated and retrained, and it was one of Fedotov's tasks to see to it that I was educated in the right manner and in the right spirit. I was not too sure that it suited Fedotov that a special deportee such as myself had the task of educating and bringing up his daughter. However, my visits to the home of Fedotov proceeded without friction, and the parents gave expression to their satisfaction with Nina's achievements in school.

One day, however, I met Fedotov under other circumstances. All of the teachers of the school took turns, for a week at a time, to look after all of the practical items, which had to be arranged and organized. One day during my week of duty, I received a call from the local NKVD officer, asking me to see to it that all of the senior students stayed after the last class to hear a lecture by one of the NKVD officers in Pokrovsk.

I got the students together as requested and was rather surprised to see that the lecturer was Fedotov himself. On his arrival, Fedotov shook my hand and smiled, thanking me for my help. Fedotov's lecture concerned the watchfulness that Soviet citizens always had to display.

He talked about the great progress achieved by the Soviet Union despite many difficulties. He paid the obligatory tributes to Stalin and talked about the great triumphs of the Soviet economy in developing the communist society that would ensure all people and races a magnificent and happy future.

However, the enemies of communism lurked everywhere, endeavoring to put a stop to the victorious progress of the Soviet society. Enemies did not sleep, Fedotov pointed out, for they were always searching for an opportunity to harm the young Soviet state. That is why it was the duty of every Soviet citizen always to be on his guard against the undermining activity of the enemies of socialism. Every Soviet citizen had to be a patriot and protect his fatherland as the most sacred thing in life. One of the most important virtues was alertness, and Fedotov urged the young students always to pay attention to what was going on around them. If they encountered something suspicious, they would have to report it immediately to the NKVD office, where NKVD officers would always be prepared to listen to them. Imperialist agents were everywhere, he stressed, and they worked in devious ways. Even the most innocent actions could conceal serious crimes against the Soviet state. As an example of how cunning such agents could be, he mentioned an incident that, according to him, had taken place quite recently. In an office that handled classified material, a sheet of carbon paper was thrown into the wastepaper basket. It had been used for copying a very secret report. It later on turned out that the cleaning woman of the office was an imperialist agent. She had, of course, found the used carbon paper in the wastepaper basket, and in that way a state secret had leaked out and become known to the imperialists. Be on your guard and help the NKVD destroy the enemies of the country, Fedotov concluded.

As he left, he once more shook my hand, smiling in a friendly manner. With some effort, I managed to force a smile, for after that lecture there was not much to smile about for a man in my position. It was, among others, people with my background whom Fedotov had indirectly asked the students to keep an eye on. Now I had to be even more careful about what I said and did in my classes and in the teachers' lounge. While such alertness campaigns were in progress, there was bound to be someone wishing to impress the authorities by catching one of the agents of imperialism "in the act."

Rachel · Israel

Pokrovsk was more pleasant than Yakutsk, because there were no swamps or thick fogs. The climate was quite severe but healthier than in Yakutsk.

During the latter half of May, usually around May 20, the ice on the Lena broke. It was an impressive natural phenomenon and an event anxiously awaited by everybody, for it meant that spring, sunshine, and warm weather were on their way. The Lena was approximately four to four and a half miles wide at Pokrovsk. The ice that had formed in the course of the winter could become as much as ten feet thick, and when these huge masses of ice broke, enormous natural forces were released. When the ice broke and the pieces pushed together in the most incredible formations, the sound was like the thunder of guns. "*Lena tronulas! Lena tronulas!*" it was shouted everywhere in Pokrovsk when the ice began to break and slowly start moving. The young and old then rushed down to the river to watch more closely the struggle of the Lena with its masses of ice. If it happened during school hours, the students were given the rest of the day off. It was impossible to carry through any instruction on such a day, for the school was located close to the river, and it was impossible to keep the attention of the students.

Each year at around the same time, we saw large flocks of various migratory birds flying in well-ordered formations toward their breeding places still farther to the north. The most beautiful time of the year was approaching. It usually took about six weeks for the Lena to become entirely free of ice. Spring and summer more or less coincided, and the transition was always sudden and overwhelming. Suddenly everything became green, the flowers opened, and everybody got busy digging and planting in his garden.

There were several collective farms and small villages on the other side of the Lena opposite Pokrovsk. In the winter, crossing the river was no problem—we walked or drove over the ice. In the summer we crossed the river in a fairly large motorboat, towing a barge. However, during the period just before the Lena broke and until the river became free of ice, it was too dangerous to cross. Consequently, many of the students whose parents lived on the other side of the river were cut off from their families for nearly two months. But when the sheets of ice floating down the river with the current started to melt, it was possible to begin crossing the river by boat, and the students started once again to go home over the weekends.

In the latter part of the summer, Schneur and his friends often sailed to some of the islands in the Lena to collect wild chives. They returned home with huge quantities of the delicious chives, which were cut into tiny pieces and pickled in salt and other spices to last far into the winter.

The Lena was of great importance to all of us. A large part of the supplies from the south arrived via the Lena. As soon as navigation started, long convoys of barges loaded with all kinds of goods came from the south. The Lena, of course, also provided us with water, and in the summer there was quite a lot of fishing. The Lena had a rich stock of fish, and in Pokrovsk a small fish resembling the anchovy was caught in large quantities and prepared either in a marinade or fried in butter or oil. It was a great delicacy.

However, to us, the deportees, the Lena was, above all, the road back to freedom. In the past, we had sailed up the Lena on our way toward Bykov Mys, and one day we would hopefully be sailing in the other direction. The Lena was the safest and best way south, although other possibilities existed. One might fly or go by truck to Irkutsk.

There was air service throughout the year to and from Yakutsk, but only fairly small aircraft flew to Yakutsk, and they were primarily reserved for civil servants and party officials. It was, moreover, fairly expensive to go by air. The connections by truck were the ones used most in the winter. The Lena and most of the other rivers in Yakutia had no bridges in those days, and it was only possible to cross the rivers in the wintertime. An awning was pulled over the trucks to convert them into buses, and then they were ready to take off for the station by the name of Never on the Trans-Siberian Railroad. It was a long, strenuous, and very cold trip. Therefore, if we were to leave some day, it would probably be on board a steamer.

We would anxiously follow with our eyes the ships sailing down the Lena, dreaming of the day when we ourselves would be passengers.

15

---·•·---

Rachel · Israel

The 5th of March, 1953, marked the end of an era in the history of the Soviet Union and in the lives and fates of millions of Soviet citizens, including ourselves. On that day, Levitan, the announcer, stated in his well-known doomsday voice that the leader, the father, the teacher, the great thinker, the standard-bearer of Marxism and Leninism, Generalissimo Joseph Vissarionovich Stalin, had died. The announcement was read throughout the day on the radio, which only played funeral music. Portraits of Stalin, shrouded in black veil, and flags with black mourning bands were hung everywhere in Pokrovsk.

The news shocked most people. Citizens of the Soviet Union do not know anything about the private lives of their leaders, and when they die, the announcements of their deaths always take people by surprise, for they have been given no information on any illness or hospital stay.

The reactions in Pokrovsk to the announcement of Stalin's death were almost hysterical. People cried without restraint in the streets, in the shops, and at the school. A sense of doom more or less prevailed, and everywhere one heard people asking in despair, "How are we to manage? How shall we be able to live without Stalin?" Memorial ceremonies were held at the school and in other organizations throughout Pokrovsk. The sorrow of people was spontaneous and genuine, and what happened in Pokrovsk was, of course, nothing compared to the scene in Moscow and the other major cities. Only a long time afterward did we hear about the scenes of horror which took place in Moscow during Stalin's funeral, when panic erupted in the huge crowds and many people were trampled to death.

Stalin had come to symbolize an almighty father figure—it was he who decided, who gave, and who took away, and his role seemed to be in full agreement with the expectations and requirements of a leader

185

among the people. The desire to subject oneself to and to worship a leading figure seems deeply embedded in the Russian people and is, of course, not a characteristic that has developed since the Soviet Union was formed but goes far back in history to the autonomous czars and their brutal regimes. The personality cult of Stalin had exceeded all bounds and had led to the people's uncritical admiration of their leader and father, as he was also called. Such a father and leader figure creates security in the minds of people and gives them the feeling that as long as he is there, they will be taken care of, and nobody will threaten them or leave them in the lurch. Now that he was gone, people were seized with real anxiety and sorrow, for they felt that the basis of their entire existence had vanished.

Even if Stalin had caused the physical sufferings and deaths of millions of people and the emotional tragedies of still more, only a relatively small number of people knew the terrible truth about his role in all of the events that had spread horror and fear throughout the country for such a great number of years. If anybody had tried to reveal the truth about Stalin's crimes at the time, people simply would not have believed it.

The sorrow and despair at Stalin's death, however, did not spread to our family and our home. We had long before identified Stalin with the disasters that had descended upon us. To us, his appearance—the sly look in his eyes and the false smile concealed in his big moustache—had come to reflect evil. Therefore, if not a genuinely happy event, his death became an event we hoped would herald changes, especially in our status as special deportees. We felt that the death of Stalin would have to bring about something good. Even if our presentiment proved correct, the changes came but slowly, for even though Stalin was dead, his spirit lived on and would continue to do so for a long time. We got proof of this only five weeks after his death.

DECREE

Ministry of Education of the Yakut Autonomous Soviet Socialist Republic

Yakutsk   Register No. 7-109   April 10, 1953

Concerning Appointment of Teachers at the Schools in
The Ordzhonikidze District
in the School Year 1953–54

At the end of the present school year and the end of the standard school holidays, the following appointments, transfers, and dismissals of teachers will take place:

Clause 27

Exempted from teaching as a result of failure to comply with the requirements:

1. Rachlin, Israel Semyonovich, foreign language teacher at the school in Pokrovsk.

S. Savin
Minister of Education
The Yakut Autonomous Soviet Socialist Republic

Witness:
P. Skryabin
Director of Education of the Ordzhonikidze District

Israel

When I received the decree, I had to read it several times before I realized what it said and what it involved. But I still could not understand why I had been dismissed and what was meant by "failure to comply with the requirements." I had now been teaching at the school in Pokrovsk for six years without having received a single rebuke or reprimand from the principal or the party secretary. I had no reason to doubt that everybody was satisfied with myself and my teaching. The atmosphere around us had become relaxed, moreover, to such a degree that I had started to believe that after twelve years of deportation, we would finally be left in peace and placed on an equal footing with other Soviet citizens. But this, evidently, was not the way it was going to be.

My dismissal was to be our last greeting from Stalin, for there was, of course, no other reason to fire me than a new wave of political persecution of unreliable elements. It was a campaign that had been launched while Stalin still lived and that was primarily aimed against people of Jewish origin. However, since we lived so far from Moscow, the campaign and the decree had only reached Pokrovsk after a long delay.

Rachel · Israel

Once again we were suddenly in a critical situation. We had financial difficulties as usual, and the job of a bookkeeper paid only half as much as a teaching job and could thus offer no solution. Schneur was in the tenth grade and would graduate in May. He would then start studying at the institute in Yakutsk and need our financial support, for he would not be able to manage on his scholarship. We considered our situation and after a while reached the conclusion that we had to try to get back to Yakutsk, since the possibilities of getting a job there would be greater and Schneur would then be able to live at home. But that was easier said than done. The long and difficult procedure of applying for permission to go to Yakutsk now began. We immediately contacted the NKVD office and started filling in countless forms and questionnaires. We were allowed to remain in our apartment until the first of September, when the school holidays would be over. After about one and a half months, numerous applications to the NKVD, and a number of personal talks with some of the NKVD officers, we were told that we would be allowed to move to Yakutsk.

The last couple of weeks in Pokrovsk were very unpleasant. The family who was to take over the apartment pressed us to get out, but we had nowhere else to stay and were unable to go to Yakutsk immediately. Schneur had gone to Yakutsk ahead of time to prepare for the admission test at the institute where he had applied. He was staying with some friends.

It was no easy task to find a car to take us and our possessions to Yakutsk. After much persistent effort, we managed to reach an agreement with a driver from the brickworks. He demanded an exorbitant amount of money for the trip—half a month's salary, but we were in no strong bargaining position and accepted his charge. We were happy to leave, for we could not bear to remain in Pokrovsk any longer. Among the articles we took with us to Yakutsk was a rather extraordinary present we had received several years earlier from Klimov, the manager of Selektsionnaya. Klimov had left Pokrovsk in 1948, and before his departure he had given us a metal relief of Joseph Stalin himself. The picture was the size of a large dinner plate and was very heavy, so it was quite understandable that Klimov did not want to drag it around with him. Several people witnessed Klimov presenting us with the showpiece, and we thus felt we had to hang it somewhere. We did not want to risk being accused of lack of respect for the leader of the country and the father of the people. It hung on one of the walls of our small apartment and remained there throughout our many years in Pokrovsk. Considering our feelings with regard to Stalin, it did not especially please us to have him hanging on the wall of our living room, where we were forced to look at him every single day. But what could we do?

In leaving, we dared not, as Klimov had done, give the picture of Stalin to somebody else. Such an act might be interpreted as an expression of contempt for the deceased leader of the country and be used against us. After some reflection, we decided to take the "heirloom" to Yakutsk, and Stalin joined us on our trip.

Only in Yakutsk did we manage to get rid of him. While we stayed with some friends, we put the picture in a shed with various other things. When we left, we "forgot" Stalin in the dark corner where we had put him. From then on, we did not have to look at his abhorred profile and had in every respect been relieved of a heavy and troublesome burden.

Rachel

On a glorious September morning, we stood with all of our things outside the house, waiting for the truck to pick us up. We did not have much by way of furniture, and all of our clothes, kitchen utensils, and other household articles were contained in a chest and a few suitcases. In addition, we had eight bags of potatoes and, of course, the chicken coop with the chickens inside it. We had become so used to having chickens that we could not conceive of parting with them.

In this time of transition, we once again began to evaluate our past experiences and our present situation. We had been deported for twelve years, and nine of those years had been spent in Pokrovsk. Whatever we might say about the years there, Pokrovsk, like most of the people we had met in the town, had been good to us. There is no knowing how we would have managed for all those years if we had ended up somewhere else. In Pokrovsk we had, after all, begun to lead a normal and relatively stable existence, and even if we were often in straitened circumstances, we had managed and survived. Somehow or other, we had felt more protected there than anywhere else during our deportation, probably because Pokrovsk was located in such a remote area, but certainly also because people had often been good and helpful to us.

That poor small town in the wilds of Siberia will forever remain in our hearts, another reason being that it was there that Smauel was born, becoming the ray of sunshine for all of us at a time that was often gloomy and dark. Together with his older brother and sister, he spent the first six years of his life in Pokrovsk, growing up a healthy and happy little boy.

Our departure from Pokrovsk was associated with insecurity and uncertainty, since we did not know where we would be living in Yakutsk and, more generally, what would become of us. I could not help wondering how long we would still be moving and traveling before our trials would be over, and whether the day we would leave for Denmark would ever come.

As always, my heart beat more quickly at the thought that we might one day begin a trip that would take us all back to Denmark. The dream was as fantastic and wonderful as ever, but there was nothing in our situation to indicate that we were any closer to its realization. We were merely faced with another of the many upheavals that had been forced upon us over the years.

The truck arrived, and with the help of the driver and some neighbors who had come to take leave of us, we managed to load everything into the back of the truck. With the children, I sat down on top of the bags of potatoes. Samuel held a braided basket with his cat, Pusyok, and its newborn kittens on his lap. There were six other passengers on the truck, and Israel had to sit on top of the chicken coop. It was a very awkward position, and he had to cling either to the chicken coop or to the side of the truck during the whole trip.

The driver was very busy, for he had to collect certain things in Yakutsk and return with them to Pokrovsk immediately, so he drove like mad along the bumpy, dusty road. As Pokrovsk disappeared behind us in a cloud of dust and we drove toward Yakutsk at full speed, we did not realize that we had begun the first stage of our long trip back to Denmark.

16

Rachel · Israel

When we arrived in Yakutsk, we immediately visited our old friends, the April family, who had informed us that we could stay with them for a while. The Aprils had a small house in the center of town, and there were three rooms for the four members of the family, Tanya and Isaak and their two grown sons. We were given one of the rooms, in which Isaak and Tanya assured us we could stay until we found a place of our own. The decision was not discussed much, being quite in keeping with what was normally done. We had similarly opened our home to friends and acquaintances who came to Pokrovsk.

As we knew Yakutsk rather well from our first stay, we had no major problem adjusting and getting used to the new environment. We immediately started looking for a place to live and after about three weeks managed to find a house for rent. The house was located on Lomonosov Street, not far from the center of town, and belonged to a retired teacher, who, preferring to live under more pleasant conditions, had moved to a warmer part of the country. The house was now managed by her brother, who offered us a lease for a year on very reasonable terms. After having inspected the house, we decided to rent it.

The house, which had a floor space of approximately 650 square feet, was very run down and in need of repair, for it had been neglected for a long time. However, for the present we were unable to undertake such repairs. The house stood somewhat removed from the others on the street, and there was a small lopsided house in front of it. Like all the other houses, our new house was surrounded by a wooden fence on the three other sides.

We moved in shortly after having signed the lease and were happy to finally be on our own. We had in time grown to dislike sharing kitchens.

Harrietta started school, Schneur was in full swing with his studies at the institute, and Samuel soon found a lot of new friends (he was not to start school until a year later).

Israel

As soon as we had arrived, I started looking for a job. Taught by my experience of nine years ago, I immediately approached the Ministry of Education to find out whether it might be possible to get a job as a schoolteacher. It turned out that there were no vacancies left in Yakutsk, but I was offered a job as a German teacher in a small town about fifteen miles north of Yakutsk. I had to turn it down, as we did not feel like moving again and also did not want to leave Schneur alone in Yakutsk.

It is true that I had had similar experiences many times before, but I still could not help wondering at the unpredictability of the system: in April, I was fired because of failure to comply with the requirements, and by September, I had somehow become competent enough to once again be employed as a teacher.

Shortly afterward I was offered the job of bookkeeper at Yakuttorg, a state organization that supervised all retail trade. I became bookkeeper in the training division, which trained, among others, shop assistants, cashiers, stockroom workers, and restaurant personnel. The apprenticeship system did not exist in the Soviet Union at the time, and all instruction and training took place in such special courses.

A few weeks after having started my job as bookkeeper, I was offered the job of teaching a few mathematics courses, using the abacus. When I had first arrived in Siberia, I did not know how to use the abacus, but I had now become so good at it that I could easily teach others how to use it.

When the next school year started, I got the job of German teacher at School No. 8. And at times I worked as a substitute at two other schools as well; I also had some classes as language teacher at a forestry institute, taught an evening course several times a week, and, finally, had private students. The private students were all sons and daughters of high-ranking civil servants and party officials, who were concerned about their children's poor grades in German and hoped that tutoring would improve their performances and restore them to their proper position among the best students in the class.

I had to hold all of these jobs at once to earn enough income for us to make ends meet, for salaries were so low that it was impossible to manage on one alone.

My students in the evening courses were between the ages of eighteen and fifty. Many of them were in high positions, but their education was inadequate, and they therefore wished to supplement it with intensive instruction in an evening school. Other students had had to interrupt their schooling and education on account of the war and now wanted to catch up.

Among my students was a couple—the husband was an NKVD officer and attended the seventh grade, and his wife was a shop assistant and attended the sixth grade. They were both very much interested in each other's progress and would often come up to me after class to ask, "How is my wife doing?" or "Is my husband able to keep up?" Lieutenant Mamotenko was better at German than his wife, who had difficulty keeping up with the other students. On the other hand, she worked hard and ended up doing quite well in the course. Whenever her husband asked me about her work, I would always answer that she was doing very well, thus making sure that the German course would not be the cause of any marital problems.

Rachel · Israel

Twelve months after we had moved in, the house we were renting was offered to us for sale. We were allowed to own a house, provided the area did not exceed sixteen hundred square feet. No family, however, could own more than one. The price of the house was extremely reasonable at fifteen thousand rubles, and we wished very much to buy it. We had only about two thousand rubles ourselves, however, and the house had to be paid for in cash. There was no possibility of borrowing the money from the bank or getting some other kind of credit. Only our friends could lend us the money. When it was rumored that we needed money to purchase the house, it did not take long for the remaining thirteen thousand rubles to be raised by our good friends. They had painstakingly saved up that money for themselves, but when they heard that we needed help, they did not consider twice—we were to have their money to purchase the house.

As soon as we had become homeowners, we started putting the house in order. Some of the work we were able to do ourselves, while we left the rest to workmen. We had a new, built-in stove put up in the kitchen, and new *zavalinki*—a special kind of Russian insulating material—was installed on the exterior of the house. All the way around the house, an extra hollow space was made by means of beams, which were erected at a height of nearly three feet, and the hollow space between the house and the beams was filled with soil. Rotten beams were replaced, and the entire house was refurbished on the outside. There was no cement or mortar to be had, so we used a local recipe, calling for a mixture of clay, horse manure, and a small amount of straw, and that worked perfectly. Finally, the entire house was whitewashed and came to look quite nice.

Inside the house, the living room was covered with red wallpaper, the only kind available in the shops. The woodwork of the entire house was painted green, for green paint was the only paint available in the entire town. However, we had a bit of white paint and found that we could add a little variation by mixing a bit of the white paint with the green paint to come up with different shades. The doors and the stove in the kitchen were painted dark green, while all of the window frames, windowsills, and other woodwork were painted light green. It is doubtful that the result would have been approved by an interior decorator, but we were all very happy and even quite proud of our achievements.

We could not afford to live in the house alone and had to rent one of the small rooms. During the entire period that we lived in the house, this room was occupied by lodgers, so we were always a total of seven people. That gave us about a hundred square feet each. There were no major problems, however, for everybody was used to living under such cramped conditions.

We often spent very pleasant evenings with our lodgers. During the first year, the small room was occupied by our acquaintance, Harry P., a pianist, and a physician from Moscow by the name of Sasha Veksler. We spent many happy hours with them, and we especially enjoyed the company of Sasha, who was very cheerful and knew a lot of stories and anecdotes, with which he liked to entertain us. Sasha had a fantastic memory and impressed everybody with his ability to remember large numbers, names, and various combinations of words and figures, which he was able to reel off hours after he had memorized them. His retentive memory, moreover, made him the most feared cardplayer in our circle of friends. He was simply able to memorize all the cards that had been played, enabling him to win practically every time. Sometimes we played for money, but after some time, Sasha was no longer invited to join in the card games. Incidentally, he had a very beautiful voice and got an extra job as announcer at the local radio station. His work at the station was always in the evening, and he often got back very late at night. In the winter it was still dangerous to go out after nightfall—as during the war, there was still a lot of crime in Yakutsk, and assaults and robberies were quite common. Therefore, when he left in the evening, Sasha always took along a big kitchen knife, which he put in his breast pocket. Each night he gave it back to us, thanking us for the loan and noting that it had not been used and need not be washed.

When Harry and Sasha left, two young women moved into the small room. Their names were Valya and Rita, and they were both from Moscow. After completing their studies, they had been posted for three years at the Geodetic Institute in Yakutsk. They, too, soon became close friends of ours, and Valya, in particular, became fond of Samuel. On her days off she would always take him along shopping, to the market, to the museum, or to the stadium to watch a soccer game or other athletic competitions.

Financially, we were in fairly good shape in Yakutsk. We did not have an abundance of anything, but our situation was nevertheless considerably better than it had been in previous years. We still received parcels from Sweden and Denmark, and they made a very important contribution to our financial resources.

We got good prices for the used clothing in the parcels, and we sold it either privately at our home or went to the flea market, which was located on the outskirts of town and was held every Sunday.

Israel

One day in 1955, I was suddenly summoned to appear before the NKVD, where an officer told me that my deportation was now over, and that my status as a special deportee had been revoked. The officer provided me with a letter for the militia, requesting it to issue me a passport to replace the identity card that was the only personal document a special deportee was allowed to have. I asked for a corresponding letter for Rachel but was told that I was the only one whose deportation had been revoked, since there had been a new provision to the effect that all special deportees working as schoolteachers could now have their deportation revoked. Although we had been deported together, family members were not included in the new provision. That I was primarily the one who had been deported in the first place and that Rachel had merely accompanied me as my wife was, of course, not considered. But it was no use asking questions or becoming angry—it was simply another of the many absurdities to which we were subjected.

After some time, I received my passport and went to register at the national register. Here I was told, however, that I could not become registered without submitting the necessary military papers. I was still under fifty years of age and therefore had to present papers testifying to my military competence. The result was that I had to come up before the draft board, and after lengthy negotiations, examinations, and interviews with various committees, I was registered as a soldier in the third category. The draft board experts had figured out that they could use me as an interpreter on account of my knowledge of various languages. There was a lot of enthusiasm at home when I told the children about their father's new military rank.

The revocation of my status as a special deportee naturally was a major event that gave rise to expectations on our part that more and even greater changes were on their way. The fact that I was the only one who had been liberated, however, darkened our joy. It meant that we were still unable to leave Yakutsk and had to wait for Rachel to be covered by the new regulation revoking, among certain individuals, the status as a special deportee.

Schneur had become a Soviet citizen as soon as he had started studying at the institute in Yakutsk because of a regulation to the effect that all children of special deportees would have their status as special deportees revoked as soon as they started studying at a university.

One day in early winter, one of our acquaintances, a young woman by the name of Lea Leybov, came running into our house, red-eyed and horror-struck. Her hands and arms were covered with blood, and when she got into the house, she told us in tears that her father had committed suicide. He had hanged himself in the cow shed next to their house, and she had just found him. Not being able to enter the cow shed, since the door was locked from the inside, she had therefore had to break a windowpane, cutting her hands and arms. Lea was completely beside herself with sorrow and shock, and we did what we could to console and calm her.

Two days later, Leybov was buried. He was one of those who had become separated from their families during the first days after the deportation from Lithuania. He had been placed with other men in a special railroad wagon, which at some point was disengaged from the other wagons. Leybov was sent to a labor camp, and only after having served for ten years was he reunited with his family. The long, exhausting stay in labor camps had weakened his nerves, and he suffered from a compulsion neurosis and delusions of persecution. It must have been in one of these desperate moments that he could no longer stand the pressure and decided to take his own life. In the course of the years, there were quite a few suicides among the deportees. Not everybody had sufficient strength to carry on, and to some, suicide became the only way out of the hopelessness and despair.

There were also instances of failure on the part of the deportees to live up to the high ethical standards required by the situation. The NKVD was constantly on the lookout for people who would be willing to cooperate with them and inform them of what was going on among the deportees—what they talked about and the plans they made. Everybody knew that the NKVD attempted to hire people either by means of promises or threats, and some succumbed to the pressure, either because they were weak or because they allowed themselves to become trapped. Unfortunately, there were several such cases, and some of those who had been tempted or threatened into becoming informers brought disaster on their friends, who had to spend long periods of time in prisons or labor camps.

Most people had gradually become quite weak from their stay in the harsh climate. Many were ailing, and several had developed mental problems. After a certain period of acclimatization, people seemed to adjust to the severe winters and the abrupt transitions between the seasons. However, after a certain number of years, it nevertheless became increasingly difficult for us to cope. It was as if the reserves in one's system were being depleted.

After fourteen years in Siberia, our strength seemed to have run out, and we both experienced increasing difficulty coping with the cold weather. When the temperature dropped lower than forty degrees Fahrenheit below zero, we both had great difficulty in being outside and had problems with breathing and with our hearts. The winter of 1955–56 was exceptionally severe, and our longing for the summer and the warm weather seemed stronger than ever.

We kept informed of events in the outside world through the newspapers as well as the radio. On rare occasions some of our friends managed to get a foreign radio station on their shortwave radios and thus break through the information monopoly of the Soviet media. However, it was not easy to get these stations from abroad, for the jamming stations usually surrounded the towns with impenetrable sound screens.

In early March of 1956, we heard in the news from Moscow that a Danish government delegation, headed by Prime Minister H. C. Hansen, would be paying an official visit to Moscow. By this time, our correspondence with our relatives in Denmark had become quite regular.

Rachel

We wrote quite frequently to my family, and I learned from the letters from Copenhagen and Göteborg that my family was in contact with the Danish government, which would try to arrange exit permits for us. They were trying to obtain permission for us to visit our family in Denmark, for it was apparently easier to obtain tourist visas than direct exit visas. The Danish government had already granted us entry permits some time earlier. Although we were not too optimistic that the efforts of my family would lead to any positive results, the news of Prime Minister H. C. Hansen's visit gave us new hope.

A few days after we had heard the announcement on the news, we received a visit from one of Israel's former evening school students, Mamotenko, a lieutenant of the NKVD.

We were rather surprised at his unexpected visit and especially at the interest he showed in myself and my family during our conversation. Mamotenko asked me very detailed questions about all of our family relations, about my mother and my brothers and sisters, where they lived, how old they were, and what they did. I answered him as well as I could, and, finally, he asked me whether I missed my family in Denmark. "Of course I do," I answered. "I have been missing them every single day during the fifteen years we have been here, and I shall continue to long for my country and my beloved ones till I die. Anybody in my situation would do the same."

Mamotenko thanked us for the interview and was about to leave when I could not restrain myself any longer and said, "You have got to know something or other concerning my family. What is it all about?" However, NKVD people had still not changed and gave no answers to questions. Mamotenko shook his head but could not help smiling. It was a good-natured, ambiguous smile.

Rachel · Israel

Although Mamotenko had not revealed anything at all, we were able to draw the conclusion ourselves that his visit reflected the authorities' desire to test our feelings and to find out how we would react to the possibility of becoming reunited with our family in Denmark.

Only two days after Mamotenko's visit, we received a long cable from the Danish Embassy in Moscow. The embassy informed us that the subject of our departure had been discussed during Prime Minister H. C. Hansen's recent visit to Moscow and in his talks with the Soviet leaders. It had been indicated on the part of the Soviets that they would consider an application for exit permits from us favorably, and the embassy therefore recommended that we start applying for exit permits immediately and keep the embassy informed of the course of events.

The Danish delegation had apparently succeeded in persuading the Soviet leaders to promise that we would be allowed to leave the country, but our experience had taught us that a long, even infinitely long, time might elapse between the time that a promise was made and the time it would be redeemed. However, on receipt of the cable from the Danish Embassy, we immediately began the long and difficult procedure of applying for exit visas.

We first approached the OVIR, the office concerned with the issue of visas and permits for foreign travels. We were handed a stack of long questionnaires with detailed questions about our lives, educational backgrounds, travels, and memberships in political, cultural, or sports organizations. We also had to indicate in minute detail who our relatives were and where they lived.

Schneur had already for a number of years been a member of the Komsomol, the Young Communist League. Like all other members of the Komsomol, Schneur had become a member more or less automatically. Young people who refused to join were certain to run into a lot of difficulties, and it was most unlikely that they would be allowed to complete their education.

Members of the Komsomol were to support the party actively and participate wherever they were needed. Help was always needed within the agricultural sector, especially during the harvesting season, when young members of the Komsomol were ordered to go to the collective farms to help gather in the harvest. After his first stay at such a collective farm, Schneur told us of the way they had been packed together in a yurt infested with vermin and how they had had to live under the most filthy conditions and toil away from early morning till late evening gathering potatoes. The farmers of the collectives regarded the students more or less as substitutes who gave them the possibility of taking a vacation. Consequently, they did not feel like doing anything themselves and left all the work to the "activists."

The next summer Schneur decided to stay at home and did not report to the Komsomol when the students took off for the collective farms to help the farm workers.

One of the Komsomol secretaries came to our house several times to talk to Schneur, but he was never at home. Instead, Schneur managed to get a job as assistant teacher in a Pioneer Camp. He made a good contribution to the Pioneer Camp, and when the summer vacation was over, he received a letter of thanks from the Komsomol organization of the camp for his efforts.

After the new school year had started at the institute, the Komsomol organization had a meeting, and one of the secretaries criticized Schneur sharply for having let his comrades down and for failing to fulfill his obligations by staying away from the collective farm. Schneur, however, was prepared and gave the secretary the letter of thanks he had received for his work at the Pioneer Camp, asking him to read the letter aloud. Schneur did not receive any more reprimands from the Komsomol.

Gradually, all of the deportees from Lithuania gathered in Yakutsk. We were quite a Jewish community now and often gathered to celebrate the Sabbath and the Jewish holidays together. Everybody talked more and more about the things that were about to happen and how everybody's situation would be affected by the changes we felt were under way.

Our questionnaires, applications, and letters of recommendation from employers had to be submitted to the OVIR with eight photos of each family member. We immediately proceeded to fill in the application forms, procure all of the necessary information, and have all of us photographed.

A Chinese saying has it: "Even the longest trip begins with the first step." To us, the first step on our long trip was handing in all of the papers, documents, and photos to the OVIR.

We hesitated to tell anybody about our plans. Only our closest friends among the deportees knew. We realized that it would still be a long time before our exit permits would be granted, and we expected to remain in Yakutsk till the end of the school year.

Israel

The first positive result of our application for exit permits was the revocation of Rachel's status as a special deportee. We were now able to move to any place in the Soviet Union (except for the major cities and the Baltic States). We put the house in order so that it could be sold at short notice. The money from the sale of the house would go to pay for the trip, but we did not, of course, want to sell it until we had obtained our exit permits.

As soon as the school year was over, I resigned from my teaching job. Harrietta and Samuel were withdrawn from the school and Schneur from the institute. Two months after we had been to the OVIR to hand in all of our papers, I went back to find out how things were going with our applications and when we could expect to leave. I was told that we would be informed as soon as they received a reply from Moscow.

One day in late August, as I was sweeping the street in front of the house, it suddenly occurred to me that we should leave Yakutsk as soon as possible to get to Irkutsk. The day we got our exit permits, it would be much easier to leave from Irkutsk, since there was a direct connection by train to Moscow via the Trans-Siberian Railroad. If we remained in Yakutsk, our departure would involve considerably more time and difficulty.

Rachel agreed with my decision, and we immediately made preparations to sell the house. It did not take us long to find a buyer, who bought the furniture as well. One of our acquaintances purchased our chickens, and we were then ready to leave. After having paid back the money we had borrowed from our friends when we purchased the house, we had a small amount left over to cover the costs of traveling to Irkutsk.

With some difficulty we managed to obtain tickets for the voyage from Yakutsk to the town of Ust-Kut, from where we were able to continue by a newly built railroad to Tayshet and from there the approximately 620 miles to Irkutsk. We would remain in Irkutsk until we received our exit permits.

Rachel and Israel Rachlin

Before leaving, we had to arrange for a place to stay in Irkutsk until we found our own place.

One of our close friends, Leyzer Shimberg, had moved to Irkutsk with his family sometime before and was living in a rather large house. I called Leyzer at his workplace, telling him about our problem. He told me at once to come to their house and that we could stay with them as long as we needed to.

The day before our departure, we all went to the Jewish cemetery behind the old stadium on the outskirts of the town to visit Baba's grave for the last time. It was a sorrowful moment for us, and we felt as strongly then as when we had buried her how tragic it was that Baba should die and be left in a distant and foreign world.

Rachel · Israel

Our departure from Yakutsk became a great and unforgettable event. A period of fifteen years of deportation was drawing to a close, and we were perhaps starting our trip home to Denmark.

We arranged for a horse-drawn carriage to take us and what little luggage we had down to the steamer in the harbor. Several of our friends and acquaintances had come down to wave good-bye, and some of them admitted that they envied us. The road, however, was open to everybody, and it was merely a question of time before all of our closest friends, with very few exceptions, left Yakutsk to settle down under brighter skies. When the ship started sailing, the handkerchiefs came out of the pockets, and we could see that our friends used them both to wave to us and to dry the tears from their eyes.

It was a rather strange and unfamiliar feeling for us to start out on that trip. We found it difficult to understand that it had not been necessary for us to inform the commander of anything at all and that we could move freely wherever we wanted. We had obtained excellent cabins on board the ship and enjoyed the trip. We sailed past Pokrovsk and recognized all the houses, but then, of course, we had spent nine long years getting to know everything in that town. We also saw the house where we ourselves had lived in the last few years in Pokrovsk and where we has so often dreamed of the day when we would be sailing past it on board a ship taking us away from there and back to Denmark. The time when we could leave Yakutia and perhaps continue to Denmark not much later had now finally arrived.

After a week of sailing, we arrived at Ust-Kut, which was the last har-

202

bor in the southern part of the Lena and the point of departure for the newly built railroad line to Tayshet. The station was located about two and a half miles from the harbor. Some soldiers helped us take our luggage from the harbor to the station. They had finished their military service in Tiksi and were now on their way home. They were happy that their service was over and had entertained the entire ship with singing and dancing all the way from Yakutsk to Ust-Kut. There were several Jewish boys among the soldiers, and we had invited them into our cabin to celebrate the Jewish New Year, which happened to fall on one of the days that we were sailing on the Lena.

Even with the help of our soldier friends, it took us a long time to reach the station. When we finally arrived, the train to Tayshet had left, and we had to wait for another twenty-four hours for the next one. With the soldiers and several other passengers who had missed the train, we spent the night in the waiting room of the railroad station, sleeping on the floor and on the benches. Taught by bitter experience fourteen years before, when a sack of flour had been stolen from us, we did not want to risk being robbed again and took turns keeping an eye on the luggage gathered around us. The next day, for the first time in fourteen years, we got into a train, and even if we had to sit on the so-called "hard seats" in the second class, the trip, compared to our experiences in the cattle class, was almost luxurious. It was the first time in his life that Samuel had seen a train, and it was a great experience for him. He ran everywhere, though he preferred to stay with the locomotive engineer in the driver's cab. We had great difficulty restraining his excitement.

Like many other railroad lines, the line from Ust-Kut to Tayshet had been built by people from the Gulag Archipelago. Part of the line had not yet been completed, and the train had to travel very slowly on those stretches. Several times we saw prisoners putting sleepers or rails in place under the strict surveillance of soldiers armed with machine guns and holding German shepherds on leashes.

On other stretches we also saw the unmistakable prison barracks, barbed wire fences, and high watchtowers.

Israel

I was standing in the corridor looking out the window as we were passing still another camp. Next to me was another passenger, and I

203

said to him that it was to be hoped that we would not have to see any such towers in the future, and that it was not a good idea to show such ugly buildings to foreigners. My fellow passenger, however, did not quite agree with me. "One never knows," he said. "Perhaps we shall need such prison barracks and watchtowers again some day." I did not want to get involved in any discussion with him but thought to myself that he was probably right.

The next day at around 5:00 P.M. we reached Tayshet, where we had to change trains and go on to Irkutsk. This last stretch, however, carried a great deal of traffic, and we had been warned that it might be difficult to buy tickets for all five of us. It became Schneur's task to get the tickets. When the train approached the station and had slowed down, Schneur jumped off and rushed to the ticket office. It worked perfectly—Schneur got seats for all of us, and we had only to wait for two hours for the arrival of the express train from Moscow.

Some of our soldier friends again helped us carry the luggage outside, and a short time afterward we took leave of all of them. We had come to know them very well on the long trip and were a little sad to take leave of our new friends, whom we knew we would never see again.

From Tayshet we again had to travel east to get to Irkutsk. The express train from Moscow was equipped in the manner of the best international trains, with spacious compartments and clean berths, with nice warm blankets and white sheets. These were luxuries we had not known for many years. There was a friendly conductor in our railroad car. She brought warm tea for all of us and saw to it that we were comfortable. It did not take long for any of us to fall asleep, and the next morning we did not wake up until the train was approaching the station of Irkutsk.

17

Rachel · Israel

At the station of Irkutsk, we were met by Leyzer, his wife, and their son. It was wonderful, for the first time in all the years of our deportation, to be met by somebody we were happy to see. For fifteen years we had not been travelers but people who had been transported from place to place without any idea of our destination or our future. Now we had, for the first time, decided our destination ourselves and had slowly begun to adjust to feeling like almost entirely normal human beings. We went straight to the house of the Shimbergs, where we were given a room to ourselves. The house of about one thousand square feet now accommodated a total of eleven people. Although the Shimbergs were unbelievably hospitable, we could not stay with them for any length of time and immediately began looking for a place of our own.

Irkutsk was a beautiful town with lots of opportunities and attractions we had not known for many years. It was over three hundred years old and had about four hundred thousand inhabitants. It was one of the most important towns in Siberia, with large industrial enterprises, several universities, a branch of the Academy of Sciences, and a rather varied and active cultural life. The Angara River ran right through town, and with its broad streets and many green areas, Irkutsk looked very beautiful and friendly.

The people in Irkutsk actually looked quite European, and we clearly remember the impression it made upon us to see a couple walk together arm in arm, for it was a sight we had not seen in all our years in Yakutia. The children were all very happy to have come to Irkutsk. They adjusted very quickly and all of them made new friends. Samuel especially was very enthusiastic about the new world he could now explore. The very day after our arrival in Irkutsk he disappeared for several hours. He told us afterward that he had been riding back and forth on the streetcar from one terminal to another. It was the first time in his life that he had seen one, and wanting to try it out immediately, he had run off without asking for our permission. When several hours had passed and he did not return, we began to worry that something might have happened to him. However, he returned in high spirits to tell us with enthusiasm about his free rides. He soon showed us that he was as good at coping in a big city as in the taiga.

After hunting for a couple of weeks, we found an apartment with one room and a kitchen and rented it on reasonable terms.

The small apartment was located in an old wooden house not far from the center of town in a street by the name of Ulitsa Oktyabrskoy Revolutsii. Across from the house on the other side of the street was a huge factory. Harrietta and Samuel started school immediately, and Schneur resumed his studies at the institute. We did not expect to stay in Irkutsk very long, and Israel did not look for work since we would be able to manage for still some time on the money we had received from the sale of the house in Yakutsk. We hoped that we would not have to wait too long.

The climate in Irkutsk was considerably milder than in Yakutsk, and winter arrived much later. We were thus much more comfortable even if our housing conditions were not too good. The apartment was damp, low-ceilinged, and barely large enough for the five of us. We bought two cots for Harrietta and Schneur, who slept in the other end of the room. As for our water supply, a water carriage periodically drove into our courtyard, and people from all over the neighborhood came to collect water in their buckets.

We were also able to collect water from a small pumping station nearby. Food supplies in Irkutsk were incomparably better than in Yakutsk, even if certain goods were similarly often in short supply. In the summer and the fall months, the market received supplies of fruit and vegetables from the southern regions—the vendors often came all the way from the Georgian Republic to sell their precious fruit at high prices.

Time went by, however, without anything happening. When November arrived, we felt that something had to happen soon. On our arrival we had reported to the local OVIR office, so they knew how to get in touch with us. In mid-November we received a small postcard from the OVIR, inviting us to their office. All our hopes were dashed, however, when we got to the OVIR office, where we were presented with a letter from Moscow rejecting our application for exit permits. It was a hard blow for us, since we had hoped very much that we would now be able to get it all over with and leave for Denmark. But it was not to be so simple to escape our years of difficulty and trouble. We were disappointed and depressed when we returned to the children, who knew without having to be told what had happened.

The rejection of our visa applications meant that we would have to be prepared to remain in Irkutsk for a long time. We did not give up hope but understood now that we would have to fight till the end before the Soviet authorities would release their hold.

Israel

I now had to find a job, and after looking around for some time, I was able to add still another title to the fairly long list of professions I had accumulated—I became a translator at a scientific research institute, which specialized in the construction of machinery for chemical industries. My new place of employment was called Niikhimmash, one of the abbreviations which have become so widely used in the Russian language.

The institute was located in the center of town, and the distance was short enough for me to be able to walk back and forth to work every day. The task of the institute was to project and prepare the construction of chemical works that were to use the power of the large hydroelectric power plants to be built in that part of the country. Along with another translator, who had been employed at Niikhimmash for a number of years, I was to check scientific magazines from the United States, Great Britain, and Germany. I translated the lists of contents for the management, and if one of the managers was interested in one of the articles, I had to translate it. The people working at the institute were chemists, engineers, and constructors, and I soon felt at home among them, becoming good friends with several of them.

Rachel

The time after our visit to the OVIR office was a difficult one. Our departure had seemed so near, and still it had not worked out. We were again left to uncertainty and had to find new sources of strength to endure it and persevere. For the first time in all those years, I began to doubt whether we should ever succeed in getting out. Both psychologically and physically, we had gradually become run down after the many years in Siberia; our nerves were becoming frayed and our health failing.

Sometime after the rejection of our visa applications, I sat down to write a letter to the embassy to find out what had happened and what we could do.

Irkutsk, November 5, 1956

The Royal Danish Embassy
Moscow

Dear Sirs:

As I have not yet received a reply to my last letter of October 7, 1956, I have decided to write you once more. The local authorities have informed us that the Soviet Union has rejected our application for exit permits to Denmark. I do not understand anything at all anymore. In your cable of March 9, you informed us that the Soviet government had given us permission to leave for Denmark. It was our understanding that the permit had been granted and that only formalities were left to be settled, and we ourselves acted according to your directions. I should like very much to know the cause of this sudden change. Of course, I do not give up hope, and I still trust that we shall be granted permission to leave despite the rejection of our applications. I hope that the authorities will take into consideration my husband's poor physical health, which makes it difficult for him to work at present.

So many people are returning to their native countries, and I should like very much to be among them and finally see my mother, my brothers, and my sisters, who are all yearning to see us.

I ask you kindly to inform me whether we should submit another application and, if so, to whom, or whether the embassy will want to take the necessary steps itself. If I knew whether it would serve any purpose, I would be prepared to go to Moscow either alone or with my husband. Could you please tell me what you feel about it? I do not know how to convey the latest news to my mother, my brothers, and my sisters—it will be a severe blow, especially to my dear old mother. I hope to hear from you soon and ask you to confirm the receipt of my letter.

With kind regards,
Rachel Rachlin

N.B. Our new address is Ulitsa Oktyabrskoy Revolutsii 10, Apt. 3

Shortly afterward we received a reply from the embassy, which wrote that they would continue to work on the matter and that we should not lose courage. It encouraged us to know that there were still people who wanted to help us.

The Royal Danish Embassy
Moscow, February 25, 1957   File No. 35.J.1

Mrs. Rachel Rachlin
Irkutsk

Dear Mrs. Rachlin:

I hereby acknowledge receipt of your letter of December 5, 1956, and wish to write you a few words, as I know that you are anxiously awaiting news of your application for exit visas. I regret very much that, at the present time, I am unable to give you the information you wish, namely, that the Soviet authorities have granted your application. Some unexpected difficulties seem to have arisen, which we are unable to understand, considering the promise previously given by the Soviet leaders, and which I feel must be due to certain misunderstandings. It may take some time to get these misunderstandings clarified, but I wish you to be patient and not give up hope.

With kind regards,
Alex Mørch
Ambassador

Rachel · Israel

It had become easier keeping in contact with our relatives in Denmark after our arrival in Irkutsk. The letters were not long on the way, and the parcels, of which we received several, took only two or three weeks to reach us. Since the distance from Copenhagen to Irkutsk was five thousand miles, that was quite an achievement. We prepared ourselves to spend the winter in Irkutsk, but all the time we had only one thought—getting on the train to Moscow and leaving for Denmark. So far, there was nothing for us to do but wait and hope that we would finally manage to leave.

We soon got together with our friends, and time did not pass as slowly, for we were able to do a lot more than in Yakutsk. We went to the theater and to concerts and quite a lot to the movies. Samuel was probably the most ardent moviegoer of the family, and he did not miss many films during our time in Irkutsk. Despite our disappointment at the rejection of our visa applications, we felt better and happier than before, since our environment was considerably friendlier and calmer than in the previous years.

We naturally talked a great deal about the possible reasons for the rejection. We had received no explanation from the OVIR, nor did we ask for one. Only after our arrival in Denmark did we learn that events in Hungary had played a decisive role. Danish criticism of Soviet intervention in Hungary had not been well received in Moscow, and the deterioration of the international climate in the wake of the Hungarian drama became the indirect cause of a second rejection of our application for exit visas.

The winter in Irkutsk was not nearly as severe as in Yakutia, even if the temperature on colder days did drop to between twenty and forty degrees Fahrenheit below zero. However, there were many sunny days in the course of the winter, and as early as February, the sun became sufficiently warm for the windowpanes, which had been covered with ice ferns throughout the winter, to start thawing. The time had then come to undertake the same drainage arrangement we used every year upon the approach of spring.

The ice that had formed on the windowpanes and around all of the cracks in the window frames started melting when the weather became warmer, and the water ran down onto the windowsill and threatened to flood the floor unless we did something about it. The method used in Yakutia was to place a piece of cloth rolled up into a thin strip along the windowsill and to put its ends into two bottles hanging from strings on either side of the windowsill. The rolled-up cloth absorbed all of the water and carried it down into the bottles, which we would empty when they were full. This was a simple and efficient method for collecting the melting ice of the winter. Each year, this drainage procedure was a happy augury that spring was on its way.

To be certain of finding supplies in the grocery stores, we had to get up early in the morning and stand in line before the stores opened. We might then be lucky enough to come home with milk, butter, and eggs, and extra lucky to return with frozen Chinese chicken. At the time, relations between the Soviet Union and China were still very close and friendly. We often saw Chinese students who studied at the various universities in Irkutsk.

Rachel

The 28th of May, 1957, started out as quite an ordinary day. Israel and the children had left, and I was in full swing cleaning the house.

Our mailman usually arrived at around ten o'clock, but it was not even nine o'clock when, through the kitchen window, I caught a glimpse of him making his way to our house. He was not carrying his usual bag. It turned out to be a special mailman who had come to deliver a cable. The cable was from the Danish Embassy, which informed us that the embassy had now received word that the entire Rachlin family had been granted exit visas. We were now to contact the Soviet authorities in Irkutsk to take care of the formalities. My heart started beating very hard, and I was beside myself with joy at the absolutely fantastic message I had just read. I had waited so long for that message that I found it difficult to grasp that it had actually arrived and that it was true. At the same time, I felt doubt and skepticism gnaw at me, whispering to me that nothing was certain until we had left the country.

In any case, I was not able to carry on with the cleaning of the house—I had to let it all out by telling Israel what had happened. It was not yet ten o'clock when I stood outside the gate of Niikhimmash. I asked the guard to contact Israel and tell him to come outside to meet me, for without a special permit, one was not allowed to enter the institute.

Israel was frightened when he saw me, believing that something terrible had happened. But I was quick to calm him down, telling him that I brought only happy news. His fears now gave way to joy mixed with some disbelief and skepticism, as had been the case with me. In the few minutes we had available, we immediately agreed not to report to the OVIR for the time being. We were afraid that the OVIR might not have been informed by Moscow, and we might then risk that they would tell us to come back in six months. In that situation, it would be of no use coming back until the six months had passed.

On my way home I wondered how it would feel to return to Denmark after so many years. Much was bound to have changed in Denmark in the twenty-two years I had been away, and it might be like returning to an entirely different country. Of course, I myself had changed too—the many years could not have gone by without leaving their trace on me; my habits and my attitude toward life were bound to be entirely different from those of my family and of everybody else in Denmark. I understood that we would have to brace ourselves to meet new problems and that the transition would not be entirely without problems.

I also wondered about the financial difficulties we might encounter and how we would cope with having to start all over again. We would, for example, have to see to it that the children got a proper education, enabling them to manage on their own later in life, and I wondered how Israel would be able to manage that task. He was now fifty years old and did not speak a word of Danish.

When Israel returned home from work, it turned out that he, too, had entertained the same thoughts and considerations, and he asked me whether I realized the kinds of problems we would encounter on our arrival in Denmark. "If we were able to manage in Siberia," I answered him, "I am sure we shall also do so in Denmark."

When a week had elapsed, I decided to go to the OVIR. After having been kept waiting for a while, I was shown into an office, where a middle-aged man gave me a searching look and asked me what I wanted. I answered that I had come for information about our application for exit visas to Denmark. With a lazy movement he took out a folder, flipped through it, took out a document, and said, "We have received word from Moscow that if you apply for exit visas, we should inform you that they will be granted."

It was a very strange way of putting it, but the idea was that the OVIR would not have given us any information unless we ourselves approached them. I was now told that we were to fill in additional questionnaires and pay an amount to the bank as a deposit for our passports. We had to pay a total of twelve hundred rubles, which was quite a lot of money, considering that Israel's monthly salary was eleven hundred rubles. The man finally told me that the OVIR would contact us as soon as they received our passports.

It finally looked as if our trip home had become a reality. However, we had had too many disappointments in the past to start rejoicing ahead of time. We would take one step at a time and not make any further preparations until we had received our passports.

Rachel · Israel

In the following days, there was much talk in our home about our upcoming trip and what it would mean to us to be transplanted to Denmark after so many years. The idea of settling in Denmark had until now appeared entirely abstract and unrealistic, but now that it seemed real, we both had to consider thoroughly what to do and how to prepare ourselves. We fully realized that we would have to build up an entirely new life from the very start and that it would not be an easy task. Schneur asked us whether he would be able to complete his studies, and we promised him that we would do everything we could to arrange that. We had not been able to tell the children too much about Denmark and life in the West. Rachel had taught the children a few Danish songs, and they knew, of course, Hans Christian Andersen's fairy tales in Russian translation, but apart from that, they did not know any Danish or anything about Danish cultural life. The children, however, were all very intent on leaving—the idea of Denmark and meeting the family attracted them a great deal. All three felt that it would be wonderful to suddenly have a grandmother, uncles, aunts, and cousins. During all those years, they had not known of any family ties beyond our own small family circle, and they were looking forward to meeting and being with the rest of the family.

While we were waiting, we wondered whether the authorities might, at the last minute, find a new excuse to prevent us from leaving. We could not exclude the possibility that they might say that only Rachel would be allowed to leave with the children, while Israel had to remain. They had done something similar in Yakutsk, and we would not be surprised if they did it again. They might demand that Schneur do his military service. They still had quite a few possibilities of keeping us, and we would not be certain of anything until we had left the country.

We did not say anything about our traveling plans to anybody except our friends among the deportees. The news of our trip became a sensation within the colony of deportees, to whom our example became of great importance, because it was an omen that they, too, would be allowed to leave Irkutsk and go back to Lithuania and perhaps continue to the West. Many of our friends among the deportees had for many years made fun of us because we kept applying for permission to leave for Denmark. They had regarded it as an entirely hopeless cause and advised us to give up our attempts and save ourselves the trouble. They now came to congratulate us and tell us that they admired us for our courage and perseverance. They all said that our impending trip would be the starting signal for all of them to break up and move back to Lithuania.

We started talking about what to take along from our wardrobe and what to sell in the flea market. We were certain that we did not need to take our winter clothes—our felt boots, padded jackets and pants, fur gloves, and fur hats. All of these things were put aside, ready to be sold at the flea market the next day, as we were certain that we would no longer need them.

The month of June passed without anything happening. We anxiously awaited word from the OVIR. The day we had been longing for finally came in early July. In the morning the mailman brought us a card from the OVIR, asking us to come to their office. We went there a few hours later and received our passports. It did not take long to settle the formalities, and when, a little later, we stood in the street again, we embraced each other, laughing and crying with joy. The joy and happiness we felt at that moment was immense. To both of us, it was one of the greatest moments in our lives—our efforts and the efforts of our family and the Danish government during so many years had finally paid off. We were able to begin preparing for our journey.

Israel

The first thing I did was to resign from my job. The manager did not quite understand what I meant when I came up to him to say that I wanted to resign because I was moving away from Irkutsk. He knew that I had come from Lithuania and believed that I would be returning there with my family. He immediately said that I should not expect to get as good an apartment in Lithuania as the one Niikhimmash had promised me for the fall. I then told him that we were going to Denmark and not to Lithuania. He looked at me in surprise and said that we would need foreign passports to go to Denmark. I showed him my newly acquired passport, and that convinced him that it was no use trying to persuade me to stay. He congratulated me, adding that he was sorry to lose me as his colleague.

The administrator at Niikhimmash was Ivan Ivanovich, and one of his tasks was to get air and train tickets for the employees of the institute. We had already discussed how to solve the problem of getting tickets for the train to Moscow, for this was quite a difficult task. It now occurred to me that Ivan Ivanovich would be the right man to help us. He had once held a much higher position but had been degraded because of his drinking problem. I immediately went to him to tell him about my problem. I let him know that if he took his contacts at the ticket office out to lunch, I would be prepared to pay for it. He responded with a deprecating gesture, insisting that we were friends and that he would be most happy to help me get the tickets for the train.

214

The following Sunday, Rachel and I went to the flea market to sell our winter clothing. All of the clothing was in a bag, and in less than one hour we had sold all of it. Selling our furniture was just as easy. The two beds, two cots, five stools, and a table were sold to neighbors and acquaintances, who came to collect all of it the day before our departure.

Ivan Ivanovich had asked me to come to the ticket office, where we would arrange the matter together. Rachel was not too sure that my "good friend" would keep his word and wanted to come along if it should prove necessary to stand in line to get the tickets ourselves. When we got to the ticket office, Ivan Ivanovich immediately took me to the manager, introducing me as an employee of Niikhimmash going on a trip to Denmark with his family. Ivan Ivanovich presented the matter in such a way that the manager was led to believe that it was Niikhimmash which had asked me to go to Denmark with my family. However, the end of the matter was that the manager told us to go to the cashier with a note from him to get the tickets.

A little later, I stood with five tickets in my hand—they had cost me seventeen hundred rubles, and in my pocket I still had two hundred rubles, which I gave to Ivan Ivanovich. He at first declined to accept the money, but I managed to persuade him, saying that it was merely for a modest lunch in thanks for his help. Rachel had followed the whole thing at a distance and afterward came up to Ivan Ivanovich, took his hand, and thanked him for his wonderful help.

The last day at Niikhimmash passed without any special occurrences, although it was a very special day for me—it was my last day at a Soviet workplace. I acted, however, as if nothing had happened and calmly took leave of my colleagues, who all wished me the best of luck. The thing that made the greatest impression on me that day was a small incident that happened as I was on my way to Niikhimmash early in the morning.

As usual, I walked to work with my colleague, Lyudmila Nikolayevna, who lived in the house next to us. She was a very cultured and wise woman, and we had had many interesting talks on our way to work. Lyudmila Nikolayevna told me, among other things, that she had known many Danes who had come to Irkutsk in the past on behalf of the Great Nordic Company, which had had many projects in Siberia. Lyudmila Nikolayevna told me that she recalled her Danish acquaintances, most of whom had been technicians and engineers, as being tall and handsome men who were very attentive and courteous toward Russian women.

That morning I told her that it was the last time that we would be walking to work together, for our family would be moving to the homeland of the handsome engineers and technicians, which was also the homeland of my wife. Lyudmila Nikolayevna stopped abruptly, looked at me, and said, "Never in my fifty years of life have I been jealous of anybody, but I envy you. I would love to see Denmark one day!" I do not know whether it was Lyudmila Nikolayevna's Danish acquaintances who caused her to react so strongly or whether she had other reasons for it. I was merely surprised at her frankness, for it was not common at all to give expression to such frank opinions. The small episode was the last sign I received that new times were on their way in the Soviet Union. The thaw started by Nikita Khrushchev had begun to be felt. We were to see the consequences later on, but by then we were in Denmark and no longer affected by it.

Rachel · Israel

We got tickets for July 12, and on July 11, we went to the Shimbergs with all our luggage to spend the last night with them, just as we had spent our first day in Irkutsk in their hospitable home. In the evening quite a few of our friends from Lithuania gathered for a farewell party at the Shimbergs. They made speeches to us, and the atmosphere was somewhat sad, for after all the years we had spent together, we had come to be good friends, brought close together by a common fate and the problems we had always solved together. It was late when we went to bed that night. The next morning we left for the railroad station by a horse-drawn carriage, with our suitcases stowed away in the back. Several of our friends had come to the railroad station to wave good-bye to us. One of them, Wollik Bernstein, had brought a present along for us— a Russian-Danish dictionary, which, in some inexplicable manner, he had managed to procure in Irkutsk and which we later on used quite diligently.

We had problems with the female conductor, who would not accept one of our suitcases on the train because it was too big. We knew, however, how to solve that problem—ten rubles changed owners, and suddenly the suitcase had become smaller, and everything was in order.

We took leave of our friends, thanking them for the help they had given us and promising to write as soon as we had reached Denmark. After many embraces, kisses, and quite a few tears, we got into the train, but we kept talking with our friends through the open windows till the very last minute. With a small jerk, the train slowly started, and our trip home had begun. We kept waving to our friends until the train rounded a bend and we could no longer see them.

It was a well-equipped and comfortable train, and we felt at ease. We were incredibly happy and full of expectations, and when we had traveled a distance from Irkutsk, we all sat down in the compartment and had a glass of wine, drinking to a happy trip and arrival in Denmark.

It was probably the most wonderful trip of our lifetime, for we were all equally relieved to finally be leaving Siberia. We spent the time during our trip relaxing and discussing how we would handle things in Moscow and, later on, in Copenhagen. There was a lot to talk about, but we both had difficulty imagining what life in Denmark would be like, for many years had gone by and much could have happened in the meantime. We did not worry that the children would not be able to manage. All three were well equipped for the impending transition, and although they did not speak Danish, they had no problems with German, which had been the language we had always spoken among ourselves. All three of them understood German without difficulty and were able to make themselves understood. Instead, the difficulties in Denmark would be in finding a job and a place to live and in getting everything to function in the manner of a normal family life.

Through the windows we saw all the towns we had passed sixteen years before. And when we saw the names of stations such as Krasnoyarsk, Novosibirsk, Omsk, and Sverdlovsk, we invariably recalled the time when we were transported in the other direction, crowded together in a cattle wagon. It seemed an eternity ago. Now we were traveling in the opposite direction as free people, without guards and toward a destination we ourselves had decided. Behind us was a life that had given us a lot of experiences, bitter as well as useful. Our present situation was far too close and overwhelming for us to be able to get an overall picture of it, to organize in our minds all that we had been through to find out what it had meant to us and what we had become. All of this had to wait till later, when we would be able to look at it all from a distance. At the moment, we had to prepare ourselves for the impending changes, which might still hold surprises for us.

In the vicinity of Sverdlovsk, we crossed the border between Asia and Europe. We again touched glasses as we crossed the border and put Siberia behind us.

After more than five days on the train, we reached Moscow. Before the train had even stopped at the railroad station, we were in contact with "Denmark" through the window. There were many people on the platform, but we immediately caught sight of a man who was taller than most of the others and who was dressed in Western clothes. Most conspicuous, however, was his bow tie—no Russians wore bow ties—which was thus an immediate indication that the person was a foreigner. Rachel said immediately that the man was a Dane.

When we got out of the railroad car, the man with the bow tie came up to us, introducing himself as Levald of the Danish Embassy and welcoming us to Moscow.

Rachel

I was beside myself with joy when I suddenly heard somebody talk Danish for the first time after all those years. It was quite strange to hear Danish again, and somehow I had to adjust to the sounds and words so well known and so foreign at the same time.

We wanted to know at which hotel we would be staying during our stay in Moscow. We expected to remain for a few days until we could continue our trip to Denmark. Levald, however, told us that no hotel reservations had been made for us but that, instead, reservations had been made on the train to Helsinki at 10:00 P.M. the same night. The children were disappointed, for they had been looking forward to sightseeing in the Soviet capital, of which they had heard so much from the time they were quite small. However, we were to remain in Moscow for only twelve hours as guests of the embassy. Levald told us very diplomatically that the embassy found it best that we continue our journey as soon as possible. We had no objections and understood quite well why the embassy did not want our stay in Moscow to become unnecessarily prolonged.

We were to leave from the same railroad station and therefore wanted to leave all of our luggage in the checking room. Again, we had problems getting the staff to accept all of our luggage, but the matter was solved in the usual manner, whereupon we left for the Danish Embassy. I had no desire at all to go into town and felt much safer at the embassy. I therefore said immediately that I did not want to go outside the embassy at all until we were to return to the railroad station. I spent the day reading old Danish newspapers and studying the telephone directory to find the telephone numbers and addresses of my family and old friends in Copenhagen.

Israel

There were quite a few practical things to see to before our departure. We had to collect the tickets to Helsinki, money had to be changed, we had to have a Finnish transit visa inserted in our passports, and, finally, we had to redeem our state bonds. Schneur and I attended to these tasks. One of the secretaries at the embassy, Miss Bay, looked after Harrietta and Samuel and took them on a tour around town, so that they got to see the Kremlin, the metro, and some of Moscow's other tourist attractions, which had been some kind of fantastic dream to them throughout their childhood.

We encountered no problems in getting the tickets, which had been ordered ahead of time by the Danish Embassy. Changing our rubles into Danish kroner, however, was more complicated. Under Soviet law, one could only exchange five hundred rubles per adult family member prior to a trip abroad. According to the current exchange rate, we would get about sixteen hundred kroner for the fifteen hundred rubles. We went to the Foreign Trade Bank, where we were told to hand over our passports and come back two hours later. There was nothing we could do without our passports, and so we spent the time sight-seeing.

When we returned to the bank for the money and our passports, I received only six hundred Danish kroner and told them that a miscalculation had been made. The cashier looked at me in surprise, saying that the calculation was correct and that the rate used in the conversion was different from the one I had seen in the paper. The bank simply had different rates, depending upon the person who was to have the money exchanged and the purpose for which it was intended.

We continued to the Finnish Embassy for our transit visas. There were complications here as well, for when we reached the embassy, the consular office was closing, and the ambassador who had to sign our visas was at the airport to receive the Afghan king, who had arrived on an official visit to Moscow. An obliging secretary, however, helped us arrange everything, and somewhat later we went to her apartment near the embassy to collect the passports with the Finnish transit visas inside.

The last item on our program was going to a special bank where we would be able to redeem the bonds that I, like all other Soviet citizens, had accumulated over the past fifteen years. At the bank we encountered a lot of red tape as the bonds were counted and the numbers taken down in various registers. I had to sign an endless number of papers and was ushered from table to table, from desk to desk. The climax came when I was to get the money and my passport, and the bank clerk suddenly could not find my passport. It took quite a lot to make me lose my composure, but this was not what I needed at the end of a long and strenuous day. For a moment I was afraid that it might be a provocation and that they had deliberately concealed my passport to prevent us from leaving the country. We had heard quite a few stories in the course of time about the way the authorities and the NKVD played tricks on people, either to harass them or to involve them in some affair or other. I could not exclude the possibility that the NKVD, which, incidentally, had changed its name to the KGB some years earlier, might want to play a trick on me at the last minute. However, judging from the expression on the face of the bank clerk, I realized that the passport had really disappeared and that he was upset about it. Papers were flying all over the place while he rummaged about on his desk. In the meantime, I went outside for Schneur, who was waiting in the street to watch the Afghan king and his company drive past in a convoy. Schneur came back with me and started helping the bank clerk look for my passport. As always, Schneur was completely unaffected by our anxiety, and it did not take him more than a few seconds to catch sight of the passport under a typewriter. I breathed a sigh of relief, and we were now at long last able to return to the embassy.

We got a taxi and went back to Pereulok Ostrovskogo, where the embassy was located. Here we were received by Rachel, who had become very concerned because we had stayed away for such a long time. However, she soon calmed down again when she heard of our experiences and found that everything was in order. We spent the rest of the day together at the embassy.

Rachel · Israel

One always remembers new experiences for a long time, and there was a good deal we saw for the first time at the Danish Embassy. We were asked whether we wanted to watch television—none of us had watched television before, so of course we wanted very much to do so. The news program was put on, and it was a great experience for all of us suddenly to see the leader of the Soviet Union, Nikita Khrushchev, appear on the small screen.

Being invited to dinner at the embassy, where we were served Danish food with Danish beer and soft drinks, also made a deep impression on us. The children gazed in wonder at it all, their eyes almost rolling out of their heads. The very way the table had been laid—with nice plates, glasses, and cutlery—made an enormous impression on us. Canned beer was an equally incredible sight to us. When the children saw the bathroom and the toilet with the nice toilet paper, they could not help laughing—they felt it was simply too funny.

Before our departure, some of the employees at the embassy told us that they had been rather nervous about our visit, for they had no idea what kind of people we were, and they had become somewhat cautious after rather unfortunate experiences with other guests. They told us that, before our arrival, they had been afraid that they would be admitting some Siberian savages into the embassy. They told us of their fears in a smiling and somewhat apologizing fashion, at the same time giving clear expression to their sympathy for us. We took leave of them, thanking them for their help and support throughout the years and for their hospitality during our stay in Moscow. We arrived at the train station with plenty of time to spare. After finding our luggage and seats on the train, we were ready for the next stage of our trip.

We got five good seats on the train from Moscow to Helsinki, and the next morning, after a ten-hour ride, we arrived in Leningrad. The train stopped for fifteen or twenty minutes, and we then proceeded to the border town of Vyborg, which, until 1940. had been a Finnish town by the name of Viipuri. When we reached Vyborg, only about twenty passengers remained on the train for Helsinki.

Our stay in Vyborg lasted for nearly two hours. All of our luggage was carefully examined piece by piece. The customs officers felt the hems of our clothing to find out if anything had been sewn into them, all of our books were leafed through, and everything else was carefully scrutinized. It was our last encounter with the Soviet authorities, but it certainly reminded us of the first searches of our home in Kybartai just before our deportation. It seemed like ages ago, and now we were so used to the treatment that we did not feel particularly annoyed by the customs officers' offensive manner. We were merely happy that it would soon all be over and that we would never again be subjected to such humiliations.

Rachel

I was not particularly nervous about the customs check, but I feared till the last minute that some trick or other might be played on us to prevent us from crossing the border. Right from our departure from Irkutsk, I kept saying that I would not believe anything until we were on the other side of the border. The sixteen years in Siberia had taught me not to take anything for granted and certainly not when dealing with the official Soviet authorities. The many years of disappointments and the constant insecurity under which we had lived had created within me a healthy skepticism with regard to the Soviet authorities. Moreover, over the years we had heard quite a few stories about people being fooled in similar situations and being prevented, at the last minute, from leaving the country. We did not know whether all of the stories were true, but it was enough for me to retain my skepticism till we had, at long last, crossed the border and left the Soviet Union. I simply dared not be happy until we were on the other side of the border.

Rachel · Israel

The passport check followed the customs check, and when that was over, we sat down to wait for the train to continue. The children ran in and out of the compartment, clearly impatient and excited about all that awaited them. The train was under strict supervision by an armed border soldier standing at the door of each railroad car. Finally, the train started, driving the entire distance to the border at a very slow speed. We now all stood at the windows—to preserve in our minds our last impressions of Soviet territory and to gaze ahead toward the Finnish side of the border. The soldiers guarding the doors of the railroad cars did not jump off until right before the frontier line. A few seconds after the soldiers of our railroad car had jumped off, the train rolled into Finnish territory. Jubilant, we all kissed and embraced one another. The joy we had kept back for such a long time now came rushing forth, breaking the tension within us and even making us all a little dazed and

222

dizzy. Our dream had come true—our impossible, incredible dream of one day leaving Siberia and going to Denmark was now a reality. Our feelings and experiences in those moments were among the happiest of our lives. We had just passed a national border separating two states and two nations, but it was also a line that separated two different worlds and, as far as we were concerned, heralded our reunion with the world from which we had been cut off for seventeen years and an entirely new life. We drank to all of these things and congratulated each other. The embassy in Moscow had given us a few cans of Danish beer for the trip, and it was this beer which we now used to toast each other—to us, it tasted like the finest champagne.

After the Finnish passport check and a quick customs check, we had a few minutes left at the station. A Finnish girl came wheeling a small ice cream carriage along the platform, and we wanted the children to become acquainted with the delicacies of the West, but the girl was unable to accept Danish money. An American reporter with whom we had talked on the way came up to us, offering to pay for the ice cream with a dollar note. But the girl did not want to accept that either, and only when a Finnish fellow passenger detected the currency problems and took some Finnish money out of his pocket was the ice cream problem solved. Later on after the train had started again, we asked both the American and the Finn into our compartment to join us for a glass of beer—we still had a couple of cans left.

All the way to Helsinki, the children could not leave their positions at the windows. They were completely absorbed in observing all of the new and interesting things that passed by outside the windows.

When the train pulled into the station in Helsinki, we were met by a secretary of the Danish Embassy. We were to continue by boat from Helsinki directly to Copenhagen—but since the boat would not leave until two days later, we had time in Helsinki to sightsee and get used to the new environment. We were happy about the stay, for it gave us the opportunity to collect ourselves a little after the many overwhelming impressions and made the transition less abrupt. The Danish Foreign Ministry paid for the hotel and the trip to Copenhagen. It was a loan, which we had to pay back as soon as we were able to do so. The six hundred Danish kroner for which we had exchanged our rubles in Moscow were, of course, not sufficient to cover all of our expenses.

While we were filling in the necessary arrival forms at the reception, Samuel left to explore the large lobby of the hotel. Shortly afterward, he came running back, looking very surprised and upset. He told us that he had seen a very strange sight and asked us to follow him. He had seen a small room, and a lady and some men had entered it. When, somewhat later, the door opened again, the room was empty, and other people entered it. A short time afterward, entirely new people got out of the small room. It was the biggest mystery of his life. We laughed at his surprise. It was Samuel's first encounter with an elevator.

The hall porter did not quite know who we were or how to address us. Our rooms had been booked by the embassy, and an embassy secretary had taken us to the hotel, but on our arrival forms we had not indicated any profession. He solved the problem, however, by simply addressing Israel as "Mr. Diplomat."

The two days in Helsinki were full of experiences. Only Schneur was able to remember vaguely what a bathroom looked like and how it worked. To Harrietta and Samuel all of these things were new discoveries, and it was an indescribable joy for them to test it all. They spent hours in the bathtub and under the shower and were beside themselves with excitement.

A visit to a large department store in the vicinity of the hotel was an equally great experience for us and the children. We had been gone too long to remember the enormous supply of articles of many different designs and qualities, and we were completely overwhelmed and amazed to see all the things one could get without having to stand in line, without having to wait for hours, and without any other difficulties. It was simply too difficult for us to comprehend the enormous supply of goods available to the customers, and we looked with wonder at the brisk business going on everywhere. The goods were not only put on display to be admired—they were indeed sold, and people were able to purchase as much as they liked.

The children experienced other "miracles." *Chewing gum* had a wonderful ring in their ears—they had heard about it in Siberia but had never tried it, as it was not available there. Instead, they had chewed a substitute made of various things such as resin, and they now wanted very much to taste real chewing gum. It turned out that the vending machines in the streets of Helsinki held chewing gum. By putting some coins into the vending machine and turning a handle, they could get a few sticks. The children had never seen vending machines before either, and Harrietta and Samuel found it the world's best invention, of which both made diligent use during the two days we stayed in Helsinki. The children, however, realized that we did not have much money for exciting purchases and did not ask us to buy anything for them. Samuel was very excited about a small Finnish sheath knife he got in memory of his visit to Helsinki. We bought a few other small items as presents for the family in Copenhagen. Most of the time, however, we spent walking around sight-seeing—everything was extremely interesting and exciting to us. We also took the opportunity to tell the children about the way the systems worked in Finland and the other Western countries. Samuel had difficulty understanding the ownership conditions of the West. He could not accept that one man might own a house, while another man might own a movie theater, a large department store, or a hotel—this was beyond him, and it was not easy to explain such things to a boy who had spent the first ten years of his life in a socialist country.

To us, it was a remarkable experience not having to take into consideration where we were or whom we were standing next to when talking to one another. It took us a long time to get used to it and to feel entirely safe, no matter where we were. We were all extremely happy and completely overwhelmed by the new impressions. Once in a while, it was hard to understand that it was true, and we had to assure one another that it was all real and not merely something we were dreaming.

Rachel

Naturally, we phoned Copenhagen. I was in an agony of nervousness when the first call to Copenhagen came through. It was difficult talking to my brothers and sisters and my mother after all those years—there was so much to tell them that we did not know where to begin, and we merely exchanged a few words about our trip, the time of our arrival in Copenhagen, and the state of health of each person. It was not easy to pick up the thread with one's beloved ones after all those years, and we promised each other that we would discuss it all when we reached Copenhagen. The children were extremely eager to meet their grandmother, aunts, and uncles, about whom they had heard a great deal—all three had their turns to say a few words to my brothers and sisters and my mother on the other end of the line.

Rachel · Israel

After two wonderful days as tourists in Helsinki, which we found to be an extremely beautiful and hospitable town, we boarded the *Ariadne*, which was to carry us on the last stretch of our long trip to Denmark.

Rachel and Israel Rachlin

It was a beautiful voyage and lasted for two days, helping to make the transition from the one world to the other more harmonious and calm. We had plenty of time to discuss the impending problems and to get used to the idea of a life under entirely new conditions, which would be considerably more pleasant than those to which we had been subject in our sixteen years in Siberia but which nevertheless would make heavy demands on each of us. Although the *Ariadne* was not an entirely new ship and had probably seen better days, we were all equally enthusiastic about the cleanliness, the modern comfort, and the good and friendly service on board—to us the trip was a luxury.

Although we stayed by ourselves on board the ship, it was soon rumored who we were, and people displayed a great interest in us. Our first talk with some of our fellow passengers began on the deck right after we had got out of the harbor of Helsinki. An elderly Swedish couple started talking to us about the weather, Helsinki, and the voyage to Copenhagen. After these few introductory remarks, the man said that he had immediately noticed that we came from the Soviet Union. We could not understand why, for we felt it was difficult to see any difference between us and the rest of the passengers—we were certainly dressed in Western clothes, which we had received in packages from our family. The man smiled, saying it certainly was not our clothing that had betrayed us. It was the way we talked to one another that showed where we came from—he had noticed that we both looked around in all directions before starting to talk to each other. We could not help smiling at his keen perception and said to him that it would probably not be too easy to get rid of that bad habit, since it had developed into some kind of reflex in the course of our sixteen years in Siberia.

Our trip was now drawing to a close. We had traveled a total of 129 days and had covered a distance of approximately 15,500 miles from June 14, 1941, the day we were sent off to Siberia, till July 22, 1957, when we arrived in Copenhagen. During the sixteen years, we had had twenty different homes and lived in six different places all over Siberia. It was easy enough to take stock of all that we could measure in figures. But how were we able to judge what the deportation had done to us as human beings? We were now forty-eight and fifty years old. How were we to evaluate the effect of the sixteen years, which measured one third of our lifetime, on our lives and our development as human beings? What had we missed in all those years, and what had we gained? We did not know the answers to the questions that kept cropping up. More time was needed for us to understand all that had happened and to evaluate it in its right context. We had undeniably learned a lot during our stormy life in Siberia—from bitter as well as useful experiences, which had contributed to shaping us as human beings and teaching us about life and our fellow men as other circumstances might not have. In the midst of all the sadness, we had also experienced bright and happy hours and had many joys. We had made friendships we knew would last forever, even if we never saw our friends again. We were now faced with another major transition, though, for the first time in all those years, it was one we had chosen and decided for ourselves and one we were looking forward to with indescribable joy. Still, it would be a transition, and we now had to brace ourselves for the new tasks and challenges that lay ahead of us. We knew that the task would not be entirely simple, although we would no longer be subject to the unfriendly and hostile environment.

When the *Ariadne* went alongside the quay of Langelinie in the harbor of Copenhagen on July 22, the entire family stood there to meet us. As soon as the gangway had been put up, we were the first ones to be allowed to go ashore, and a few moments later, we were reunited with our family in long and warm embraces, while our crying and laughter intermingled and random questions and answers flitted through the air. Shortly afterward, we were on our way by car to the apartment of Rachel's brother, Fyzik, who lived on Blaagaardsgade, where the family had prepared a festive reception for us. It became a long, long day of rejoicing and drinking to one another, and questions were asked and answered till late in the night.

After the welcome celebrations and the initial days of euphoria, we had a busy time finding out how to live, where to live, and how to earn our living.

One of the first things we did after our arrival in Copenhagen was pay a visit to Prime Minister H. C. Hansen to thank him for his help in getting us out of Siberia. All five of us went to Christiansborg, where H. C. Hansen received us and, during a brief conversation, asked us about our trip and the plans we had for our future life in Denmark. We told the prime minister how grateful we were for all that the Danish government had done to help us and that we were now full of hope and not at all afraid to start a new life in Denmark.

However, before really starting to settle down, we spent a few weeks in Smidstrup in a small summer cottage our family had rented for us. Here we were to relax, recover our strength, and make plans for the future.

Rachel

Our return to Copenhagen and reunion with my family and my world had all been wonderful. I felt happier and more relieved than ever and felt that there was nothing more wonderful than getting home. When, twenty-two years earlier, I had left Copenhagen to go on a honeymoon with Israel, I had not dreamed of the detours I would have to make to get back, nor of the happiness I would feel the day I would again be in Copenhagen. The joy of recognition on seeing the familiar streets, shops, and houses, of looking up old friends and places, and the feeling of security in being in one's own city and surrounded by friendly, smiling people—these were all things which made the strongest impression upon me during the first period after our return. How can I begin to describe the joy and thankfulness I felt at being able to be together with my beloved mother again and having the opportunity to do something for her during her last few years?

Sometime after our arrival in Copenhagen, I sat down to write a letter to the Danish Embassy in Moscow.

Copenhagen, July 31, 1957

The Royal Danish Embassy
Moscow

Dear Sirs:

First, I wish to thank you for the wonderful reception you gave us—we shall never forget it. We had a pleasant trip home and were met by the entire family. I cannot tell you how happy we all are now. In a few days we shall receive our temporary passports. We are staying with my brother E. Lachmann and ask you kindly to write to us at that address if you need to contact us. Once again, thanks for everything and many, many friendly regards to everybody at the Royal Danish Embassy.

Yours,
I. and R. Rachlin

I sent the letter via the Ministry of Foreign Affairs. It became my last letter to the embassy, and it probably closed the embassy's file on the Rachlin family.

228

Rachel · Israel

Not until many years later did we learn a little more about how the Danish delegation had succeeded in persuading their Soviet hosts to permit us to leave the Soviet Union and go back to Denmark. Julius Bomholt accompanied Prime Minister H. C. Hansen on his trip to Moscow, and in one of his books he describes the course of events.

The Danish delegation arrived in Moscow on March 5, 1956, a week after Nikita Khrushchev's "secret speech" at the twentieth party congress, on which occasion he had given the go-ahead to the showdown with Stalin and his terrorist regime. This was probably the first Western government delegation to meet with Khrushchev after his epoch-making speech. At the time, the Danish delegates did not know what had happened at the congress, but according to Julius Bomholt, judging from their talks with the various leaders, they definitely felt that something or other was about to happen. A large number of Soviet leaders attended their first round of talks in the Kremlin. Among them were Party Chief Nikita Khrushchev, Premier Bulganin, Foreign Minister Molotov, First Deputy Premier Mikoyan, and a large number of other ministers and high-ranking party and state officials.

Bomholt describes the situation as rather tense when they sat down in front of the Soviet leaders, who regarded them with somber and stern expressions, which did not bode well for the negotiations. The subject on the agenda concerned some tankers that Denmark had contracted to deliver to the Soviet Union, but which, in the meantime, had been put on NATO's list of commodities that were not to be exported to the East-Bloc countries. They were trying to solve the painful problem.

Bomholt writes that, in the tense situation, H. C. Hansen decided to talk about minor things first in order to break the ice before proceeding to the really explosive issues. He therefore started talking about a family's tragedy, which had begun in one of the Baltic republics. A Danish woman and her family had been unable to obtain permission to leave the Soviet Union to go back to Denmark and be reunited with the rest of her family.

H. C. Hansen's move caused surprise and aroused the curiosity of the Soviet leaders, who found it difficult to comprehend that they were to sit and talk about a woman, a single human being, a single human fate. Khrushchev asked impatiently if it were not tankers that were on the agenda for their talks. But the prime minister did not give up very easily and kept explaining the matter and the many fruitless attempts that had been made to get the family out. When he had finished talking, Bomholt goes on to say, Bulganin made a reassuring gesture with his hand and said, "We shall attend to the matter and seek to find a solution."

H. C. Hansen's persistence and Bulganin's gesture decided our future, even if the final permit for us to leave for Denmark was only obtained after another series of complications and a painful period of waiting.

Israel

Even though Rachel's brother, Eyzik, and his wife, Minna, had been extremely helpful and hospitable, we could not, of course, continue to stay with them, and we soon started looking for our own apartment. In October we were able to move into our own apartment in a newly constructed apartment building complex in Rødovre. The apartment became our base in our efforts during the following years of creating and adjusting to our own independent life.

Every beginning is difficult, even in a friendly environment. I had to find a job as quickly as possible to be able to support the family, and after some time, I succeeded in getting a job as bookkeeper in the firm of Titan on Tagensvej.

It took me some time to understand the Danish mentality and get used to the Danish life-style, which was so different from what we had been used to in Siberia.

A remark I heard soon after our arrival jarred my mind and made a deep impression on my memory: "Here in Denmark, everybody lives his own life." Both Rachel and I were astonished at these words and wondered at the underlying mentality. In time, however, as our insight into the Danish patterns of behavior and life increased, we came to understand that this was actually the way things were, that the better off people were materially, the less they seemed to need other people. Self-sufficiency, isolation, and dependence on material goods were some of the things that impressed us, and which we studied with both surprise and curiosity during our exploration of Denmark and the Danes. We found that many people felt lonely and suffered from lack of contact and companionship. We ourselves had difficulty getting used to the new ways of dealing with people and the tone the Danes used among themselves, both within the family and among friends and acquaintances. We have never missed Siberia, but we have to admit that we have missed our friends and our time with them during our deportation to Siberia.

The most important thing for us on our arrival in Copenhagen was our newly gained liberty, which enabled us to open up and live as we pleased. We no longer feared arbitrary persecution or reprisals and no longer felt insecure about the future. We soon adjusted to life in Denmark and came to feel at home there. We again started feeling like normal human beings with the same opportunities and rights as all other people and with a newly gained feeling of human dignity and its inviolability.

Little by little, we established a daily routine. Samuel started school and was the one who managed the transition easiest. Schneur and Harrietta continued their educations as chemist and laboratory assistant, respectively, and I myself kept my job as bookkeeper for about twelve months. After that, I started translating for Danish firms doing business with the Soviet Union, and in the evening I taught Russian at evening schools. When Russian was introduced as an elective in secondary schools, I was appointed teacher at Gladsaxe Secondary School, where I remained till my retirement.

We felt that we managed to create a meaningful life for ourselves and our children. We felt well equipped for the new challenges, for we had sound backgrounds and, in the sixteen years we had spent in Siberia, had learned a good deal about adjusting to life.

Rachel · Israel

Today, twenty-five years after our arrival in Denmark, we can look back at the years in Lithuania, Siberia, and Denmark through a perspective that only time can convey. It often happens that memories crop up, and we talk about them, helping each other to revive them. There are many such memories, and we have covered some of them in this book.

Fate gave our lives a somewhat crooked course, which we traveled along together and which, perhaps for that reason, has a special coherence and meaning for us. We were able to cope with it all because we always had each other and each other's love. Wars and political systems have intervened in our lives with violence and force and thrown our family back and forth like a small insignificant pawn in a big game, in which the individual and his fate are of little consequence. As we now live in quiet retirement, keeping up with the unsettled conditions in the world and watching the way games are played with human lives, we are filled with wonder at how it was possible to survive and eventually greet the opportunity to start a new and happy life in Denmark.

And when we then look back at all of the years that have gone by and think of our children, who long ago have gone their own ways and established their own families, we are sometimes filled with even greater wonder and understand that we are looking back on an entire life.

Bagsværd, 1979–81

Appendix to Foreword

Instructions of the Soviet Deputy Commissar for Public Security, Serov

I.—INSTRUCTIONS

Regarding the Procedure for carrying out the Deportation of Anti-Soviet Elements from Lithuania, Latvia and Estonia

STRICTLY SECRET

(Translated in London from the original Russian Text)

1. GENERAL SITUATION

The deportation of anti-Soviet elements from the Baltic Republics is a task of great political importance. Its successful execution depends upon the extent to which the district operative "troikas" and operative headquarters are capable of carefully working out a plan for implementing the operations and for anticipating everything indispensable. Moreover, care must be taken that the operations are carried out without disturbance and panic, so as not to permit any demonstrations and other troubles not only on the part of those to be deported, but also on the part of a certain section of the surrounding population hostile to the Soviet administration.

Instructions as to the procedure for conducting the operations are given below. They should be adhered to, but in individual cases the collaborators engaged in carrying out the operations shall take into account the special character of the concrete conditions of such operations and, in order correctly to appraise the situation, may and must adopt other decisions directed to the same end, viz., to fulfill the task entrusted to them without noise and panic.

2. Procedure of Instructing

The instructing of operative groups by the district "troikas"* shall be done as speedily as possible on the day before the beginning of the operations, taking into consideration the time necessary for travelling to the scene of operations.

The district "troika" shall previously prepare the necessary transport for conveyance of the operative groups in the village to the scene of operations.

On the question of allocating the necessary number of motor-cars and wagons for transport, the district "troikas" shall consult the leaders of the Soviet party organized on the spot.

Premises for the issue of instructions must be carefully prepared in advance, and their capacity, exits and entrances and the possibility of intrusion by strangers must be considered.

Whilst instructions are being issued the building must be securely guarded by operative workers.

Should anybody from among those participating in the operations fail to appear for instructions, the district "troika" shall at once take steps to replace the absentee from a reserve which shall be provided in advance.

Through police officers the "troika" shall notify those assembled of the Government's decision to deport a prescribed contingent of anti-Soviet elements from the territory of the said republic or region. Moreover, they shall briefly explain what the deportees represent.

The special attention of the (local) Soviet party workers gathered for instructions shall be drawn to the fact that the deportees are enemies of the Soviet people and that, therefore, the possibility of an armed attack on the part of the deportees cannot be excluded.

3. Procedure for Acquisition of Documents

After the general instruction of the operative groups, documents regarding the deportees should be issued to such groups. The deportees'

* "Troika"—a body consisting of three members.

234

personal files must be previously collected and distributed among the operative groups, by communes and villages, so that when they are being given out there shall be no delays.

After receipt of the personal files, the senior member of the operative group shall acquaint himself with the personal affairs of the families which he will have to deport. He shall, moreover, ascertain the composition of the family, the supply of essential forms for completion regarding the deportee, the supply of transport for conveyance of the deportee, and he shall receive exhaustive answers to questions not clear to him.

Simultaneously with the issuing of documents, the district "troika" shall explain to each senior member of the operative group where the families to be deported are situated and shall describe the route to be followed to the place of deportation. The roads to be taken by the operative personnel with the deported families to the railway station for entrainment must also be indicated. It is also essential to indicate where reserve military groups are stationed, should it become necessary to call them out during trouble of any kind.

The possession and state of arms and ammunition of the entire operative personnel shall be checked. Weapons must be in complete battle readiness and magazine loaded, but the cartridge shall not be slipped into the rifle breach. Weapons shall be used only in the last resort, when the operative group is attacked or threatened with attack or when resistence is offered.

4. Procedure for Carrying Out Deportations

If the deportation of several families is being carried out in a settled locality, one of the operative workers shall be appointed senior as regards deportation in that village, and under his direction the operative personnel shall proceed to the villages in question.

On arrival in the villages, the operative groups shall get in touch (observing the necessary secrecy) with the local authorities: the chairman, secretary or members of the village soviets, and shall ascertain from them the exact dwelling place of the families to be deported. After this the operative groups, together with the representatives of the local authorities, who shall be appointed to make an inventory of property, shall proceed to the dwellings of the families to be deported.

Operations shall be begun at daybreak. Upon entering the home of the person to be deported, the senior member of the operative group shall assemble the entire family of the deportee into one room, taking all necessary precautionary measures against any possible trouble.

After the members of the family have been checked in conformity with the list, the location of those absent and the number of sick persons shall be ascertained, after which they shall be called upon to give up their weapons. Irrespective of whether or not any weapons are delivered, the deportee shall be personally searched and then the entire premises shall be searched in order to discover hidden weapons.

During the search of the premises one of the members of the operative group shall be appointed to keep watch over the deportees.

Should the search disclose hidden weapons in small quantities, these shall be collected by the operative groups and distributed among them. If many weapons are discovered, they shall be piled into the wagon or motor-car which has brought the operative group, after any ammunition in them has been removed. Ammunition shall be packed and loaded together with rifles.

If necessary, a convoy for transporting the weapons shall be mobilized with an adequate guard.

In the event of the discovery of weapons, counter-revolutionary pamphlets, literature, foreign currency, large quantities of valuables, etc., a brief report of search shall be drawn up on the spot, wherein the hidden weapons or counter-revolutionary literature shall be indicated. If there is any armed resistance, the question of the necessity of arresting the parties showing such armed resistance and of sending them to the district branch of the People's Commissariat of Public Security shall be decided by the district "troikas."

A report shall be drawn up regarding those deportees in hiding or sick ones, and this report shall be signed by the representative of the Soviet party organization.

After completion of the search the deportees shall be notified that by a Government decision they will be deported to other regions of the Union.

The deportees shall be permitted to take with them household necessities not exceeding 100 kilograms in weight.
1. Suit.
2. Shoes.
3. Underwear.
4. Bedding.
5. Dishes.

6. Glassware.

7. Kitchen utensils.

8. Food—an estimated month's supply for a family.

9. Money in their possession.

10. Trunk or box in which to pack articles.

It is not recommended that large articles be taken.

If the contingent is deported from rural districts, they shall be allowed to take with them small agricultural stocks—axes, saws and other articles, which shall be tied together and packed separately from the other articles, so that when boarding the deportation train they may be loaded into special goods wagons.

In order not to mix them with articles belonging to others, the Christian name, patronymic and surname of the deportee and name of the village shall be written on the packed property.

When loading these articles into the carts, measures shall be taken so that the deportee cannot make use of them for purposes of resistance while the column is moving along the highway.

Simultaneously with the task of loading by the operative groups, the representatives of the Soviet party organizations present at the time shall prepare an inventory of the property and of the manner of its protection in conformity with the instructions received by them.

If the deportee possesses his own means of transport, his property shall be loaded into the vehicle and together with his family shall be sent to the designated place of entrainment.

If the deportees are without any means of transport, carts shall be mobilized in the village by the local authorities, as instructed by the senior member of the operative group.

All persons entering the home of the deportee during the execution of the operations or found there at the moment of these operations must be detained until the conclusion of the operations, and their relationship to the deportee shall be ascertained. This is done in order to disclose persons hiding from the police, gendarmes and other persons.

After verification of the identity of the detained persons and establishment of the fact that they are persons in whom the contingent is not interested, they shall be liberated.

If the inhabitants of the village begin to gather around the deportee's home while operations are in progress, they shall be called upon to disperse to their own homes, and crowds shall not be permitted to form.

If the deportee refuses to open the door of his home, notwithstanding that he is aware that the members of the People's Commissariat of Public Security have arrived, the door must be broken down. In individual cases neighboring operative groups carrying out operations in that locality shall be called upon to help.

The delivery of the deportees from the village to the meeting place at the railway station must be effected during daylight; care, moreover, should be taken that the assembling of every family shall not last more than two hours.

In all cases throughout the operations firm and decisive action shall be taken, without the slightest excitement, noise and panic.

It is categorically forbidden to take any articles away from the deportees except weapons, counter-revolutionary literature and foreign currency, as also to make use of the food of the deportees.

All participants in the operations must be warned that they will be held legally accountable for attempts to appropriate individual articles belonging to the deportees.

5. Procedure for Separation of Deportee's Family from Head of the Family

In view of the fact that a large number of deportees must be arrested and distributed in special camps and that their families must proceed to special settlements in distant regions, it is essential that the operation of removal of both the members of the deportee's family and its head should be carried out simultaneously, without notifying them of the separation confronting them. After the domiciliary search has been carried out and the appropriate identification documents have been drawn up in the deportee's home, the operative worker shall complete the documents for the head of the family and deposit them in the latter's personal file, but the documents drawn up for members of his family shall be deposited in the personal file of the deportee's family.

The convoy of the entire family to the station shall, however, be effected in one vehicle and only at the station of departure shall the head of the family be placed separately from his family in a car specially intended for heads of families.

During the assembling (of the family) in the home of the deportee the head of the family shall be warned that personal male effects must be packed in a separate suitcase, as a sanitary inspection of the deported men will be made separately from the women and children.

At the stations of entrainment heads of families subject to arrest shall be loaded into cars specially allotted for them, which shall be indicated by operative workers appointed for that purpose.

6. PROCEDURE FOR CONVOYING THE DEPORTEES

The assistants convoying the column of deportees in horse-carts are strictly forbidden to sit in the said carts. The assistants must follow alongside and behind the column of deportees. The senior assistant of the convoy shall from time to time go the rounds of the entire column to check the correctness of movement.

When the column of deportees is passing through inhabited places or when encountering passers-by, the convoy must be controlled with particular care; those in charge must see that no attempts are made to escape, and no conversation of any kind shall be permitted between the deportees and passers-by.

7. PROCEDURE FOR ENTRAINMENT

At each point of entrainment a member of the operative "troika" and a person specially appointed for that purpose shall be responsible for entrainment.

On the day of entrainment the chief of the entrainment point, together with the chief of the deportation train and of the convoying military forces of the People's Commissariat of Internal Affairs, shall examine the railway cars provided in order to see that they are supplied with everything necessary, and the chief of the entrainment point shall agree with the chief of the deportation train on the procedure to be observed by the latter in accepting delivery of the deportees.

Red Army men of the convoying forces of the People's Commissariat of Internal Affairs shall surround the entrainment station.

The senior member of the operative group shall deliver to the chief of the deportation train one copy of the nominal roll of the deportees in each railway-car. The chief of the deportation train shall, in conformity with this list, call out the name of each deportee, shall carefully check every name and assign the deportee's place in the railway-car.

The deportees' effects shall be loaded into the car, together with the

239

deportees, with the exception of the small agricultural inventory, which shall be loaded in a separate car.

The deportees shall be loaded into railway-cars by families; it is not permitted to break up a family (with the exception of heads of families subject to arrest). An estimate of twenty-five persons to a car should be observed.

After the railway-car has been filled with the necessary number of families, it shall be locked.

After the people have been taken over and placed in the deportation train, the chief of the train shall bear responsibility for all persons handed over to him and for their delivery to their destination.

After handing over the deportees the senior member of the operative group shall draw up a report on the operation carried out by him and shall address it to the chief of the district operative "troika." The report shall briefly indicate the name of the deportee, whether any weapons and counter-revolutionary literature have been discovered, and also how the operation was carried out.

After having placed the deportees on the deportation train and having submitted reports of the results of the operations thus discharged, the members of the operative group shall be considered free and shall act in accordance with the instructions of the chief of the district branch of the People's Commissariat of Public Security.

DEPUTY PEOPLE'S COMMISSAR OF PUBLIC SECURITY
OF THE U.S.S.R.

Commissar of Public Security of the Third Rank.

(Signed) SEROV.

Original Reference

U.S. Congress. House. *Report of the Select Committee to Investigate Communist Aggression and the Forced Incorporation of the Baltic States into the* USSR. Third Interim Report, pp. 464–68. Washington: G.P.O., 1954. (Original, U.S. House of Representatives, files of Baltic Committee, Exhibit 16-H of 12.X.53.)

Personal Reference

Kaslas, Bronis J. *The USSR-German Aggression Against Lithuania*, pp. 327–34. New York: Robert Speller & Sons, Publishers, 1973.

Index

Index

Index

Index

Index

Index

Index

Index

Index

Index

Index

sians, 149; Shamanism among, 149; war against Soviet regime, 92

Yakutsk, 53–54, 56, 74–80, 83–86, 90–95, 97, 102, 107–10, 113, 115, 118, 120–21, 123–25, 127, 147–48, 151, 164–66, 172, 174, 176, 179–80, 182, 184, 186, 188–92, 195–96, 200–202, 206, 209, 213; colony of deportees from Lithuania in, 95, 200; communications of, 183; crime rate in, 94–95, 195; employment of deportees in, 54, 95; founding of, 92; Jewish community in, 200; history of, 92–93; housing of, 93; permafrost of, 93

Yakuttorg, 192

Yaroslavl, 27

Yegorov, 125–26

Yekaterinoslav, 6

Yermolayev, 37–40; first Russian friend, 40

Young Pioneers, 174, 176, 200; summer camp of, 176–77; weight-growth plan of summer camp, 177

Yurt, 62–68, 76, 200; building of, 62–65

Zakrytyye magaziny (closed shops), 131–32, 139. *See also* Shopping

Zavalinki (insulating material), 194

Zavkhoz (school attendant), 100–101

Zayarsk, 51–53

Zemlyakov family, 64

Zion, land of, 55

251

The Rad
June 14, 194